High school's Not Forever

Jane Bluestein, PhD.
and
Eric Katz, M.S.A.C.

HCI TEENS

Health Communications, Inc.
Deerfield Beach, Florida

www.hcibooks.com

We would like to acknowledge these publishers and individuals for permission to reprint the following materials:

Excerpts from *When Gifted Kids Don't Have All the Answers: How to Meet Their Social and Emotional Needs* by Jim Delisle, Ph.D. and Judy Galbraith, M.A. ©2002; *The Teenagers' Guide to School Outside the Box* by Rebecca Greene ©2001; *GLBTQ: The Survival Guide for Queer and Questioning Teens* by Kelly Huegel ©2003; *How Rude!*™: *The Teenagers' Guide to Good Manners, Proper Behavior, and Not Grossing People Out* by Alex J. Packer, Ph.D. ©1997; *What Do You Stand For? A Kid's Guide to Building Character* by Barbara A. Lewis ©1998. Used with permission from Free Spirit Publishing Inc., Minneapolis, MN; (866) 703-7322; *www.freespirit. com*. All rights reserved.

Excerpt from "Precious Things," Tori Amos, Little Earthquakes (Atlantic, 1992). Used with permission.

**Library of Congress Cataloging-in-Publication Data
is available from the Library of Congress**

Publisher: HCI Teens
          An Imprint of Health Communications, Inc.
          3201 S.W. 15th Street
          Deerfield Beach, FL 33442–8190

Cover and inside book design by Lawna Patterson Oldfield

High school's
Not Forever

To Michèle Robin,
teacher extraordinaire, who is still
a valuable and important part of my life
decades after she first inspired,
validated and, indeed, rescued me in my
ninth-grade French class.

–Jane Bluestein

To my father,
the late Dr. Jacob Katz,
who taught me to care for others,
and to my sons, Alec and Ryan Valenzuela,
who enter high school even as
I write this book.

–Eric Katz

CONTENTS

ACKNOWLEDGMENTS

We gratefully acknowledge the following individuals for their encouragement and support, with a special thank-you for those who put us in touch with many of the contributors in this book.

Betty Austin
Arlene Barlow
Nydia Benitez-Nee
Marianne Bivens
Barbara Bourne
Jennifer Burns
Tracey Carmichael
Mildred Gutierrez-
Colon
Peter Copeletti
Laurie Crotty
Lynn Duncan
Anissa Emery
Evonne Fisher
Jo Ann Freiberg
Laura Gutman

Tim Harnett
Lois Hyatt
Karen Hazan
Thomas Hill
Mike Jones
Tara Jones
Dodi and Kendra Karp
Christine Marie Katz
Bryan Keiser
John Keydash, Cmdr.
Heather Kraus
Elizabeth Kudan
Kathy and Pablo
Ledesma
Ambika Longnecker
Marcella López

Evelyn Mercur
Calvin Parent
Judith Peabody
Danielle Pearl
Gloria Sanchez
Anthony Sculley
Linda Sorenson
Nina Snyder
Jerry Tereszkiewicz
Frances Terrazas
Aaron Trummer
Gary Van Voorhis
Diane Visconti
Stephanie and Walt
Witkowski
Beth Yount

Additionally, we would like to thank the high school students and survivors—more than 2,000 of them—who graciously shared their personal stories, observations and experiences, without which this book would not have been possible. Many of the contributions were submitted anonymously and others came with requests to use only their first names. To maintain a certain degree of consistency and a more universal feel to the contributions, we have omitted the last names from the attributions. Although we were not able to use each contribution we received, we would like to acknowledge those individuals who did supply their full names, along with their permission to use them:

Norman E. Abramson

Faizah Alkaff

JoAnne Allen

Kate Allman

Joel Christian Ballezza

Lindsey Bartlett

Jena Bauer

Nydia Benitez-Nee

Sonia V. Borges

Michael Borrello

Melissa Breau

Rachelle Brennan

Lynne Brownlee

Elisabeth Carroll

Natasha Carroll

Jordan P. Casson

Rachel Chandler

Michael Cimorelli, Jr.

Natashia Cooper

Chris Corrales

Philissa Cramer

Cristal Crisostomo-Girón

Carey Cronkright

Dorraine Denton

Colleen Ferguson

Omar Fernandez

Tara Frady

Joe Gbolo

Yanquoi Gbolo

Emily George

Jennifer Gillespie

Amber Gleave

Michael Gonzales

Amber Grant

Alexandra Hackett

Kari-Lyn Hansen

Clara Hartman

Judy Hernandez

Irisdalia Hernandez

Kristen Hoyer

Paul Ireifej

Carol Jáquez

Chad Jarvis

Nida Javaid

Chelsey Jensen

Ashley Jones

Read Judah

Christine Katz

Bryan Keiser

Shali Keiser

Nancy Knickerbocker

Hannah Kohl

Daniel Kripke

Jesse Kumicinski

Lisa Kuney

Adam Kupersmith

K'asha Lindsley

Arianna Lonkewycz

Line Lorenzen

James Mahoney

Alex Markey

Emily Maxwell

Brian McCabe

Casey McCormick

Alex Mendes

Mark Mendoza

Lisa Danni Messer

Judy Milburn McGraw

Nancy Morales

James Nani

Ngoc-Quynh Nguyen

Samantha O'Neill

Caitlin O'Neill

Amanda Otten

Ana Park

Danielle Pearl

Mike Permar

Sharon Phillip-Peters

Vianey Ramirez

Josh Reagan

Sandi Redenbach

Delisa Reed

John Regan

Bryan Rice

Princess Rodriguez

Andrew Rodriguez

Jan Rogers

Stephen M. Romm

Hannah Romm

Chauncey Rowe

Andrew Ruiz

Erik Sanchez

Krysta Scalzo

Andreas Schobel

Meghan Schroeder

Alessa Shaw

Sean Sivrais

Stefani Solarez

Linda Sorenson

Kyle Spurrier

Kelly Kamrowski Starwas

Allen Talbot

Ashley Taylor

Jon Tereszkiewicz

Justin Thomas

Donald Tillman

Aaron Trummer

Chelsea Udell

Kristofer Valadez

Jason Vazquez

Sue Oakes Verlaan

Peter Volkman

Celia-Ann Wagner

David E. Webber

Bobby Wetjen

Rachelle Williams

Matthew Witkowski

Laura Young

Mark Zampano

INTRODUCTION

Whether you sailed, slithered or slogged through middle school, or just barely survived, here you are in a new environment called high school, probably with a lot of people you don't know very well. And, as you may or may not have noticed, this environment has its own set of rules and peculiar reality—emphasis on the word *peculiar*.

Now you may be clear-headed or sophisticated enough to realize that the rest of the world operates by different rules, in a different reality, one that can be far more forgiving and accepting than even the best high-school experience. Still, that may not help much when you're in the middle of this fun-house ride. For most of us, when we're there, in the middle of it, it can be easy to forget that the high school reality isn't really *real*. It feels real enough. And pretty soon, it's easy to start believing that certain things, like the labels on your clothes or where you sit at lunch, are a lot more important than they really are.

This book is about perspective. It's a look at life in high school today, the good and the bad, and how life after high school can be different (and often, better and more sane), and what you can do now to make this time more pleasant, positive and productive.

HOW TO USE THIS BOOK

Good news. You don't have to read this book cover to cover. And there's no test at the end.

This book is designed like a buffet at your favorite all-you-can-eat restaurant. Take a quick look around, see what's being offered and pick whatever you're hungry for at the moment. Remember, you can always go back and take more when you need it, and what you want today may be different from what you want tomorrow.

WHAT'S WITH ALL THOSE *S?

We received input for this book from over two-thousand high school students around the country. Many of them did not include their names. Rather than try to guess their age or gender and assign a reference accordingly, or write "student" time after time, we decided to use a kind of shorthand to note the source. If you see a quote or a story followed by an asterisk (*), you can be sure it came from a kid in high school. We just don't know which one.

CHAPTER ONE

Delusions, Distortions and Daily Struggles: The High-School Reality

EVERYONE experiences high school differently. Some love it, some hate it, and some are just doing time. Here are some examples of how rules, restrictions and realities play out in high schools around the country. Take a good look and see if you recognize your own high school experience.

THE DAILY GRIND

©Zits Partnership. Reprinted with special permission of King Features Syndicate.

1

> In the mornings, I'm already not in a good mood knowing that all I have to look forward to is going to a class to learn about dead guys and math formulas that I will never use again.
>
> —Anthony, 15

Today, when I woke up, my heart was an emotion darker than black. I bet it's going to be a bad day. Why do I have to be me? I hate myself. I'm ugly, stupid and unlucky. I'm so unlucky that if I picked a fortune cookie out of a box of a hundred, I'd pick the only pessimistic one. Life is frustrating, complicated and confusing. It's 6:30 A.M. so I better go take a shower and shave my legs, not like it's going to help my appearance.

Figures, I missed a couple spots. I got a lot of bloody slashes from the blade. Oh well, a few Harry Potter Band-Aids will fix that. Next, what should I do with my hair? The only thing I like about it is the black gleam to it. Oh man, the curl is coming in the back. I better brush my hair before the curl discovers a counterattack. Finally, my face, wow . . . when did that get here? I'll need some concealer for that. I reach in the cupboard and pull out some shimmery powder the color of vanilla and dust it on top of my freckled cheeks.

This is as good as it's gonna get.

Mom made breakfast for me—some chai tea and two eggs, looking at me. They seem to mock me.

Okay, I'm at school for first block . . . oh wait, did I brush my teeth? Damn it! I'm so tired, I'm getting paranoid. Why do some days I feel like I want to cry? It's probably just a hormonal/mental thing; something else to add to my list of problems. Anyway, I have to go to next block.

The day is only half over.

Oh wait, my friend is up ahead but when I call her name and wave, she must not see or hear me, but the rest of the hallway does and now they're staring. I look like a complete idiot. Ummm . . . . was that the final bell or warning bell? Gotta run.

I'm in Non-Western World and we are learning about Asian rulers. I can't concentrate. I wish I were an empress—ahhhh! No, bad Emily, bad. Focus on the teacher. Unfortunately, the teacher has a case of voxophilia (love of hearing one's own voice). As a result, the rest of the class was blah blah.

Getting through the hallways is hell with people who can't walk and talk at the same time, the "popular" people who act like they are gods and the rest of us are untouchables, and the very tall ones you can't see around no matter what angle you crane your head. They should really put traffic lights in here because I'm beginning to feel herded. Dang it, I missed my freakin' class door. I'll get it in the next round I make. Cool! I think that cute guy just smiled at me. Nope, wait one sec. He was smiling at the pretty blonde behind me.

I'm at lunch, and I still feel like crying. I spilled salsa on me and now I wanna burrow into a hole and die.

After lunch, I got my math test back from Tuesday. An F! Why doesn't the teacher just put "You're a stupid cow" or "How did you make it to high school?" on the front of the test? The girl next to me says, "Man, this test was a killer!" I look down at her score, and she got an A.

Shut up! I think to myself. I just glare at her.

Whew! Last class of the day. Thank God. Today, nothing special happened . . . again. I wake up each morning hoping that maybe, just maybe, a guy will actually take interest in me or I'll get no homework. But who am I kidding? That won't ever happen, but I hang on to those ideas by a thread.

When my mom picked me up and drove home that day with the windows down (but in the "loser cruiser" so I sat in back with the tinted windows), I feel . . . I feel . . . like an exotic princess—beautiful and full of passion. Maybe I won't go home and blast Rob Thomas's song "Living Dead Girl" because no longer do I sense an oncoming mood swing screaming at me to slowly back away from humanity before I blast off. I actually feel quite good. The only problem I have now is how to last until the weekend.

—Emily, 17

> What makes you
> a success in high school
> is the exact opposite
> of what makes you a
> success in life.
>
> —JoAnne Allen

What I remember best about high school? Not fitting in. Having so-called friends I could never trust. Having a chip on my shoulder about a mile high. Not feeling visible except for all the wrong things, like being fat or not having the right clothes. Humiliation on a regular basis. Having people use me or avoid me. Having the people I needed support from simply tell me what they thought was best for me or how my behavior, grades or looks affected *them*. Having teachers I hated and teachers I loved, and feeling like I would have done anything for any adult who treated me with the least bit of dignity and respect for my intelligence. Counting days until graduation. Calculating daily, once I got accepted into the college of my choice, exactly how much or how well I had to do just to pass the classes I didn't like. The glorious elation when they gave me that stupid little piece of paper. It says something like "diploma" on it, but for me it still reads, "Free at Last."

> Whoever called high school "the best years of your life" must have started college at thirteen.
>
> —Ralph Keyes[1]

—Beverly

LIFE IN THE EYES OF A LOSER

Why am I forced to wake up in the early morning?
All I do is go to classes that are boring.
I sit here and realize I still have a year to waste.
The school food has one bad taste.
We've shared the good, we've shared the bad.

We frown on others when we are mad.
The lessons we learn in this damn pit:
"You'll succeed in life if you're rich, popular or a jock."
In my opinion, I say, "F*** that shit."
I pick on some, get harassed by others,
I have even had to kick the shit out of a couple people's brothers.
All my friends are either losers or class snoozers.
We band together and with that I say:
Enjoy school—it's only a four-year stay.

—Alex, 18

Well, I despise today fairly vehemently, and it's only 11 A.M. Isn't that some sort of a record? Technically, it's the first day of school, but it's just assembly, registration and a bunch of papers from homeroom. Tomorrow classes begin. I'm feeling pretty down right now. I've come to the conclusion that no matter where you go, really, high school is quintessentially the same: It's typical in all the same ways; it's frustrating in all the same ways; it's scary in all the same ways; it's good in all the same ways . . . although not so much of the latter for me since I've been here. Yet at the same time, life can differ so much from one school to another. Don't ask me how that works—I haven't come close to figuring it out.

> School's gone from being a place of education to a place where competition and fighting for the top come before learning. We have to deal with the continual pressure to keep up the pace, stay in the game, be the best at all times, never settle for less than the ultimate. . . . It's exhausting for a teen to always be fighting. Fighting grades, teachers, other people's attitudes, society . . . the list just goes on.
>
> —Katie, 18

> High school can be a blast for some kids. But if it sucks for you, you are not alone. I thought everybody in my school was a lot happier than I was. That really wasn't true, but I didn't know that at the time.
>
> —Clare

I've been to three high schools in four years, and I'm tired. I'm tired of being new; I'm tired of never being surrounded by anyone of my caliber; I'm tired of "giving it a chance" and "making the best of the situation;" I'm tired of most people my age; I'm tired of this country; I'm definitely tired of being tired of all the above, and the worst part, actually caring. But I am, and I do, and I hate it.

I've said it many times before, and damn it, I'm going to say it again. High school: Call me when it's over.

—Rachelle, 17

WHOSE BRIGHT IDEA WAS THIS ANYWAY?

> High school is an oppressive place, rooted in antiquated systems and traditional practices that neither promote excellence nor provide a safe and nurturing environment for the vast majority of students.
>
> —Aaron Trummer, high school principal

The summer before I started high school, a lot of people told me, "Oh, you're just going to love it. It will be some of the best years of your life!"

I didn't really believe this, because, honestly, if you peak when you're about sixteen, that's pretty pathetic. I did think I'd have a good time, though. I thought that it would be just like junior high, except more kids, and kids that were four years older than me.

Now that I've actually started high school, though, it isn't anything like I expected. Most of my friends and I are split up in different classes, and we don't even see each other at lunch. Plus, these classes are *hard*. I have all honors classes—just like last year—but the difference is huge. Unlike junior high, there is no week of "easing into academics." And the teachers grade a lot harder than before. I've learned this the hard way. See, English is my strong point, and I had never gotten less than an A– on an essay. So imagine my surprise when I got back my first essay and saw that the grade was a B–. I was so upset that I almost cried.

—Morgan, 14

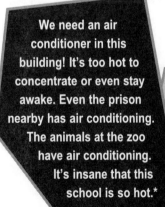

We need an air conditioner in this building! It's too hot to concentrate or even stay awake. Even the prison nearby has air conditioning. The animals at the zoo have air conditioning. It's insane that this school is so hot.*

Turn on the heat. It's really cold. I have three shirts on, and I'm cold. Seriously, turn the heat on.*

I think the institution of high school encourages a here-and-now mentality by only addressing critical present issues: if your clothes are up to dress code, if you're thirty seconds late to class, if you have the right pass to get to your locker, if you're waiting in the right line. I remember very few people ever saying, "This doesn't matter. Focus a little forward, and your perspective will undoubtedly turn brighter." If I'd heard that a little more, I think it would have made all the difference.

—Joel, 21

THE FACTS

Ever wonder why, in so many high-school classes, we sit in straight rows of desks, with everyone doing the same things at the same time? Well, if you go back a few years—when schools were training large numbers of kids to go to work in factories—an emphasis on uniformity and behaviors like compliance, conformity, hard work and obedience made sense. Now, things like individuality, independence, initiative, freedom and flexibility, which, back then were seen as threatening and were strongly discouraged, are the very traits many business leaders are looking for in today's information society! Schools just haven't caught up.

I wish the school would stop focusing on sports and do something for the arts like drama and dance. They just built a brand-new gym, but the stage is a mess and needs to be fixed. The curtains are falling apart and just painting the stage isn't a solution.*

We need interesting things to do. Boredom is at the bottom of a lot of problems in school.*

Some of the myths (lies) I was told about high school when I was in junior high were: high school is very easy; teachers don't really care if you miss class; just show up and they will pass you to the next grade; females have to change their appearance to have a boyfriend; we have to have sex to fit into a certain group.

—Dorraine, 20

I think that every so often there should be an *interesting* assembly when someone our age comes in and talks about an experience that changed his or her life. The only way a kid will listen is if someone on their level had it happen to him.*

TOP 10 LIKES AND DISLIKES ABOUT HIGH SCHOOL

LIKES

10. Open campus, being able to leave or get lunch off campus

9. Learning new things, getting an education

8. Meeting new people, making new friends

7. Career opportunities, work internships

6. After-school or extra-curricular activities, clubs and sports events

5. Social life (including dances, parties, the prom)

4. Vacation days, half days, early-release days

3. Certain teachers

2. Spending time with friends, socializing

1. Phys ed, specific sports activities and classes

DISLIKES

10. Classes are too long, sitting too much

9. Bad food, school lunches

8. Homework

7. Waking up early, not getting enough sleep

6. Annoying, mean, hypocritical, backstabbing, narrow-minded or interfering students

5. Tests, quizzes, finals

4. Standardized tests

3. Dress codes

2. Projects (class projects, senior projects, projects required for graduation)

1. Bad, mean, rude, angry or unfair teachers and administrators

By the time I get to school, the first bell's ringing. I'm already late, and I haven't even been to my locker. With just five minutes between the bells, I can never get to class on time. So I rush through the door, and my teacher sends me to the office because I'm late. By the end of first period, I'm almost asleep because I've been in the same chair for 100 minutes, and my teacher just puts notes on the board and doesn't explain what anything's about. Sometimes she reads the notes, but she never gives us something creative or hands-on. It seems like school is where we come to copy notes and get lectured. I can't use the restroom at all, and I get gum stuck to my leg because our campus is filthy. It's like the principal wants us to suffer. I can never talk to her about the problems at school because I've never even met her. You see her in the beginning of ninth grade, and then she vanishes. Everyone is so noisy. By the end of the day, I'm wired.

> Classes are too long. Half the time we're not doing anything in class. We're there so long that we get bored and usually end up falling asleep.
> —Jason, 16

—Clara, 15

> I wish we had more time between classes.*

Rivaling modern torture, my recollection draws on moments of anxiety, fear and wedgies. With clichés of gangsters, jocks and Barbie dolls, social integration is hard when your face is spotted with acne. This, though, was not my greatest difficulty.

I felt trapped in high school's bureaucracy. Never feeling free and often squeezed by what seemed like useless procedures, I lost interest in the primary reason for going to school: learning.

—Joel, 21

Walking through the halls can actually be scary. First of all, the halls are really crowded, so there is bound to be trouble. A lot of kids are impatient and just shove their way through, which leads to physical violence. There's the natural screaming and cursing every second. People throw stuff at random. Even if you're walking when classes are in session (when no one is in the halls), you can still run into the troublesome kids who are skipping class.

—Paul, 19

My first year in high school's been a lot different than I expected. I like the overall excitement. Since I've started high school, I'm always busy! I like the open-campus lunch. I think it would get a little boring staying at school every day, and it's nice to go out and eat good food. I also like block scheduling because I only have three classes a day. The tutorial gives me time to catch up if I ever forgot to finish work or anything happens to it. I also like the extra privileges, although they come with responsibility. But that's a good thing. Overall, I'm having a really great time.

It's easier to go outside and smoke than to use a computer for class.*

High school does not prepare you to grow up. It only prepares you for high school.
—Ralph Keyes[2]

—Mickie, 14

High school really isn't that bad. All you have to do is play the teachers' games. Do what you got to do and then get out.
—Justin, 15

WE'VE GOTTA DO WHAT?

> Students look at school as a place they *have* to go. It is not an option. They don't come to learn. They're here because they *have* to be here.*

I can't believe this place. Everybody says it's such a good school, but it's a lot smaller than my old school and doesn't have half the classes my other school had. I used to love school. Now, I'm stuck with classes I don't like, learning stuff I'll never use. The teachers like giving detentions more than they like teaching. They're so busy looking to bust kids who are chewing gum or kids who are coming in three seconds late that even if you're not the one getting in trouble, it's so stressful that you don't learn anything. I'm starting to hate subjects I used to love. I wish we had never moved.

—*Toby, 17*

> This school is like a prison. I can't eat when I'm hungry, sleep when I'm tired or go to the bathroom when I have to pee. It's hot and stuffy and something in here smells really bad.
>
> —Monica, 17

> Every student in this building, no matter what kind of student they are, gets treated with a serious lack of respect by the teachers and monitors. Students are working off the staff's example, and being treated like a second-class citizen is beyond frustrating.*

Ever have something strike you as being a lot funnier than it actually is? That happened to me today. My friend Terri showed me a cartoon— a silly comic that just hit me as being hysterically funny. (I guess compared to this endless, boring study hall, anything would have seemed entertaining!) Well, I started giggling, and then she started. We'd gain control for about three seconds, and then we'd just explode with laughter. We tried keeping it quiet; you would have had to have been pretty close to us to be disturbed (or infected?) by it. But we both got detention anyhow. Do you believe it? You can't even get away with being happy in this school!

—Janie, 15

> I like the freedom we have at this school. We are treated like young adults—sometimes.
> —Nicole, 14

> Besides the standardized tests and immature students, high school is very enjoyable. I enjoy having four block classes a day and the privilege of driving to school. My past two years of school have been the best two years of my life.
> —Damitra, 15

The high school I attend has a lot of rules I disagree with. One of them is our dress code. Three and a half months ago, I gave birth to my baby girl. Coming back to school my senior year with a baby to take care of was—and is—the hardest thing I have ever had to do. I am responsible for another human being's life. Everything she does, eats, says and wears is all my responsibility. I have to be there for her at all times, no matter what the school says or wants me to do. So when I wake up in the morning, the last thing on my mind is what I should and shouldn't wear to school. I can't believe the expectations schools have for children or adults.

—Amber, 18

> What's with the computer lab? Even when you have free time, you're usually not allowed in there. And if we try to use the facilities after school to play sports or have fun, someone always comes and throws us off the field.*

THINGS THAT MAKE
SCHOOL SUCK

Rules:

✓ Not having enough choices or input in decisions that affect you

✓ Rigid rules and punishments

✓ Being wrongly accused or punished

✓ Not being allowed or able to express feelings without fear of negative reactions or consequences

✓ Not being able to go to the bathroom when you need to go

✓ Not having any privacy

Adults

✓ Adults who don't treat you with respect

✓ Adults who act impatient, annoyed or disgusted with you

✓ Adults who ignore you or don't take you seriously

✓ Teachers who favor some students over others

✓ Unpredictable, inconsistent or "explosive" teacher behavior

✓ Not being recognized or acknowledged for positive behavior, achievement, effort, cooperation, etc.

✓ Not being supported or protected by adults when they see other students or adults mistreating you in any way

Class

✓ Unclear directions; not knowing what you're supposed to do

✓ Not getting enough help when you need it

✓ Not having enough time to answer questions or process information

✓ Having to sit too long

✓ "Gotcha" tests, pop quizzes, useless tests or evaluations

✓ Being told you're not applying yourself

✓ Feeling afraid to share, speak up or say anything in class

✓ Having your grades read in class (whether low or high)

✓ Too much noise, visual stimulation or movement in the classroom

Other Kids

✓ Not being able to speak or understand the language

✓ Judgment and rejection based on your clothing or appearance

✓ Any kind of prejudice or discrimination

✓ Feeling that no one really cares about you

✓ Being picked last

✓ Being bullied, harassed or intimidated by other students

✓ Going to a new school; having to make new friends

Which three of these bother you the most?

_____

_____

_____

_____

_____

What else would you like to add to this list that is not already there?

_____

_____

_____

_____

_____

RULES, RESTRICTIONS AND REPRESSION

The rule book weighs more than I do.*

We don't need metal detectors. We need *mental* detectors.
—Braulio Montalvo

The first thing I hate is the dress code. I hate it. I can't believe we can't wear hats. I feel naked without my hat. It doesn't make sense. The second thing I dislike is the ID cards. What's the purpose of them? It slows the line up. It makes it a million times slower. Then I only get like five minutes to eat because I was waiting in the line the whole time.
—Andre, 15

It's always been hard for me to sit quietly. I would get fidgety or start to doodle on my book covers. Chewing gum helped, but of course that wasn't allowed. I was always in trouble in school.
—Dale

We need to be guided, not ruled.*

About the dress code: We have too many girls who wear absolutely nothing. We need to do something more than just talk and say over the loudspeaker that they have to wear more clothes. It's too distracting.*

We can't wear spaghetti straps, but our boobs can hang out. Hmmm . . .*

There are too many rules. Having cameras everywhere is ridiculous. You can't pick a wedgie without being watched.*

There are many rules that keep us safe, but some just don't make sense.
—John, 15

Get rid of the stupid little rules. Whoever wrote in the handbook that we shouldn't bring ninja stars and swords to school is a moron.*

Look at your student handbook.

Which rules might trip you up?

_____

_____

_____

_____

_____

_____

_____

Which rules might you try to change?

_____

_____

_____

_____

_____

_____

_____

Which rules are actually there to help?

_____

_____

_____

_____

_____

_____

_____

ACADEMICS

I wish my school system had encouraged the art of thinking and learning, as opposed to memorizing and regurgitating.

—Lisa

One thing I really don't like about school is the state-mandated standardized test. We get tested on stuff that we don't know, so how are we supposed to do well? The school gets graded on how well we do, so the only reason they want us to study and teachers to work with us is so *they* can get a good grade.

—Caitlyn, 16

The pressure to pass a test in order to graduate, I think, makes people not want to come to school and learn. This will mean that many people will drop out of school. I think that if we could get rid of that test, many people would be more successful in school.

—Colleen, 15

High school is not as hard as some people say it is. All you have to do is listen and do your work.

—Robin, 14

It is hard to be a team player when you are competing with peers for an A grade on the class curve. It is difficult to remain honest when so much in school depends on appearing alert and prepared, and when there is too much work to do and too little time in which to do it.

—*Denise Clark Pope*[3]

Social Life

High school has been a good and bad experience. I enjoyed spending time with friends, meeting new people, being involved in a plethora of extracurricular activities, being Senior Class President, creating memories, dances, being irresponsible one last time

> They think there won't be any outcasts if we all dress the same.
>
> —Hamidah

and learning about what life is really about. I hated the whole being-judged-by-the-exterior scenario, people talking behind your back, people thinking they are better than you, the high-school social ladder (popular, losers, etc.), having to care about what other people think of you, the glorification of some sports while others are totally disregarded, and the teachers who don't have the heart to teach.*

> Parents really need to know how much violence, substances, sexual references and profanity high-school kids are fed on a daily basis.
>
> —Ashley, 19

High school has probably been the biggest source of stress in my life. It's really the last place I want to be. I don't like coming here every day to sit through classes—most of which are really uninteresting—and lunches where we're all crowded down in the basement. I especially don't like almost all of the people around me. I don't understand their interests and their constant need to be either putting someone down or be the center of attention with their idiotic antics. The only people I can stand are my friends (of which, in this school, I have few). They're the only ones I can talk to without getting severely annoyed.

—*Sammi, 17*

Honestly, I feel very safe at my school. I mean, we have had our share of fights and whatnot, but maybe I don't feel like I'm in danger because I don't hang out with those crowds. I'm happy here for the most part. I play sports; I'm in clubs; I have a great group of friends; I get decent grades. I'm expected to do well in school, and I want to do well. I am provided with what I need and am pretty happy.*

I wish I knew that high school gets better. When I was a freshman, all I wanted was to get out, but now that I am a senior, I have three really close friends and I have been extremely successful. If I had known it was going to be this great, I wouldn't have been so miserable before.

—Velicia, 17

The girls in high school are a lot better-looking than last year in junior high. The sports are a lot more exciting here, too. There is more adrenaline. I like the high-school atmosphere. It's like it's your second home. And your friends get more attached because you have to stick together.

—Alex, 14

What I liked the most of my freshman year was meeting a lot more students. Everyone was nice to me. I didn't get into any fights, and I didn't start any drama, which is good. Maybe my friends and I didn't get along here and there, but it all worked out.

—Wendy, 14

What surprised me about life after high school is how much more civil people were in the real world, after the completely, horribly dysfunctional social world of high school. The emotional cruelty that takes place there is unparalleled in any other environment.

—Lisa

Things have been great for me here. The first day was kind of scary because I worried that I was going to get lost going to my classes. But it wasn't a problem. What worried me the most was if people were going to make fun of me or call me names. It wasn't as bad as I thought it would be. It was fun being in high school with other people older than me.

—Susanna, 14

THE UNWRITTEN RULES OF HIGH SCHOOL

The following "rules" reflect the experiences and realities of the contributors and may well be real for large numbers of students. However, they are not suggestions for how to survive high school. In fact, many of these "rules" can limit your joy and success and may diminish the high-school experience.

✓ Don't do anything to really make you stand out from the norm. Care about grades, but not too much, and don't overachieve. (Getting an A or better is not a good thing in many students' eyes.)

✓ Do not piss off the popular kids. Age or grade level does affect your degree of "coolness." Be different, but not too different. Be smart, but not too smart. Be opinionated, but not too opinionated.

✓ If you show that teasing or rumors get to you, it never stops! Always act confident. <u>Never</u> let them see that they are getting to you. Keep to yourself, keep your legs closed, and everyone will get along.

✓ Keep the stories of drinking and drugs to yourself.

✓ NEVER RAT! Keep your mouth shut, and you'll be just fine.

✓ Don't wear the same outfit more than once a week.

✓ If you have nothing worth saying, don't say anything at all.

✓ Make as many friends as you can and keep on everybody's good side.

✓ Mind your own business, avoid trouble.

✓ Try not to take anything seriously or you'll never make it out alive.

✓ Fit into a group.

✓ There's no such thing as "blending in" or being invisible. Everyone's watching everybody, looking for weaknesses to exploit or strengths to emulate.

✓ You're gonna get picked on as a freshman. Just deal with it because you're gonna pick on the freshmen when you get bigger. It's just sort of a rite of passage.

SOCIAL PRESSURES ARE STILL STRONG

	MAJOR PROBLEM	MINOR PROBLEM
Pressure to get good grades	42%	38%
Pressure to look a certain way	16%	37%
Family pressure	15%	38%
Financial pressure	12%	40%
Loneliness or feeling left out	9%	28%
Pressure to do drugs or drink	8%	27%
Pressure to have sex	7%	24%

What are the major pressures that you face in high school?

1. _____

2. _____

3. _____

4. _____

5. _____

CHAPTER TWO

Religion, Race and the Look of Your Face: Image, Identity and Individuality

THE HIGH-SCHOOL EXPERIENCE can challenge you to face issues of identity, image and individuality. When is it best to stay true to yourself? When is it best to conform? Who decides who you are? Is it your friends, your teachers, your parents? Or do you get to decide? What if you don't all agree? Are you being challenged by the same concerns as the teens below?

REPUTATION AND STATUS

I was a popular kid in high school. Everyone wanted to be my friend, to be seen with me, to say that they knew me or to re-state anecdotes about me, whether true or not. I really didn't deserve all of the power that I had, but it came upon me starting in junior high.

It was then that I became bigger, faster and stronger than my peers, and I gained instant fame among the masses. It was interesting to me that I could be relatively unknown and ignored in grade school, and then because I was a good athlete, I gained the "respect" of those who previously shunned me.

By the time I got to high school, my reputation had preceded me, and I was immediately loved by the girls and feared and hated by the boys. The presupposition that I was stuck-up and cocky, beautiful, gifted and a party animal confused the hell out of me. I never tried to live up to anyone's ideas of me (a typical jock), but found great amusement in seeing some of my jock friends embrace the role and forget themselves. Idiots.

I did, however, relish some of the entitlements that I was given. I could get excused from class by my coaches; I was never marked tardy; I could get any girl I wanted; I could see the crowded halls part in front of me to let me pass; I heard amazing tales about myself that I had never known; I could always get into parties free and park wherever I wanted in the high school lot. None of this was deserved or earned really, just given to me as a jock along with the transparent, foundationless tower of power upon which I was placed. I felt bad for those people in band and drama who, I felt, had more talent, but were considered second-class.

After I became captain of both the football and wrestling teams, people wouldn't dare cross me for fear that I might smash them, even though I was a nice guy and very gentle when off the playing fields. I grew up fighting my older brother and fighting people off my older brother. I knew what I could do to someone and had nothing to prove, nor found any joy in pummeling people. When I was a sophomore, I refused to fight an upperclassman who was dared into confronting me. I just walked away while he and his friends mocked me—the truth being that I did not want to hurt him. For weeks I endured jeers from him and his friends until they finally gained enough confidence to jump me after school in front of all of their cronies—three on one. It didn't last long. For me, fighting was for survival, not for show. I seriously injured all three of them and cried on my way home because I hurt them so badly.

To my dismay, now I was the bar upon which wannabes and rival school jocks would make their names. I must have busted one hundred heads and never threw the first punch. Each time I wanted to cry or run away because I didn't want to fight. It scared the hell out of me.

People finally started getting sick of being beaten up, I guess, because by the time I was halfway through my junior year, the assaults had stopped, but my "fame" had grown.

There was this one kid crippled with disease who always sat alone in the cafeteria in his wheelchair. I sat by him one day, and he was so grateful that he almost started to cry. Every day I would talk with him at lunch, and people would follow me to the table and talk with him, too. He never ate alone again for the next two years because I had "noticed" him. He had become part of the culture.

> It seems to me that every activity in this school is political, especially sports. I don't think most people get fair chances. Students who are liked more or have been doing the sport longer come first, even if you work harder than them. I'm told I'll get to play in gym, but I never do. I sit on the side all period.*

A smaller kid on our football team was being hazed by some upperclassmen and I stood up for him in the locker room and swore that if anyone hurt him, I would bring the ruckus to them. He was never picked on again. I did countless acts of kindness and hoped that people would notice me as a caring person, not a muscle-head jock! To little avail.

The only one who really knew me other than my best friend was my girlfriend. She turned out to be the prom queen, and this perpetuated my image, so I figured, screw it! People will think what they want regardless of reality.

High school is a false reality, really. Popularity in high school does not always transcend graduation. It is a place where you're thrown together with people you may have nothing in common with other than proximity. When you get to college or pursue your own interests elsewhere, you are surrounded by people with whom you can relate on other levels. It is then that we realize how plastic high school really is, even for the superheroes.

—Bryan

I spent most of my time in high school hanging out at the "freak wall" with other kids who were generally rebellious, indifferent to school, sexually active, and involved with drugs and alcohol. We were careful to steer clear of the athletes, cheerleaders and homecoming court who hung out at the "jock wall." It was like "we're united here," bonded in not being able to make it in the functional world. When I see kids in gangs and groups of outcasts, I understand wanting to be a part of something, even if that thing is bad, unhealthy or harmful.

—Lori

When I was in the eleventh grade, I left the private school I had attended my entire life to go to a much larger public school and found myself in shock. I didn't understand why there were campus police, random searches and security cameras everywhere, which was quite bizarre to me. We never had those things at my old school.

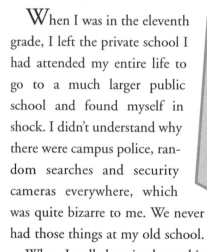

You can walk into school feeling the best you ever have in your life and dressed really good, yet there are kids who have to come up to you and bring you down and make you feel like you never want to be around people again. Not one single day goes by that a group of kids don't bring down another because he's not cool enough or he doesn't dress in clothes that are good enough or simply because that one kid is poor.

—Sean, 18

When I pulled up in the parking lot with my brand-new, fully loaded car, I felt out of place. I often got picked on for that. The kids there all had used, beat-up cars. Where I came from, it wasn't a question of whether you were going to get a car, but whether you were going to get Mommy's old Mercedes or a brand-new one. I didn't know that all teenagers did not get brand-new cars when they turned sixteen or that they didn't all have cell phones. A lot of the kids in my new school had to ride the bus and did not have new clothes and accessories to match.

I didn't realize how sheltered I had been. This new school opened my eyes to how the rest of the world was and made me more aware of the outside world. Before I would have judged people who were different from me. Now, I'm more open.

—*Kate, 20*

I am a senior at my high school and one of the students with the lowest status in the school. The kids with the lowest status, like me, are often judged by their family. Like in my case, I have many brothers and sisters and am judged in school on how they acted before me. We are people who normally like to be alone and are more intelligent than people realize.

Money and last names play a big part in the status we have in our school. Those with less money and less expensive clothes are often considered below notice by others.

—*Sarah, 17*

Honors history. Man, I love history, but I can't stand this class. It's not the teacher, even though he wears the same brown suit every day! It's the rest of the class. They're the little goody-goody kids, and here I am, the only pothead in honors history. You know, all through elementary school I was friends with most of these kids, but now I am somehow the target of their all-too-witty, sarcastic comments

There is an incredible disparity in the rules and privileges at my school. The rich kids are in sports, student government and gifted classes. Even stupid rich kids are in AP classes! This double standard just exaggerates the gap between the "haves" and the "have-nots." It makes the poor kids hate the rich kids even more.

—Hannah

One of the most fascinating things was to see how many of the kids who everyone thought were "cool" dropped out of college and returned home because they were no longer the "it" kids in the big world. They had to return to the place where they were somebody.

—Jena, 23

and jokes. Yeah, I don't wear the same preppy clothes they do and I am not going to be showing up at the country club, but I am an honors student. The school didn't just go, "Hey, let's throw one pothead in the class just so the other kids will have someone to bust on."

I can't believe this crap. The teacher never steps in, so the kids never back off. I know the material as well as any of these brainiacs, yet I get no credit from the teacher and nothing but crap from the "good kids." All because of a reputation. Yes, I get stoned, probably way too much. But I am a very good student and a nice person. I have not said a bad word to or about any of these kids, ever! I just want to be treated like a person.

—RICKY, 16

The game of "us versus them" starts fairly innocently. You begin to compare yourself. *Are my clothes as nice as hers? Can I lift as much weight as him? Did I get a C– when my friend got a B+?* You feel resentful being on the low side of the comparison, yet being on the high side brings no peace either because there's no such thing as being better all the time.

—Deepak Chopra[4]

WHICH KIDS HAVE THE
HIGHEST STATUS IN YOUR SCHOOL?

✓ The ones who have wealth, beauty, well-known parents or
   a certain last name

✓ The "thugs"

✓ The ones with bottle-blond hair and an Abercrombie & Fitch tee

✓ The kids who accomplish something of value, like awards or scholarships

✓ The jocks

✓ The ones who keep their mouths shut, hand in their work on time, and
   don't cause trouble with teachers or other students

✓ The ones who get good grades

✓ The ones who are <u>in</u> something, whether it's student government,
   cheerleading, drama, the football team. They're the ones who have the
   most status and recognition. They also get away with a lot more than
   the rest of us.

WHICH KIDS HAVE THE
LOWEST STATUS IN YOUR SCHOOL?

✓ Surprisingly, the ones who do drugs and drink heavily

✓ I don't think it is one specific group of kids. It is just whoever is
   weaker and smaller than the person doing the teasing, whoever is in
   their way at the moment.

✓ Poor kids, kids with a certain last name or kids who come from a family
   with a bad reputation, ugly kids or kids who are <u>way</u> too different

     ✓ The druggies and the hoes

      ✓ Less motivated kids

      ✓ Kids who don't participate in activities

       ✓ The kids in band

✓ The kids in math club

✓ Shy, smart kids

✓ Students who keep to themselves and don't hang out with anyone

✓ The kids who get suspended every week for doing something stupid—
skipping class every day, not doing any work

✓ Conceited people

✓ The ones who are not in style, who wear white socks outside of gym.

✓ The preppie kids find the non-preppies disgusting

✓ The gangstas think the preppies are idiots

✓ Everybody looks down on everybody else

KEEPING IT REAL

High school is a melting pot of teenagers, each with his or her own religious or moral background. Sometimes in a sea of what seems like millions of students, you find yourself in the minority. Such was the case of my high-school career.

I grew up in a large, ethnically diverse school district with approximately seven hundred in my graduating class. In such a heterogeneous multitude, it is difficult and rare to find a person with whom you share the same values. Throughout my high-school years, I witnessed many of my peers either claiming religion as part of their culture but never bothering to keep its customs, or disregarding the subject altogether. Naturally, being a devout Christian, I stood apart from the secular student body. Watching my friends take part in stereotypical, often depraved, teenage activities, I faltered now and again, as I am not claiming flawless righteousness, but I stood firm on my Christian foundation.

At times feeling isolated, remaining faithful to my convictions was not an easy task. I never considered abandoning my beliefs to become more like my peers, although I knew it might have been a quick—yet eventually futile—solution, considering my desire for more friends. As a matter of fact, the solitude didn't bother me much. I had a supportive family, a wonderful, irreplaceable boyfriend, a small yet close group of school friends and an encouraging church congregation. Having Christian relationships provided an essential ingredient to my morals and integrity. Church fellowship had been an established part of my life since birth. Being raised in church, it became second nature to me. However, it did not become binding or ritualistic; it was very much alive and very much my own choice, as I had grown to love and fear my God.

> Just remember, you don't have to be what they want you to be.
>
> —Muhammad Ali

My predicament concerning secular adaptation only came from that desire we all secretly share: the desire to fit in with the group. Thankfully, that desire was subdued in my life. Praying to God not only as my Heavenly Father, but as my friend, I asked Him to help me with my carnal struggles. As I continued my walk in high school, the desire to assimilate became even paltrier as I began to see that my acquaintances appreciated me as a fellow student and respected me for my strong Christian character. I didn't involve myself with petty high-school nuisances; I was able to live a pleasing and rewarding life.

Like everyone else, I experienced hard times. Not a single human being is exempt from life's harshness. Luckily, I never had academic problems, but complications outside of the classroom had a propensity to permeate the school walls. Fortunately, in adversity, I never had to carry my burdens alone. God served as my sustaining rock and foundation. In manifesting God's compassion and support, my family and friends united to form an encouraging community. I always had a set of stronger shoulders than mine that lovingly bore my yolk.

High school has the potential to be a most gratifying experience. However, it can also be a hostile environment. Holding your own can be one of the most difficult parts of getting through high school. Thankfully, I always had a helping hand.

—*Jesse, 17*

The kids in school are really stuck-up. Everybody's really fake. They just think about the next thing they want to buy. They don't care about the world. They have so much money, they don't have to work for things, and they don't think about things. They just take the education they're given—which is just meant to conform us— and think that's all there is to it. They don't question things.

I came into this school with a lot of opinions and a lot of ideas that are really off from what a lot of other people think. I get called a crack-head every day just because I have these ideas and am not afraid to talk about them. People think I'm crazy. I've made people think I do a lot of Ecstasy just so I can get away with having my own thoughts.

> If you go into high school with a mind-set that you are okay the way you are, then you have already discovered what so many people want to discover. Never let anything change your mind about your self-confidence, because that is one of the key elements you have to keep with you as you go through your journey in high school.
>
> —Jordan, 17

I don't see the point of going to school when everything I'm learning is just one person's perspective. Like in history class, they leave out a lot of things. They only teach white people's history. We learn about the great things people do, but we don't talk about the bad things they do. There's all this stuff about Christopher Columbus, but there's no day for Harriet Tubman. Asians aren't even *in* American history classes. I feel like I don't even care about school because I don't like the stuff they're feeding me. They're not teaching me what really happened. I'm not gonna try to get an A in something that doesn't mean anything to me. I just feel as though they're not educating me. They're just turning me into a product this country can use.

> For me, high school has been awesome. I'm more free-spirited and a much more outgoing person than I used to be. Definitely.
>
> —Stefani, 14

—*Simone*

When I was in high school, I was often very depressed. I knew I was gay, but I thought I was the only one. One day during my sophomore year, I went into the counselor's office and I noticed a sign that read, "If you're gay, you're not alone." I'm looking around like, *Okay, I misread the sign.*

My next step was to tell the counselor about myself. I was kind of scared and uneasy about coming out to somebody I didn't really know well. I ended up telling her about a gay cousin of mine. I thought that would break the ice because I really do have a gay cousin. Eventually I told her about myself, and she gave me a hug and was very supportive and understanding. She said, "You're not alone, and you're very gifted." She gave me some literature, a lot of encouragement and the phone number of a youth support group. I went, and it was quite interesting.

> **Although my mother didn't accept the fact that I was gay, I still felt relieved I'd told her. I had no more secrets from her. She knew who I really was.**
>
> —Craig J. Jaffe[5]

> **I'm not scared anymore to tell people I'm gay. In fact, I enjoy telling them. I don't fit the stereotypes people have about gays, and that really makes them stop and think twice. I never know when I might bump into someone who could be going through what I went through. The least I can do for them is to be out of the closet.**
>
> —Craig J. Jaffe[6]

I think I would probably still be lost if it hadn't been for her. When I came out to my family, she educated them on a lot of issues and helped break down a lot of stereotypes. She's made it much easier for my family to understand, and some friends of mine as well. She told me what will happen as I get older like, "Watch for this, watch for that." I feel very fortunate to have had this person in my life.

—Ken, 19

Maybe you've known
you're GLBTQ (gay, lesbian, bisexual,
transgender or questioning) for years.
Or maybe you're only now beginning to question
your sexual orientation or gender identity.
Either way, you're not alone. Researchers believe
that between five and six percent of youth are gay,
lesbian or bisexual. According to the 2000 U.S. Census,
there are over 49 million school-age kids in America.
That means there are over two and a half
million kids just like you in America alone.
Two and a half million!

—*Kelly Huegel*[7]

I thought that
I wasn't attractive,
smart or motivated. I
worried too much about
the here-and-now. I was
too concerned with the fact
that I had an unattractive
body and poor skin (what I
thought at the time) to
think about the future.

—Joel, 21

Gifted
kids tend to hide
their intelligence, as well as
their talents, for a very simple
reason: conformity.

—Claudia[8]

I know now that my
worth as a person doesn't have
anything to do with how many A's I'm getting
or the size of my thighs. And that the expectations and
judgments other people have about me is more
about *their* stuff than about who I really am.

—Beverly

What I remember most
about high school is my
intentional isolation because
I felt so different from everyone
else and preferred being
alone for the most part.

—Cheryl

I seem to be a mystery of sorts to a lot of the people in our school. However, not too long ago I was a bit of a mystery to myself. I had tried to be so much for everyone else that I didn't know who I was anymore. I had been told to just be myself, but there was a problem with that advice: I didn't know how to be myself. It had been so long since I tried, there wasn't much of *me* left.

—Miranda, 17

If you're not happy with yourself, then yeah, you need to make some changes. But if other people aren't happy with you, but you are? Guess what? You're way ahead of the game.

—Freddie Prinze, Jr. [9]

ADVICE

WHAT DID YOU CALL ME?

E ver do ninety-nine things well and one wrong, but only be able to think about the one you messed up?

Sometimes it seems that reminders of our shortcomings are everywhere, but what do you have that reminds you of all the great things about you?

If we really pay attention to the compliments we receive, we can collect them and look at them when we feel like all we do is mess up.

- When you receive a compliment, write it down in a journal. Every week or so reread your journal.
- When you receive a compliment, write it down on your calendar. Consider writing a note to the person who complimented you, letting them know how it made you feel.
- Think about your day and write down one thing that you feel you did really well. Learning to compliment yourself is a rewarding habit to develop.

Stay true to the morals and values that made you before entering high school, because if you do not hold true to them, it is easy to get lost in the big world of high school.

—Jordan, 17

Trust that you will never repeat the same mistakes again, but please allow yourself the freedom to make new mistakes and learn new lessons. All have value.

—Sinda Jordan

My advice for getting through high school: Stay true to *yourself* and don't go too fast.

—Amber, 17

If high school is a time for learning, which it certainly is, then one of the biggest lessons you can learn before that diploma is tucked under your arm is a solid faith in your own worth as a person.

—Barbara Mayer[10]

I was never sure how to act or what to do to get people to like me. I was very much a super student, teacher's pet, people pleaser. I always had to do things to make people notice me—good things, but I had to perform. I see now how emotionally unsafe I felt.

—Beth K. Lefevre

THE FACTS

VIRTUAL IDENTITY[11]

- 56 percent of online teens have more than one e-mail address or screen name.

- 24 percent of teens who have used IMs and e-mail or have been to chat rooms have pretended to be a different person when they were communicating online so their buddies wouldn't know who they were.

- 33 percent of these teens report having someone give them fake information about themselves in an e-mail or instant message.

I SEE YOU. DO YOU SEE ME?

> Keep in mind that before trench coats became the uniforms of murderous teens, they were just plain cool.
>
> —Ned Vizzini[12]

I have friends. I have enemies. Doesn't everyone? Am I popular? Sort of. I do know a lot of people. That's not because I am outgoing or drop-dead gorgeous. I did not run for a position in student government. I am not captain of any sports team. I am "the girl with the tattoo shop."

My parents opened a tattoo shop about six years ago. My dad has been tattooing for eleven years. The shop has been operating since I began junior high, and I am now a senior in high school. I suppose my peers regard me as an expert on what I like to call body art (tattoos and piercings). I get questions on body art all the time. I do know a lot. I know the procedures and how they heal.

At least 40 percent of the students at my high school have a body piercing (a piercing in an area other than the earlobe). It is a sign of status among one's peers. Students always ask me where

> I don't want to be original. I want to be cool.
>
> —Jenna[13]

I am pierced (my ears and my navel). I don't take it as nosy or rude. I truly don't mind. The question is to be expected when you consider my environment. I have received negative feedback about body art from a few people. Once in a very long while, the feedback has been quite rude. Once again, this does not upset me; I just hope that those people get over their fear of the unknown.

Many kids ask me why I don't have more piercings. They are shocked to learn that my parents don't want me to get a lot of piercings. My parents set limits, and I respect that. Also the question as to why I am not tattooed comes up frequently. The plain and simple fact is that I am not legally old enough. In my state, the law says you have to be eighteen to get tattooed. My family and I know I could get inked (get a tattoo) and not be found out by the law, but we choose to play by the rules.

FACT

11 percent of students say at least half of those they know have a tattoo.[14]

I cannot picture my life without the tattoo shop. I love the atmosphere. It's totally unique. I am exposed to a completely different type of art, one that most kids my age do not get to experience. Tattooing and piercing are art forms. It takes skill, precision and a steady hand to administer either one. This family business has truly altered my high-school experience, making it like no one else's.

—Krysta, 17

When you meet me, you might only see a pierced eyebrow and a bad attitude, and you might not stop to talk to me because it's easier to walk off and stare. But don't be afraid or stare at me—come right up and talk to me. You'll be quite surprised, I promise.

—Kevin, 18[15]

Behind the jocks, artists, nerds, preppies, chess nuts, heavy-metal guys, folksy guitar players, scary kids with black trench coats, neo-Nazis and what's-his-names was the general collection of bozos and rejects that I hung out with. Most of them were guys who spent their free time playing a fantasy card game. . . . It was a desperate frenzy, kids playing all the time, thinking about the cards so they wouldn't have to think about anything else.

—Ned Vizzini[16]

Because I grew up in so many different places, I was used to rumors about me. You know, I didn't have the right shoes; I didn't have the right clothes. I even had the wrong accent.

—Tom Cruise

It's like every time I go in a store, the clerk's eyeing me as if I'm some suspicious criminal. And then when I need some help finding what I want, it's like everybody else gets waited on before me. Forget going to a restaurant. They might as well hang up a sign saying, "Teenagers Not Welcome."

—Lee[17]

I know a lot of people think that all high-school jocks are into drinking or that they're not as smart, that they only like and only hang out with jocks, but that wasn't true for me. I wouldn't consider myself the most popular kid, but I was definitely known by everyone. They knew I was smart, but they weren't mean to me because I was smart. I'm not the stereotype at all, but like my own person. I think I get a lot of respect because of that.

—Matthew, 18

Positively the strangest thing anyone's ever asked me upon discovering, if you will, that I'm gay: "You're gay! So, what does your bedroom look like?"

Okay, what the f***?

So being openly gay in high school is not necessarily a special experience. Let's talk about how stupid people are, okay?

Everyone has his or her own unique sexuality, not just gays. No one should have to flaunt that they're gay. If they want to, cool. But just because you're gay doesn't mean you *have* to like Cher, the color pink or Lycra.

What I learned about myself in high school that turned out *not* to be true: that I was just like everyone else and heterosexual.

—Holly

Finding a balance in a predominately heterosexual world can be rough, especially when, wherever you look, straight people are starring in movies, holding hands in the malls and starting families. I mean, come on, who's got gay grandparents? I've never heard of them.

That's not necessarily because our generation is the first gay generation. There've always been gays. Someone's got gay grandparents, but we just don't know about it because in today's society it's still not acceptable for people to be who they are and have others leave them alone. If people today actually knew about people who were different from them, I wouldn't have to answer the question, "What does a gay boy's bedroom look like?"

—Alex, 17

What I learned about myself in high school that turned out *not* to be true: that I'm not ugly, stupid or a freak. (Okay, I'm a freak, but in a good way.)

—Jan

Being blond and pretty was a liability. I was never validated for my intellect. I was immediately labeled and limited in terms of what people thought of me, like I could either be attractive or intelligent, but not both.

—Kathy

In high school, I felt extremely ugly and insecure. I felt like no guy would ever like me. I felt like all the guys liked all of my girlfriends and never liked me. I was so insecure that I would not allow anyone to like me. I felt that I was not worthy of being liked. I now realize how confidence is probably the biggest turn-on to people, and I accept myself for what I am. I also recognize my beauty both in and out and accept my good and bad.

—Jena, 23

I went from being a flat-chested fourteen-year-old to a double D almost overnight. Kids in school used to really make fun of me. They'd assume that I was a slut just because I had a big chest. They called me names, and a lot of guys found excuses to bump into me in the hallway. I was mortified.

—Melissa, 18 [18]

When I started high school, it did not take long for other students to size me up. I was about 6'4" and my shoulders were nearly door width. On top of that, I was overweight. The pressure to be athletic was immense. What no one wanted to consider was that despite my athletic body, I was a geek: I loved art, music and programming computers. Instructors, coaches and students were consistently pressuring me to get involved in sports. The pressure took many forms, mostly a consistent effort to make me feel like I was an outcast because I did not conform to their image or view of what they wanted me to be. They resorted to insults and to harassing me every day. I was not supported by the teachers or the coaches when I was being harassed. No one would intervene, even if I asked directly. I cannot begin to express the isolation and the depression from all of their crap. I got to the point where I just wanted to blend into the walls and not be noticed (obviously impossible) with the exception of suicide, which I had contemplated *many* times.

—Donald

> I'm not the kind of girl who attracts attention. Even when you look right at me, it's easy to look past me. I'm a well-behaved, unobtrusive goody-goody, pushing every symptom of rage or desire or wild ambition down past the throat, down past the heart, all the way into my guts.
>
> —Emily White[19]

> I was in all gifted classes. The teachers enjoyed us so they let us get by with stuff, like, I never went to school in dress code. They simply did not pay any attention to me because I didn't look like someone who would cause trouble. I never had a detention for tardies. They never said anything to me when I showed up late. I often ran errands for teachers, with no hall pass, and never got stopped like many kids did.
>
> —Kate, 20

Kids who look like the stereotypical troublemakers are persecuted. Sports-playing students and kids who look like jocks can get away with a lot more.*

The trend right now is to be thin, so it's hard being the big kid in school. Everyone is cracking jokes. You try to laugh at it, but it embarrasses you. Every time the teachers talk about it, you get a little embarrassed. I play sports, exercise and lift weights, but I can't seem to drop much weight. It's hard to be the fat kid, but you do learn to control your emotions better if you don't look embarrassed or get angry. In a way, you become a better person because you are in control of your life.

—Anthony, 17

Growing up, I didn't excel at anything. I was very average and mediocre. I didn't have anything to claim for myself.
—Julia Roberts[20]

For the most part, teachers are respectful to students, but there are times when teachers judge students on their past and hold it against them.*

I hate it when they call me gay for being a cheerleader.
—Omar, 14

High school was a nightmare. People would never make fun of someone who lost a limb or was in a wheelchair. But they think nothing of making fun of you when you're fat.
—Jamie

If you need help coming to terms with being GLBTQ (gay, lesbian, bisexual, transgender or questioning) or if you just want someone to talk to, seeking therapy or counseling to discuss these issues is a good idea. But you don't need to try to fix who you are because there is nothing wrong with you in the first place.
—Kelly Huegel[21]

The only gay people society sees (or chooses to acknowledge) due to its ignorance are flamboyant drag queens, those suffering in the AIDS epidemic, or those who are obsessed with Cher, pink and Lycra. Simply because these are society's stereotypes.

Society expects that if you are, in fact, gay, you *must* fit into one of these three categories. And to make life more interesting, the hypocrites of today say that even if you're *not* gay and you fit into one of the categories, you *must* be gay.

Our generation is here to prove that wrong.

A person is a person is a person. There's nothing to flaunt, display, watch or marvel over. In the big-people world we call *reality*, there's no justification for inhumanity toward gays.

—Alex, 17

> No one but you can assign you an orientation or an identity. What you call yourself, how you identify yourself (and this may not be solid—for some, it shifts) are your choices.
> —Kelly Huegel[22]

RELIGION, RACE AND THE LOOK OF YOUR FACE

Prejudice: A word we never like to hear. We often think of skin color or race when we hear that word. However, as a student in high school, I have experienced many kinds of prejudice. I had a teacher (a male) who would only listen to the girls who were all dressed up and looked pretty, not the people like me who had no time to get all made-up before school. He would ignore all of us regular people and only pay attention to the popular girls.

—Cristal, 17

> I hate being called a terrorist just because I'm a Muslim. I don't think people realize just how mean and hurtful it is to hear that.*

At my high school, people normally had to choose a group that would be the most important to them. Even if a person was a member of multiple groups, they almost always had one that they were the most loyal to. Race was often the most important characteristic. After all, there was no way to get around what race you were, but you could always drop out of other clubs and groups.[23]

A lot of times teachers automatically assume that I am some genius because I am Asian, and I prove them wrong, which shocks them!

—Dorothy, 17[24]

The bravest thing I have done during high school was correcting an aggressive girl making racial remarks like, "Look at that Chinese girl." I would answer "Ha, ha, say it right . . . I'm Korean."

—Ana, 17

African-American men have a heavy load to pull. We're automatically categorized by society as being sports stars, high school dropouts, jailbirds, drug dealers or drug addicts.

—Marshala Lee, 14[25]

As long as people expect me to act a certain way because of the way I look, or to look a certain way because of the way I act, I will continue to be something of an outcast because I defy their prejudices. The reality is that I'm different from a stereotypical white kid from suburbia because, no matter how I act, others will see me differently. Society has different expectations for black and white people, and it becomes uncomfortable if we differ from those expectations. Just ask anyone who's ever picked me for a game of two-on-two basketball just because I'm black.

—Jamal K. Green[26]

Sometimes, I hear a lot of names being called toward different groups of people, and nothing is done by the adults, even when these names are called right in front of them. Any time you walk down the halls, you hear something about Spanish people or blacks. The racist kids are never caught, though.*

Being a young African-American female in school has been fun for me. I have expressed my opinions on topics up for debate in my classes because if I don't agree with what you're saying, I will tell you, and why. I've met a handful of peers who are similar to me and view things the same way I do. There've been days when I've gotten referrals for dressing out of dress code, which was my way of expressing myself. I've gotten ugly looks from "haters" who don't like my great sense of fashion, my car, my New York clothes and say I act too "white." But at the end of the day, I can say I'm actually glad I'm here. I am very blessed to have had the opportunity to experience public school. I know that I can take the good and bad with me as I enter the real world, learn from other people's mistakes and succeed to become something in this harsh society America has set up for me.

—Natashia, 18

It is difficult to combat xenophobia and ethnocentricity in a homogeneous community like this school, which is plagued by cultural illiteracy.*

There aren't enough minority students here. I feel uncomfortable amongst a majority of white students.*

I'm Jewish, and I'm tired of being ridiculed and stereotyped. What does my religion have to do with anything?*

Yeah, there's racial harassment, but I speculate it isn't just racial prejudice. In an argument, any difference is exploited: fat, stupid, black, white, tall, short, whatever.*

SPEAKING OUT AGAINST ACTS OF HATRED

The only way to change racist attitudes, comments and behavior is to speak out against them. It only takes a few vocal people who get upset at these behaviors to encourage others to do the same. As more people take offense at acts of hatred, those acts are, in fact, discouraged. When a "hater" encounters large numbers of people who do not hold the same prejudices, that person can change behaviors, as well as the beliefs behind those behaviors.

So there are good reasons to speak up. In the process, you may become a hero, but you may become a target yourself. Are you willing to take this risk?

We all witness acts of discrimination and hate. Which act that you witnessed bothered you most?

I was most bothered when I saw/heard _____

_____

_____

_____

_____

If I ever see or hear this again, I could _____

_____

_____

_____

_____

_____

If I take action, these are the positive things that could happen:

_____

_____

_____

_____

If I take action, these are the negative things that could happen:

1. _____

_____

2. _____

_____

3. _____

_____

Am I willing to take this risk? ❏ Yes ❏ No

CHAPTER THREE

Bonding, Buds and Betrayal: Friendship, Cliques and Belonging

FINDING A PLACE where you fit in socially can be one of the biggest challenges in high school, especially when your placement depends on luck, looks or labels. Where do you fit in? How do people in your school judge you? How do you judge others?

USERS AND ABUSERS

People in high school always seem "shady" to me. I think I know someone, then, suddenly, the friendship gets trashed. This is one of the main reasons I have a hard time trusting people. I am constantly getting hurt by so-called friends. At one point during my sopho-more year, I ignored all individuals at my school with few exceptions, trying not to start drama

> You can be popular. You just have to be yourself in a whole new way.
>
> —Marge Simpson

and hear what new rumors were being said about me by selfish, non-confident, wanna-be popular girls. I constantly feel as though people are trying their hardest to get something out of me, then, of course, I get screwed over for putting myself out there. It sucks having to watch what you say to certain people! I don't feel as though I should have to hold my tongue to make sure I'm on someone's good side.

> **We have this one group of girls who are really into hair and jewelry and certain clothing labels. The only people who get to hang out with them are the ones who wear the "right" stuff, and wear it well. Even then, you can't be too tall or too fat or too anything. If you don't look like them, they ignore you, unless they're making fun of how you look. If you're lucky, they don't even know you exist.**
>
> —Vicki, 16

This one group of girls tried to ruin my social and school life because of their jealousy. I'm not trying to be conceited, but it's true. High school is all about games with groups you usually don't care much about. Dignity, I feel, is an extreme problem in this chapter of our lives. You feel you continuously have to impress others, when really, nothing will matter after you graduate anyhow. Freshmen, sophomores, juniors and seniors don't grasp the larger reality of life. Popularity isn't all it's cracked up to be. Every person you surround yourself with is fake. Your friendships, fake. Fakeness is your personality. I see shapeless, good people morph every week, every year, into individuals who have nothing going for them. You don't get to truly express yourself because high school doesn't accept anything real. All that matters is how well you dress, what party plans you have this weekend and if you do drugs.

To keep yourself out of the pointless circle of drama, I would suggest getting involved in activities your school provides or obtaining a job to set yourself apart from others, and to realize early on that you do have a wonderful future ahead of you.

—Shali, 17

...in my peach party dress
No one dared
No one cared to tell me
Where the pretty girls are
Those demigods
With their nine-inch nails and little fascist panties
Tucked inside the heart of every nice girl.

—Tori Amos

It is interesting how things work out and how extreme things seem at this time of your life. It all takes a toll on your mind and body, especially friendships. I can guarantee almost ninety to ninety-five percent of high-school friendships go sour or drift to where you do not see them anymore. Life takes you to unexpected places, and you are never sure who you can or cannot take with you.

—Michael, 18

I am nineteen years old, a teenage mother, and I am still in high school. I have a little girl who just turned a month and two weeks last Sunday, and she is my life. School is harder since I had her because there are kids at school who make fun of me or call me names behind my back. When I found out I was pregnant, I was eighteen and in school. I quit school because the rumors were killing me. My own best friend, since we were in diapers, now does not talk to me. Instead, she was one of the girls talking about me behind my back. When we see each other, we don't ever look at each other. The rumors were like: I was a ho, there were ten guys lined up to be the father, I was nasty, etc.

This year I have made all new friends. My old friends, the ones who did not turn on me, we still talk, but not much.

—Ashley, 19

ADVICE

IF YOU'VE
HURT SOMEONE . . .

Is there someone in your school you've teased, ignored, bullied, insulted or hurt in some way? There are a number of things you can do to make things right.

- Stop the behavior! This includes how you act toward this person when you're around your friends.
- Step into the other person's shoes. Imagine how that person might have felt.
- Apologize.
- Refuse to participate in any form of meanness, including direct bullying, teasing or shutting someone out.
- Refuse to stay silent when witnessing any hurtful behavior.
- Refuse to gossip or spread rumors, even if the story is true.

A DAY IN THE LIFE OF A HIGH SCHOOL
FOOTBALL OFFENSIVE GUARD

The play is called
In the quarterback's huddle.
I intently listen—
Mistakes do not reflect well.

The play is clocked
Onside my focused temple
The animal knows
His measured responses.

"Blue 32!" "Blue 32!"
(He changed the play.)
I get to think, for just a moment,
From my cold, calm, calculating demeanor.

"Hut! Hut!" The ball is snapped.
I raise and pull, running to the left
In a search and destroy
Of the other team members—
Demolishing, devastating block to render.

Then it is back to the huddle
Another play called
And repeated all over.

After the game
It's congratulations—if winning,
For performance rendered,
Or frowns, for defeat engendered.
"We'll get 'em again next year," the coaches say.

But regarding next year, my senior year,
I refuse to play.
Then begins the peer-pressure swirl
Not so much from outer voices
But from emotions entangled
In teammates and student cohorts assembled.

This is peer pressure.

Animal pack entrapment.
The group comes first.
The group is Alpha.
The individual is non-entity,
Just a cog in the wheel.

Thus was I cast out.
No longer of the caste, left to foil and fumble
A new identity to re-mash.

A new order, a new social order
In search of, went I,
To fill the void, the vacuum inside.

—Justin

I really don't like the girls who think eating the top of a bran muffin and a diet coke is filling; who wear clothes that they can't walk, bend or flex in; who spend all their time in front of mirrors, caking on layers of makeup and helping disintegrate the ozone layer with their heady perfumes and hair spray, all the while refusing to move so you can use the sink.

And who could forget the boys? The boys who make you get up in the morning because they are so charming, boys who make or break your day, boys who only talk to you if they need a pencil.

—Emily, 17

It sucks being the new kid. Today, this girl turned around in history class and said, "We really like you. But you're not gonna get invited to everything 'cause you didn't grow up here." I don't even know what that means. I could not have felt any smaller when she said that to me.

—Darlene, 17

People are so worried about what their hair is going to look like, what they're going to wear, so worried to look cool . . . It's a rat race to see who's going to be more popular. Everybody's thinking: Am I going to look cool for the popular kids? Are they going to accept me?[27]

Sometimes I don't want to go to school because of the students in my classes. If I had friends in my classes, I would like it more.*

High school was like a big party I wasn't invited to.
—Tara, 22

The hardest thing about being an outcast isn't the love you don't receive. It's the love you long to give that nobody wants.
—Jodee Blanco[28]

If you are not a jock or a size 3 with nice hair, you are not accepted. You are teased relentlessly, and we wonder why kids shoot up schools.
—Cassie, 16

All my best friends since elementary school were a year younger than me, so when I started my freshman year I had to look for a new group of guys to hang out with. I had played soccer for a couple of years with a group of guys who were part of the "cool" group, so I decided that I wanted to be part of their clique. It was okay, but I never really felt like I was part of them. I continued to hang on the fringes of their group for my whole freshman year and about half of my sophomore year.

By this time my old friends were in high school with me, but I was intent on being one of the cool kids. My old friends were great guys, but they weren't exactly the coolest guys in school, and I decided that hanging out with them wouldn't help me achieve the status I aspired to attain. Things were okay, but overall I wasn't very happy. The cool guys weren't mean to me and didn't do anything to make me feel really unwanted, but they also didn't make me feel like I was welcome. I was just this unhappy guy hanging on to the status of other people hoping some of their coolness would rub off on me. I still hung out with my old friends, but I didn't give them the attention I used to, and I probably wasn't the best friend some of the time. At some point in my sophomore year, I realized that I didn't like the way my high-school career was going, and I didn't like the way I was treating my friends.

So I said, "Screw it." I stopped trying to be one of the cool kids and went back to my plain old, un-cool friends. It was the best decision I ever made. I was happier because I was hanging with people who made me feel like I belonged and cared about me. And do you know what? A funny thing happened along the way. It didn't happen overnight, but before I knew it, *we* were some of the cool kids. We had lots of different groups of friends, and we were well liked by other guys and, most important, by girls. I've thought about it a lot since graduating, and I think the thing that made the biggest difference for us was that we were having a good time. We were happy with who we were, and people like that. We were a great group of friends—we still are today—and I think we will continue to be for a very long time.

—Read, 24

I can't believe what an idiot I am. It's been clear all along that these girls didn't want anything to do with me, that they only wanted me around when they thought I could do something for them. I must have been so desperate to be a part of the group that I refused to see how they were using me. Like, if I was open enough or vulnerable enough, they wouldn't hurt me, like how dogs are when they roll over on their backs. But it was just the opposite. The

> You never know who you can trust. Somebody who's supposed to be your friend has a party and invites everybody except you and thinks nothing of it. Do they think you're not gonna find out? Or maybe they're hoping you will. . . . I doubt they care much one way or the other.
>
> —Dionne, 15

more I gave, the more they took, and the less they valued me for anything other than my having a car or cigarette money or something, the more they'd leave me out of stuff they did.

—Nicole, 18

ADVICE

When we feel shut out, alone or betrayed, we may act out certain roles or "scam styles" to get our needs met. Sometimes we don't even realize that we are manipulating others to get what we want. Do you recognize any of the following?

The Victims use helplessness ("poor me") to get others to take care of them, solve their problems, feel sorry for them and give them lots of attention.

The Depressed focus on the negatives and have a hard time enjoying their lives. They try to get people to feel sorry for them and take care of them.

The Blamers can identify why they are so unhappy—and it always seems to be someone or something else's fault. They use guilt and blame to get other people to take responsibility for their lives and make it up to them.

The Easily Hurt are super-sensitive and can take even the most innocent statement the wrong way. They take things personally and often act overly hurt or wounded.

The Angry control others by attacking or exploding.

The Hypochondriacs use sickness as a way to avoid coping with life. They can get people to feel sorry for them, take care of them or quit making demands on them.

The Rescuers want to cheer you up, fix your problems and "save" you so you will feel that you need them and owe them.

The Martyrs take on so many problems—yours *and* theirs. They want you to believe that you cannot get along without them and never leave them.

The Enablers feed your addictions and cover for your bad choices. They make it easier for you to avoid taking responsibility for your actions.[29]

Who do you know who uses one or more of these "scam styles"?

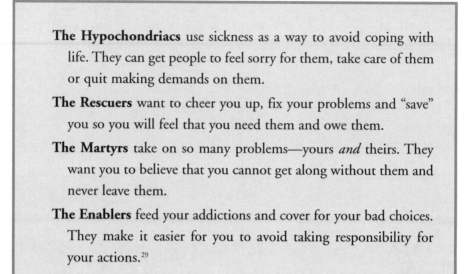

_____

_____

_____

Which one(s) do you use most often?

_____

_____

_____

_____

What do you gain when you use one of these styles?

_____

_____

_____

_____

What do you lose by using one of these styles?

_____

_____

_____

If you lose more than you gain, how could you ask for what you need (attention, friendship, etc.) without having to use a "scam style"?

_____

_____

_____

> A smile can start a friendship.
> A question can start a friendship.
> An answer can start a friendship.
> So do not always wait for somebody else to make the first move.
> Let people know you are interested in them.
>
> —*Terry Dunnahoo*[30]

MAKING FRIENDS

At times, it seems like high school has been no different from any other part of my life. I grew up in a military family, which meant I could be living somewhere as long as three years or as short as six months. My entire life has been spent leaving friends and making new ones. This high school has been the sixth school in my years of education and, like years before, I've spent my time here losing friends and making new ones.

Friendship is an awkward word when it comes to high school. It seems everyone grows in and out of relationships. It seems so fragile and yet, when high-school drama hits the best of us, friendship can be the strongest force that keeps you glued together. Being as how I've moved in and out of places so quickly, making

> No act of kindness, no matter how small, is ever wasted.
>
> —*Aesop*

friends is a skill I've mastered. But high school's made me realize that *keeping* friends is a task all in itself. I never realized how much it took, the giving and taking, the pushing and pulling, the compassion and understanding that it takes to keep a friendship going.

—Celia-Ann, 17

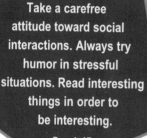

Take a carefree attitude toward social interactions. Always try humor in stressful situations. Read interesting things in order to be interesting.
—Danni, 17

Sports and clubs are a way of doing something productive and making new friends. In my case, I joined the ROTC drill team in ninth and tenth grade. In eleventh and twelfth grade, I joined the cross-country and track teams. I met all of my high-school friends through these groups.

I made no friends through my classes. I am too shy to approach people who I know already have cliques and friends. However, in the groups I joined, I had something in common with the other kids. It was easy to become close to them because we had something to talk about. Having something in common, being a part of a team, makes it easy to cross over from being acquaintances to true friends.

—Amanda, 18

One thing I really like about this school is that it's so big! I mean, it can be overwhelming at times and I don't always have enough time to get from one end to the other, but I love that there are so many kids here. We've got 4,000 students in this school, and some of them don't like me very much. I wish that wasn't true, but it is. The cool thing is, I don't always have to see them like I might if I were at a smaller school. And I guess as long as all 4,000 don't hate me, I can always find somebody to hang with, somebody to be friends with.

—Marti, 15

I make sure to confirm every single rumor about myself. Sometimes if I am bored, I spread them about myself just to have the satisfaction of laughing when they get back to me. It's like playing telephone in kindergarten.
—Danni, 17

Treat others the way you want to be treated and enjoy the friends you have regardless of how many you have, because having a few good friends is better than a ton of not-so-good ones.
—Sarah, 23

Don't make the same assumptions everyone around you is making. Be honest and open every time you look at anyone. Friends and enemies are created, not born, and the place where they are created is in your heart.
—Deepak Chopra[31]

How did I reach out to others and make friends? I just forced myself to take risks. Even if I was uncomfortable with it, I did it. It's hard to explain. I just forced myself! I knew I wanted more out of life, and I knew that breaking free of my limitations was the way to do it. I knew breaking the barriers was possible, so I just tried my hardest to do it. Of course, my friends helped me to become more social. I just hang around them more often. I was always accepted socially because I'm generally a nice person; I had to choose the right friends in the first place, though.

—Paul, 19

Some of the most valuable lessons in high school revolve around learning how to meet, get along with and resolve conflicts with your peers. Even the annoying situations are part of the education.
—Altoosa Rubenstein[32]

Personally, I'm a lone wolf. I've never liked these things [cliques] and all. I couldn't find my place, so I made one. I created the Creative Writing Club at my school, and now we're eight members strong! This is what I mean by making your place if you can't find it. You may find more like-minded people.

—James, 17

Humor is a fabulous multi-purpose tool. When used properly, it can save face, save the day and save your hide.

—Alex J. Packer[33]

I like high school because it has given me the opportunity to meet new friends. This is important to me because I like to talk to people and learn about them, especially about their background and culture.

—Michael, 17

When you are mad at a friend, do *not* seek revenge by exposing the secrets this person once confided in you, no matter what the situation. No matter how serious it may seem now, chances are you will both get over it, but things will never be the same if you tell their secrets. Second, you do not want to be known as that person who cannot be trusted with secrets. And finally, chances are, if they confided in you, you probably confided in them at some point. Do you really want those secrets to come out?

—Danielle, 22

Listening is not the same as waiting to speak.

—Anonymous

I know now that people who told me that high school was the best time of my life were lying, completely and utterly full of shit. Now I have personal skills—and friendship skills—that I wish I'd had in high school, stuff I wasn't ready to learn until a few years later. I wish I'd had a better attitude about the school, the town, the people. I'm sure I only made things harder for myself. I wish I'd picked more worthy friends, and that I hadn't needed the ones I did have as badly as I did.

—Beverly

HEALTHY VS. UNHEALTHY FRIENDSHIPS

HEALTHY

Healthy friendships are not one-sided. Both people benefit from knowing each other.

Healthy friendships are based on mutual respect.

Healthy friendships allow each person to grow and change.

Healthy friendships are not possessive.

Healthy friendships nourish you and add to your life.

Healthy friendships enable you to be accepted for who you are.

Healthy friendships allow you to have your feelings.

Healthy friendships respect differences.

Healthy friendships are safe and secure.

In healthy friendships, both people are committed to the friendship.

Healthy friendships are not about power or status.

UNHEALTHY

In unhealthy friendships, one person always seems to give a lot more than the other.

In unhealthy friendships, people ridicule one another, gossip or spread rumors, or act mean to one another.

Unhealthy friendships are threatened when one person grows or changes.

Unhealthy friendships are threatened by other people.

Unhealthy friendships leave you feeling empty and drained.

Unhealthy friendships require you to act the way someone else wants you to be in order to be accepted.

Unhealthy friendships only accept certain feelings.

Unhealthy friendships demand conformity.

In unhealthy friendships, trusts are broken, secrets are shared, and confidences are betrayed.

In unhealthy friendships, only one person is committed to the friendship.

Unhealthy friendships look to take advantage of another person's social standing in order to improve their own.

Think of your friends and the people you know. Then go through the list on the previous page. Count the number of times you would put "Healthy" next to their names.

Friend's Name	No. of Healthy Characteristics Your Friendship Has
1. _____	_____
2. _____	_____
3. _____	_____
4. _____	_____
5. _____	_____

Take a look at your role as a friend. In what ways are you a healthy friend? In what ways are you an unhealthy friend?

_____

_____

_____

_____

_____

_____

> Think about someone in your life who leaves an open space for you to be yourself. No one is more valuable. I would rather have a pillar of trust in my life than a pillar of strength.
>
> —Deepak Chopra[34]

TRUE FRIENDS

There has been one person who has guided me and helped me grasp the concept of true friendship. We met when I entered this school district in eighth grade. I can't exactly say we got along great, but we got along well enough to keep each other occupied in classes. In high school we were in a new building with new classes, new teachers and more

Good friends are always in support of another friend, no matter what. They are honest and trustworthy, and are good communicators and listeners. They act how they want to be treated by their friends.

—Ashley, 19

people surrounding us than ever before; everything seemed new and crazy.

Now our junior year is coming to an end, and we have brought each other through everything together. Many people believe soul mates are only the people that you are destined to live your life with—a romantic relationship. But I've learned that soul mates are not only for romance, but also for everyday relationships. She became a part of me. She taught me things I never had thought about regarding life, school and myself. Even in my house, she is considered a daughter to my parents. She has made me realize a friend is not someone who is there for you always, connected to your hip, but one who is there when needed the most. True friends are the ones not telling you what you want to hear, but what you *need* to hear and what you *should* hear.

—Celia-Ann, 17

Good friends stick with you through thick and thin. They will always take up for you, and they respect you. They are always there to offer a shoulder to cry on. They don't pressure you into anything that will make you uncomfortable.

—Stacie, 18

I started off last year at this school I'm at now. Halfway through the year, I transferred to the school near where my mom lives. That school had like 2,000 kids and a whole bunch of bad people, like gangs. There were so many people, nobody even realized there was a new student there. I barely saw the same people twice. They picked on me because of my accent, coming from the South, and they were stuck-up. They'd say stuff like, "I don't like you. You're different. You don't act like we do. You don't dress like we do. You're weird." They never even gave me a chance.

> High school rocks!
> I have a bunch of friends,
> no enemies I can think of, and a bunch
> of people who I don't know but who have
> somehow learned that I exist. I don't get into
> fights and stay away from drugs, although
> some of my friends have not. I make friends
> with every genre of teenager and even
> more acquaintances.
>
> —Kristofer, 14

I couldn't stand going another year at that school. I've been in a small town all my life. There were more kids in that school than there are in the whole town I came from. So I moved back in with my dad over the summer. All my friends were like, "Hey, you're back!" They were really happy to see me.

We've got about two hundred to two hundred-fifty people in the high school I'm at now. It's like I could point at everybody at my school and tell you their names and something good or bad about them. And the town that I live in, if something happens everybody knows about it.

We're like friends with our teachers. There's only so many people in the town, so you can't help but know them. In the summer you do yard work for them. We're really into sports. At my other school, the cool thing to do was drugs. Here, we'll go out in groups of fifteen and twenty and just go into town to hang out. There're gravel pits everywhere, and we just go out there and hang out, have a bonfire and chill. We don't drink or do drugs. It's just not cool. We don't think that breaking the law is fun. If there's no point in doing it, we don't do it just to see what'll happen.

Now that I'm back, I'm on the football team. I've got a whole bunch of friends. I'm friends with everybody in the school. Everybody gets along. We don't have gangs. If a new kid moves to our school, we welcome him and try to find out about him. I guess you'd call it southern hospitality. One of my friends from the next town over moved to my school. I knew him, but nobody else did. Now he's friends with all my friends. It's awesome. When I moved to my other school, I thought everybody would be like they are here. At the other school, kids were awful to teachers and to the other kids. And the day took forever when I didn't have any friends. Here I've got like two hundred of them.

—Bryan, 17

Each friend represents a world in us, a world possibly not born until they arrive, and it is only by this meeting that a new world is born.

—Anaïs Nin

I transferred to a private high school after getting kicked out of the school I had been attending. All the kids at this new school were really, really rich and really conservative as far as sex, drugs, divorce, friends dying, things like that. I'd already experienced these things, but nobody there had. So they'd look at me like, "Who is this wild girl? Where did she come from?" I was really out of place.

I was used to having a ton of friends and being really popular. Then I got to this private high school and did not relate to anybody. There was this one girl who was the complete opposite of me: She went to church. She'd never touched a guy. She didn't lie to her parents. She didn't smoke or drink. For fun, she did innocent things like go to the mall, have sleepovers, go to dances and then home right after the dance was over—being appropriate. Doing things you're supposed to do. A very normal kid, the way your parents would like you to be. I don't know how we became best friends, but we just clicked. We were in all the same classes and just ended up hanging around together. She was the only one I felt safe with. She helped me get through high school. She was always willing to see where I was coming from. And she was curious. She made me feel like my ideas were not trash. Nobody else was accepting where I was coming from.

—Simone, 21

❧

FREE TO BE ME

It had finally arrived, the last day of school. I mean the very last day, graduation day. A day I really hadn't given much thought to, or obsessed about, until my junior year.

Over the years, school's demands became more grueling. Had to have the right hairstyle, had to wear the right clothes, had to be liked by students, get good grades and not let anyone know I enjoyed the learning process, but MOST important I had to have the RIGHT friends.

Yes, picking a good social group begins early. Being Hispanic and a Californian, I felt like I had to pick a group that was assimilated. I hated the greaser, gang-member stereotypes, or as we called them "Chucos." I wanted NO part of being identified in that manner.

My friends were cheery, intelligent and most important . . . POPULAR. I found out very soon that once you lock yourself into a peer group or clique, you are pretty much in it for the rest of your scholastic career, barring some unforeseen act of God or nature. (If you are a "real person," this isn't so. I have to admit I wasn't.)

It was fun for awhile, but then I noticed there were so many other kids who were different from me/us/the group. They were from other backgrounds, other religions, and even other countries. I wanted to learn from them. I wanted to talk to them and hang out with them, but I couldn't for fear of being ridiculed. It sounds lame now, but to an aspiring kid in high school, your friends in the

> Your friends must have the freedom to live their own lives. If the two of you can share your experiences and respect each other's individuality, that's great. If not, you may be good acquaintances, but you are not really good friends.
> —Barbara Mayer[35]

> What I learned after high school: Nerds *can* have fun.
> —David

> My freshman year, I joined with my friends when they were picking on a girl because of the way she dressed and because of the people she hung out with. Eventually, she became one of my good friends because I learned to judge people by their personality, not by outward appearances.
> —Shona, 18

here-and-now seem to be your entire world. Thank God nothing could be further from the truth.

Then, graduation day was here. To me it was LIBERATION DAY and a day of mourning. It meant the end of innocence, the end of childhood and the beginning of responsibility. Total and absolute responsibility. It meant adulthood.

> Ultimately standing up to peer pressure will gain more respect than giving into it.
> —Sarah, 23

And yet, that day I cried tears of sadness and great tears of joy because I was free from the group—the mold. I had the rest of my life to be me. I made the decisions about who was cool and who I wanted to associate with and what I wanted to do. I could help pick the president, I could pay bills and pick my college, but most important I was free to be me. I love learning and socializing with all kinds of people. Yes, on graduation day I finally came out of the closet. I allowed and admitted to being a full-fledged NERD and am proud of it. Too bad I waited so long to come out.

> Trying to hold on to a friendship that has already died can only be a cause of heartache. Accept the pain, try to understand why it happened, and move on.
> —Barbara Mayer[36]

I think if I could tell what I have learned most in my life, it certainly is that high school is the here-and-now and is not your future. It really and truly isn't forever. Thank God!

—Christine

> Some things I've learned: Your smile can make someone else smile. No one *really* gets shoved into a locker, at least not all the way. People change, and the friends you have going into high school may not be the same ones you leave with.
> —Alex, 17

> One thing that I like to remember when I am up for discussion on people's list is: If people take time out of their busy day to talk about me, I must be doing something right.
> —Jordan, 17

Scar tissue is much stronger than regular skin. I believe the same is true of the human spirit. Some of the country's most successful people—musicians and moguls, authors and actors—were teen misfits, too. The heartache they endured at school defined their character and determination. Perhaps if they had it easy, they wouldn't have become who they are today.

—Jodee Blanco [37]

I was definitely preoccupied about what everyone else was doing or thinking. Now I just do my own thing, and if you don't like it, then you don't have to be my friend. I wish I would have known that I could just be myself, as corny as it sounds.

—Allie, 16

High school is still not my favorite place, but I am no longer afraid to go to school, and I am no longer unhappy. I no longer have to go to school and watch all the popular kids and wish I was one of them, and I no longer have to worry about having a few friends and being invisible to the cool people I wanted to know. I don't really care about those things anymore because popularity is a game and is not important in the long run. Today I know who my real friends are. I am glad I have a lot of friends, but the one thing I am happiest about is my realization that high school is just one small chapter in my life.

—Dan, 17

Moral courage is what enables you to stand up to your friends and say, "No, I won't show you the answers to the test. That would be cheating." This is the kind of courage that helps you stay true to your beliefs and make good choices, even when your friends tease you or snub you. It gives you the strength to admit, "I was wrong" or "I made a mistake" and to say "I'm sorry." It gives you the power to influence others when they're facing difficult decisions.

—Barbara Lewis [39]

I don't want to be friends with them anymore. I don't want them to ask me to dance. I don't want to be them. . . . I want to be me.

—Nora Ephron [38]

CHAPTER FOUR

Hookups, Breakups and Breakdowns: Sex, Sexuality and Dating

SO WHO ARE YOU going to the prom with? Few things in high school change as quickly as high-school relationships. Yesterday, we were a couple; today, we don't even speak. And for many teens, issues of sexual identity can come up for question. (Am I bi, straight or gay? What's the answer today?)

HOOKING UP

Freshman year, I went out with Brad (my first kiss), Kyle and Garry, none of which were anything too serious. I was with Garry for a week and Brad for about a month. I went out with Justin three times after breaking up with Garry. (You'd think a girl would learn after the first time.) The crazy thing is, now that I am a senior, these guys are like brothers to me, the best friends a girl could ask for.

After Kyle, I thought my life was over. No one had asked me out for a very long time, and I didn't think they were ever going to. Then Jason, a senior, asked me on a date. Wow, was I excited! Someone finally asked me out! This didn't last long, though. A guy named Derek, a senior, came into my life in November of my sophomore year. Let me tell you, he had it all: the looks, the popularity, the letter jacket and all the girls.

I was so frightened in the beginning. I had never felt this way before. Derek picked me up for school in the mornings and, if he didn't have football practice, he would take me home as well. He told me he loved me after about three months, and I said it back. I still remember it as if it just happened yesterday. I was the happiest girl in the world. I was so completely lost in him that I started to let my grades fall. As a result, I am now taking another science class to make up for the semester I failed my sophomore year.

> Dating has evolved from being just a casual get-to-know-you outing to being almost like marriage. From what I have observed with friends and from seeing other people, couples settle too fast for one another. They hook up fast, and the breakups come just as rapidly.
>
> —Katie, 18

One night at a party, he broke up with me; I was crushed. He was worried about graduating and hanging out with his friends. Funny thing is, I cried the entire night, and he was at my house the next day at noon begging me to come back. We got back together because "we loved each other."

Things were great for a while, and then we broke up a couple more times, never longer than a couple of days. About one-fourth of the way through the summer before my senior year (a year and a half into our relationship), Derek started ignoring me when we went out. We were never alone, we always did what he wanted, and he started being extremely rude to me in front of our friends. I tried to talk to him about it, but he just said, "There is nothing wrong!" and got very angry. Finally one night, we decided to end it because things were not good anymore, and he didn't know what he wanted in life. We were broken up for a week and three days, the longest time ever.

The weekend we were broken up, I made out with one of my friends whom I had been working with at the pool all summer. That was Friday night.

Saturday night, Mark, the guy I kissed, some of our friends and I went road-tripping. Mark and I made out again. Sunday night, we went on a triple date to the movies. He paid for everything and was a complete gentleman. Monday, Derek went home early from work because he was so upset about us breaking up. He called and said he wanted the promise ring that he had given me. I was supposed to meet him at his house and give it back, and afterwards I was going out with Mark. Well, things didn't quite go as planned. When I was at his house, Derek started crying and so did I. I missed him so much. We decided to give it another shot, and we both promised we were never going to break up again.

Derek was completely perfect when we got back together. He said all the right things and treated me with the respect I deserved. Believe it or not, I couldn't handle it, so I broke up with him when he went on a trip with his friends. I ended up staying the night at Mark's. The next night, Derek and I were back together again. Things went smoothly for a long time. I was in school now, and everything was fine. Mark and I were past all of the drama, so I asked him to be my escort when I was nominated homecoming queen. We are still friends to this day.

A week after homecoming, I broke up with Derek again because I was worried about what college I was going to go to and where I was going to live. I just didn't see any way for Derek to be with me unless he gave up his dreams. The night after we broke up, we talked things through and made a compromise. I plan on marrying this guy some day and having his children. I love him so much.

FACT

WHERE DO TEENS LEARN ABOUT LOVE AND RELATIONSHIPS?[40]

Friends	56%
Mother	49%
Television	41%
School	37%
Father	30%
Brother or sister	25%
Books	25%
Magazines	22%
Boyfriend or girlfriend	21%
Religion	17%
Web sites	9%
None of these	8%
Chat rooms	7%

As you can see, I have had my share of ups and downs. I wouldn't trade these experiences for anything. That is what has made me who I am today. Our relationship is ten times stronger now than it ever was because of all of the hard times.

—Julie, 17

Where did you learn what you know about love and relationships? _____

_____

_____

_____

What do you still want to know? _____

_____

_____

Where can you go for the information you need? _____

_____

_____

_____

You can either have a boyfriend/girlfriend or you can "hook up," meaning there is no commitment involved, just having fun. There isn't really such a thing as dating like it used to be, where on Friday night you can go out with one person and on Saturday you can go with someone new.

—Ashley, 19

I think dating in high school is funny. I've seen people think they are *in love* one day and *in love* with someone else the next day. It is taken a lot more lightly than it should be. I think when people overuse the word *love* it just becomes a cliché and meaningless.

—Ana, 17

It is hard knowing if guys want to date you because they think they are going to "get some" or if they truly like who you are.

—Velicia, 17

I didn't go to my prom. The guy who asked me was someone I'd been friends with for a while, but I was pretty sure he was making fun of me when he asked me to go with him. So I turned him down and went out of town that weekend. I never regretted missing the prom, but I feel bad about the way I handled things with this guy. It never dawned on me that he might have felt rejected or that it might have been hard for him to ask me.

—Belinda, 20

In my mind there was double the confusion. I liked half the guys in my senior class, but I also had a crush on two girls on my block. That's major confusion at an age when you are changing physically and mentally.

—Enrique[41]

You go to all this trouble to look good, and then some guy whistles at you and you're supposed to think it's this great compliment. Being whistled at is like being called a dog. Why can't guys just say, "Hi, how are you?"[42]

It would be a wonderful change to be appreciated for my mind, to have guys talk to my face instead of to my breasts, to have a guy look into my soul instead of into my shirt.

—Kara-Kaye, 16[43]

I can't tell you what everybody else is looking for in a girlfriend or boyfriend, but I can tell you what I want. I want friendship, a companion, someone I can sit down with and talk to for a long time.

—John[44]

Sometimes it is easier to say what is in your heart online. You can type the words and hit send instead of freezing up in person. Sometimes, in the mornings, I get love letters, and it makes me feel so good. I love hearing what my sweetie is thinking.[45]

ADVICE

Increase your chance of success when asking someone out by doing the following:

- Get to know the person first. See if you have things in common and if you enjoy each other's company.
- Ask early. Give the other person three to four days for informal dates (dinner, a movie, paintball).
- Don't ask too early—like months or years in advance.
- Choose the right moment, preferably when the other person is not upset, distracted, rushed or surrounded by other people.
- Do the asking yourself. Avoid secondhand invitations through friends to avoid possible miscommunications, gossip, rumors or looking frightened and insecure.
- Go slowly. Do something low-key and informal, maybe with a group of friends. When your comfort level and friendship grows, you can go for a date with a capital D.
- Be specific about the day and event.
- Be positive. Avoid negative invitations: "You wouldn't want to go, would you?"
- Be upfront about money and which expenses you can cover.

—Alex Packer[46]

FACT

17 percent of IM users have asked someone to go out with them through an instant message.[47]

Dating is very confusing in high school. You never date below your social class. Some people act like they don't care, but they really do.

—Elizabeth, 17

It's not just you and the other person who goes out; it seems society comes with you. You make out with your significant other one period, and two periods later you have someone who would never come up to you otherwise start to criticize your technique on the situation. Talk about no consideration of privacy.

You also lose many people close to you because of whatever your being in a relationship brings up in them. And let's not even talk about the unprecedented amount of rumors about you and what you have done, regardless of your character. I once had a girl come up to me when word was around the school that I was having some problems with my girlfriend, and she would drop clear signs that I should break up with my girlfriend to be with her. Not only do most people have no life, they become hell-bent on destroying yours.

—Michael, 18

THE FACTS

My parents have rules about how old I can be before I date:[48]
Boys 16% • Girls 34%
How about you?
❏ True ❏ False

My parents have rules about whom I can date:
Boys 8% • Girls 24%
How about you?
❏ True ❏ False

My parents have other rules for me about dating:
Boys 21% • Girls 43%
How about you?
❏ True ❏ False

My parents do not have ANY rules for me about dating:
Boys 49% • Girls 25%
How about you?
❏ True ❏ False

I was so in awe of her beauty that, even though it was expected of me as a well-respected jock to get into her pants ASAP and share the details with my friends, I was simply content holding her hand and kissing her. I confess that I kissed her with my eyes open for a long time just to watch her close to me. To the dismay and disappointment of my friends, it took us several months to actually "go all the way." Equally interesting, in terms of my friends' reaction to my relationship, was their jealousy and downright resentment of her taking so much of my time away from them! Weird!

—Bryan

ADVICE

YOU'RE GAY.
SHOULD YOU COME OUT?

The decision to come out is a significant one, especially when you're a teen. Some teens who come out are harassed and experience violence at home or at school. Some teens are kicked out of the house or are forced to run away. These things don't happen to everyone, but it's important to seriously consider your safety and well-being before coming out.

But there are many positive aspects about coming out. You can live your life openly and meet other GLBTQ (gay, lesbian, bisexual, trans-gender and questioning) people. Many GLBTQ teens say being out feels liberating. It can be very empowering to be honest about who you are.

Some teens choose to come out, but that doesn't mean you have to. In fact, in some cases, coming out might not be the best decision, at least for now.

—Kelly Huegel[49]

One year we organized a National Coming Out Day event, which consisted of putting up posters and handing out rainbow stickers. It was great. There were rainbows all over the school, on many people's backpacks who I'd never even met! But best of all, people stopped using "gay" as an all-purpose insult. When people started to realize that they knew gay people and that gay people were being affected by slurs, a lot of people stopped using them.

—Brian[50]

Some schools' policies make it difficult for supportive teachers to be vocal about their acceptance of GLBTQ people. But it's not uncommon for teachers who are supportive to let students know, in subtle or more obvious ways, their feelings. (And gradually, teachers are starting to come out at school, too.) If your school has a gay-straight alliance, the group probably has a faculty or staff advisor. If that teacher is approachable, she could be a good person for you to talk with when you need the advice and support of an adult.

—Kelly Huegel[51]

If you're lucky enough to come across an actual relationship and not just another gay boy, *congratulations!*

A common misconception is that if two boys are gay, they should date. That would be like saying just because I have two straight friends that they should get married. *Hello?* That doesn't work.

On that note, I have a best friend who is honestly a metro-area gay-boy directory. I just don't know how she does it. She knows all gay people within like a hundred-mile radius. No one really knows how, either. It's really funny. Anyway, she's naïve enough to believe that I should meet and date each one she runs into. Well, I've met a few and all of about ONE of them worked out. For a week.

Please keep in mind when dating around: *It takes all kinds.* (And first dates are actually interviews in disguise! Ha!) Brace yourself.

—Alex, 17

BREAKING UP

From what people tell me, I am a sweet, smart and beautiful young lady. In school I always had good grades, and my academic performance was always on point. But regardless of how good you are academically, friends can help or hurt you. In my case, they hurt me!

In February of last year, my life totally took a 180-degree turn. I started a relationship with this guy, and ever since then I saw life in a whole new way. In the beginning, everything was smooth sailing and I was so much happier, but I noticed that I slowly started to cut class and skip school.

Well, we fell in love, and that was when I got introduced to the drug game and fast money. I started living my life very dangerously. I moved out of my mother's house and in with my boyfriend and my brother. After that it was a wrap; school wasn't even an issue. I started smoking and drinking more than ever, coming home at all types of hours, and sometimes not even coming home at all. But somehow I felt like he was the greatest thing that happened to my life.

Now he's gone, and I realize all of this time was a waste. Now in my senior year, I'm getting grades like I've never had

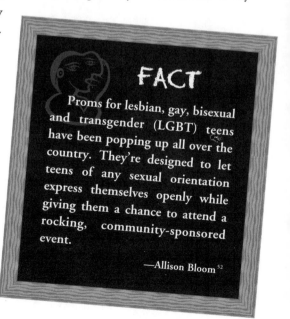

FACT

Proms for lesbian, gay, bisexual and transgender (LGBT) teens have been popping up all over the country. They're designed to let teens of any sexual orientation express themselves openly while giving them a chance to attend a rocking, community-sponsored event.

—Allison Bloom [52]

before: 20s, 30s, 40s, and now it is too late. It's the second semester, and I damn near failed *all* of my classes. I have to face the fact that I am not going to graduate.

I don't blame anyone for my downfall. I chose to do what I wanted to do. But I will say, the people around you *do* influence your decisions. My message to other people is be careful who you choose as friends. Everything is *not* always what it seems to be, and everyone around you is not always a friend. Real friends don't and won't bring you down.

—K'asha, 18

FACT

Some 13 percent of IM users have broken up with someone via an instant message.[53]

I had fallen in love. Isn't that the ultimate goal of every human being, even beyond success, fame and money? To find "true" love? Isn't that the end-all-be-all of the human experience? It was the most amazing and wonderful, fulfilling thing that had ever happened to me. Every sappy, melodramatic cliché about what love feels like is absolutely true. But when she finally left me, it was too much to deal with. I felt like I'd never be a whole person again.

—Isaac, 16

I had someone quite close to me my senior year. Everything we went through, all the drama, all the rumors, all the grudges against others, all I tried to do for her, made her break farther away from me in the end, and it has taken me over six months to try to numb the feeling I used to have when she was

around me. It was the peak time so far of my life, and we all know how someone can get to you. I do not wish that kind of pain on anyone, for you do not
know how much of a distraction this is to your focus in life.

—Michael, 18

It seems to me that losing a loved one is devastating and horrible, but having a loved one push
you away, reject you, is even worse. You have to
see this person every day, a constant reminder
of how f***ed up you are and how sad your life
is without her. You loved her, gave her everything you knew how to give, laid your soul on the
table, and she pushed you away. Not like someone
rejecting you for a little date, or being rejected for a job, but
real rejection, as deep down as rejection gets. It's as if you are saying, "Look at
me for who I am. I have chosen you of all people to truly
reveal myself to. Love me, accept
me." This person sees all of you—
you are entirely exposed—for all
your faults and all your goodness,
then she decides she doesn't want
any part of it. She doesn't want to
ever speak to you again. That's as
personal and deep down as rejection gets.

—Isaac, 16

> A boyfriend isn't a
> possession. No one can
> steal him without his
> permission.
> —Marlin Potash and
> Laura Potash Fruitman[54]

I had a girlfriend junior year.
Senior year she broke up with me because
she was afraid she'd be too attached when
she went to college. She didn't want to be
attached to anyone. We ended up going to
the same school, which was kind of funny,
but actually it was good. I started hanging
out with this other girl who was one of my
best friends, which wouldn't have
happened if we hadn't split.

—Matthew, 18

We had these exchange students from South America at our school for a couple of weeks. Some of the boys were very good looking, and they knew it. They were also pretty aggressive and more sexually sophisticated than I was used to. One day, one of them cornered me in the library and stuck his hand up my blouse. I pushed him away, but I was really freaked out. Rumors spread like crazy after that. His friends would snicker and call me *puta* (whore) when I walked down the hall, and even people I thought were my friends started to distance themselves from me.

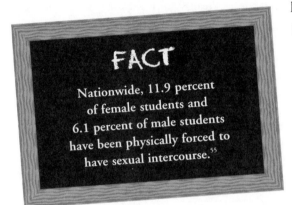

FACT

Nationwide, 11.9 percent of female students and 6.1 percent of male students have been physically forced to have sexual intercourse.[55]

I was a nervous wreck, and I guess it showed. After French class, the teacher kept me in to ask me what was wrong. I really lost it. I hadn't planned on saying anything, but I guess it all just came spilling out. She insisted that I tell the counselor. If I didn't, she would. I don't know if my experience had anything to do with it or not, but within two weeks those kids were gone and the harassment stopped. It was incredible. These people were really there for me.

—Cookie, 16

Remember that sex is always a choice. Rape is *not* your fault. Report it, even if it's a friend.

—Danielle, 22

ADVICE

SIGNS OF AN ABUSIVE RELATIONSHIP

Like any relationship, dating can be healthy or unhealthy. Here are several signs of an abusive relationship. Check those that apply to your current relationship.

Does your boyfriend or girlfriend:

Put you down in front of other people?	❏ Yes	❏ No
Publicly tease or embarrass you?	❏ Yes	❏ No
Demean your ideas?	❏ Yes	❏ No
Disregard your feelings?	❏ Yes	❏ No
Badmouth people or things you care about?	❏ Yes	❏ No
Use alcohol or other drugs as an excuse for his or her behavior?	❏ Yes	❏ No
Try to cut you off from your friends?	❏ Yes	❏ No
Take things out on you?	❏ Yes	❏ No
Get angry at you and you don't know why?	❏ Yes	❏ No
Treat you poorly, apologize, promise he or she will never do it again—and do it again?	❏ Yes	❏ No
Blame you for things he or she has done?	❏ Yes	❏ No
Deny that he or she has hurt you?	❏ Yes	❏ No
Make it clear that he or she calls all the shots?	❏ Yes	❏ No
Threaten or intimidate you to get his or her way?	❏ Yes	❏ No
Use physical force or violence against you?	❏ Yes	❏ No
Make you engage in sexual activity you don't enjoy or aren't ready for?	❏ Yes	❏ No

If you answered yes to one or more of these questions, it means that you're almost certainly in an abusive relationship. Abuse can be emotional or psychological, as well as physical. If you think you might be in an abusive relationship, get help. Talk to your parents, a teacher or a school counselor, or contact a teenage or domestic violence hotline. (See Resources at the back of this book.) Another person's bad behavior is never your fault. And you don't have to take it anymore.

—Alex Packer[56]

THE FACTS

DATE VIOLENCE

- Nearly one in ten high-school students will experience physical violence from someone they're going with. Even more teens will experience verbal or emotional abuse during the relationship.
- 10 to 25 percent of girls between the ages of fifteen and twenty-four will be the victims of rape or attempted rape. In more than half of those cases, the attacker is someone the girl goes out with.
- Girls are not the only ones who are abused physically or emotionally in relationships. Boys also experience abuse, especially psychological abuse. Boys rarely are hurt physically in relationships, but when it happens, it's often severe. Boys also can be pressured or forced into unwanted sex, by girls or by other boys.
- Violence happens in same-sex relationships, too. When it does, gay and lesbian teenagers often don't know where to turn for help. If they are not comfortable telling people that they're gay, that makes their situation even harder.[57]
- 8.9 percent of students nationwide have been hit, slapped or physically hurt on purpose by their boyfriend or girlfriend (i.e., dating violence) in the previous twelve months.[58]

SO, WHAT'S UP?

It is very possible to have meaningful relationships in high school, however, it is a good idea to learn and move on when things don't work out. Many people who date the same person all through high school often end up making sacrifices when graduation rolls around so that they can be together. This is a time in life for you to make your own decisions based on what *you* want. It is one of the few times in life that you can be selfish, do what you want, be adventurous and have no strings attached. Take advantage of this.

—*Danielle, 22*

> My sister is two years younger than I am. She dates and has a lot of friends. She's always on the phone and is very much in demand. Although I have friends, good friends, and go out with them, my parents bug me because I'm not as popular as my sister, like there's something wrong with me because I don't have a boyfriend.
>
> —Melody, 18

> I wanted a girlfriend all through high school, and when I finally got one, it was confusing and weird and stressful. But it also lived up to the hype, and that's rare. Pot didn't live up to its hype. Cigarettes didn't. Drinking didn't. The girl did.
>
> —*Ned Vizzini*[59]

> My prom was absolutely terrible. I fought with my girlfriend the whole night, and after we broke up, we never spoke to each other again. It was such a waste of money. I spent so much and had such a crummy time. I never wanted to go, but it was the thing to do, so I went. If I had to go back and do it again, I wouldn't.[60]

> High-school relationships are a horribly wonderful kind of oxymoronic, externally-driven false reality.
> Best bet is to simply look in the mirror: If you're smiling, you're doing it right. If you're not, change course to the direction of *your* bliss, not that of your compadres.
>
> —Bryan

I tried to get a girlfriend, but failed spectacularly. I probably shouldn't have set my hopes too high. My brother didn't get a date until senior year, so I have until my junior year to outdo him. I probably shouldn't have asked Monica. Everyone says she's crazy. She once tried to stab a guy with a pen. It was awesome.

—Kristofer, 14

If your friends really are having sex, you may feel left out or like they're growing up and you're not. Keep reminding yourself that what might be right for them isn't necessarily right for you. Only you can decide what you're ready for. Besides, if they're really good friends, they won't pressure you to do anything that's not right for you.

—Kelly Huegel[61]

SEX

You don't have to decide to have sex because of pressure in your relationship or socially. You are not the Last American Virgin. If you do make the decision to become sexually active, be safe. Understand the risks and long-term effects of unprotected sex. Sexually transmitted diseases are far too common. Many can stay with you your whole life. Get on the pill and use condoms. If you do not have an open relationship with your parents, contact an organization like Planned Parenthood for a responsible approach to having sex. Testing and preventative methods are free and confidential. Take advantage of this. Go to another town if you need to.

—Danielle, 22

In high school, sex is just an act to gain social status or feel better about yourself.

—Shona, 18

I was still a virgin. That was something I worried about every day; something I had worried about since I was thirteen or fourteen; something that particularly worried me because the average American male loses his virginity at sixteen. I was two years behind. I had lied about that so many times, to so many different people, that I could never keep my stories straight.

—Ned Vizzini[62]

The high school I was at wouldn't permit sex education because that would be promoting sex. That's not right. They think that if they teach about it, then that gives you a reason to go out and do it because then you think you know about it. But a lot of kids are going out and doing it because they *don't* know about it.

—Rhonda, 16[63]

BEING A KID AND HAVING A KID

It's the worst news possible. I'm pregnant. How did this happen? I mean, I know how it happened, but I don't know how I let it happen. Now I'm pregnant, and my mom and dad are going to kill me. Maybe I won't tell them. Maybe I won't *have* to tell them. I'm waiting for the counselor to come in and tell me what I can do. Oh God, I can't even think about what I'm supposed to do now.

I never thought I would get pregnant. We're in love, and I thought we were ready. We've talked about getting married some day when we get out of school, but I thought we were ready to make love now. Will he want to marry me still? I took one of my sister's birth control pills three months ago, the night my mom and dad went out of town.

Most of my friends are sexually active. I personally am not. I chose that path before I even took the first step into high school. My reason for being a virgin is because of my religious background, family background, and I feel that I am too young to have a child.

—Jordan, 17

I took one birth control pill, thinking that's all I would have to do. But the doctor who just told me that I'm pregnant said that one birth control pill was not enough. Why didn't I know this? I thought that taking one pill would make it safe to make love for one night. Oh God, how stupid can I be? But it was only for one night!

Am I supposed to just know how the pills work? I should have asked my sister. How did she know? Where did she get her pills? I should have asked her for a pill instead of just taking it. Asking my mom for help would have been humiliating and pointless. She would have yelled at me and told my dad. He would have hit me.

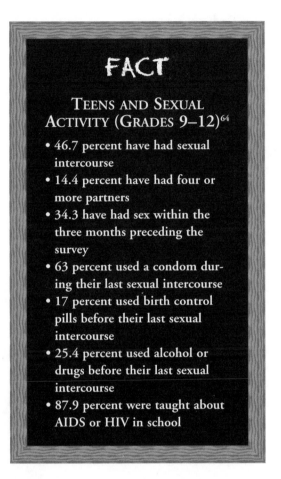

FACT

TEENS AND SEXUAL ACTIVITY (GRADES 9–12)[64]

- 46.7 percent have had sexual intercourse
- 14.4 percent have had four or more partners
- 34.3 have had sex within the three months preceding the survey
- 63 percent used a condom during their last sexual intercourse
- 17 percent used birth control pills before their last sexual intercourse
- 25.4 percent used alcohol or drugs before their last sexual intercourse
- 87.9 percent were taught about AIDS or HIV in school

Now I don't know what to do. I feel dizzy and sick. My head is swirling, and my stomach is fat. I don't want anyone to know, not even my boyfriend. I can't tell my mom. If I tell my sister, she will tell my mom. I really feel alone, and I don't know what to do. Maybe the counselor will tell me because I really don't know what to do. Why didn't I find out more about birth control pills before I needed them?

—Loretta, 16

> In school I am judged because I have a baby. I don't think that is fair at all. I don't mind the judgments because I am happy going home to my daughter and looking at her smile. That is worth everything to me.
>
> —Iris, 16

The beginning of my junior year, I found out I was pregnant. It was a nice experience, but it was also a difficult one. I had people constantly asking me when my baby was due, what sex it was, what I was going to name it and a lot of other questions. Some people asked me who the father was. Others asked me some very personal questions about my sex life. Most of the people were very nice, but there were some who were very rude. I had to deal with my grandma trying to say that my baby could be anybody's. Out of the five boyfriends I've had in my nineteen years of life, I have only kissed one of them. I also only had a sexual relationship with that same person. That person is now my husband.

—Judy, 19

Basically, I have given up everything for my daughter: my freedom, a responsibility-free world, the chance to meet new people, to go to parties without worrying about who's gonna babysit or if my daughter's gonna cry. Instead

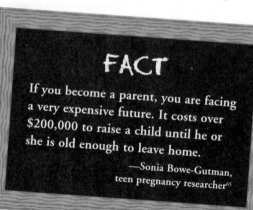

FACT

If you become a parent, you are facing a very expensive future. It costs over $200,000 to raise a child until he or she is old enough to leave home.

—Sonia Bowe-Gutman,
teen pregnancy researcher[65]

I worry if they are taking good care of her. Also, I don't get much of a chance to hang out more with my three sisters and brother. I miss the little things like just watching TV with them. That's what I've sacrificed that hurts the most.

—Cristal, 17

Throughout my life, it's been all a mess,
But the life of my baby will be a success.
I never had a mom or dad,
But my baby will have both, and she won't be sad.

I never was rich or had fancy things,
But I will make sure my baby has all of these things.
My parents were bad and never there for me,
But for my baby, I will never do any of these things.

I love my baby with all of my heart
And nothing will ever tear us apart.
She's everything to me and I love her a lot
Because she's my baby and she's all I got.

—Jennifer, 18

DO THE MATH: That $200,000 cost of raising a child works out to about $11,111 a year, $925 a month, or more than $200 a week. And that's in addition to money you might need for your car, music, clothes, hobbies or activities you're into. How would you be able to pay these bills?

_____

_____

_____

_____

_____

The consequences of unplanned pregnancies for young women and men are always life-altering. Of the nearly 40,000 teenage girls who leave school each year because they are pregnant, a large proportion never return. Teenage mothers are only half as likely to graduate from high school as girls who put off motherhood until their twenties, and only a small fraction of teenage mothers end up completing college. Teenage fathers fare no better.

—Don Nardo[66]

FACT

35 percent of girls will have at least one pregnancy before they are twenty, resulting in 850,000 pregnancies annually. Teenagers who become pregnant are less likely to finish high school and more likely to be single parents. Fewer than 2 percent will earn a college degree by the time they're thirty.

—Jill Nelson[67]

THE FACTS

TEEN PREGNANCY FACTS

- About 17 percent of sexually active teenage women report using birth control pills.
- Only half of sexually active teenagers use contraceptives the first time they have intercourse.
- Five out of six teenage pregnancies—nearly all— are unplanned.
- About 40 percent of teenage pregnancies end in abortion.

—Victoria Sherrow[68]

CHAPTER FIVE

Bloodied, Bruised and Verbally Abused: Violence and Safety in School

FOR SOME KIDS, the high-school hallways can be like going through a physical and emotional hell. Pushed, punched, slandered or slurred, each particular type of torture can leave physical and psychological scars. Do you recognize your hallway here?

A BLIND EYE

I see it happening in my head over and over again. I just remember being called ugly and a slut every day, every time I was in the hallway. It was always the same girls. In the hallways, people pretty much go to their place right before they have to go to class. They have like hangout places. You knew pretty much where everyone was gonna be after that period and, yeah, everyone is always all together. I never really understood how they got to class with all their friends with them.

The hallways were not friendly places to be. Everyone was with their stupid friends being dramatic. There was drama about anything they could start a

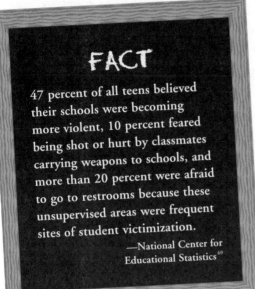

> # FACT
>
> 47 percent of all teens believed their schools were becoming more violent, 10 percent feared being shot or hurt by classmates carrying weapons to schools, and more than 20 percent were afraid to go to restrooms because these unsupervised areas were frequent sites of student victimization.
>
> —National Center for Educational Statistics[69]

fight about. Like if you were this girl who thought I liked her boyfriend, and I came up to her in a mature way and said it wasn't me who called him, then she decided to snap at me and say, "You can f***ing have him!" There were a lot of people accusing me of going after their boyfriends.

In the cafeteria, you had your table and your seat, the same people everywhere all the time. No one can ever mind their own business about anything. Girls get mad at guys and pour milk over their heads. These were the good kids, kids who played sports or got good grades. Nobody would touch them. If I was in any study halls with them, I just wouldn't go. When I tried to tell the teachers what was going on, I either got no response or they said they would take care of it or they lied and said it never happened. I was depressed and had panic attacks.

I am most angry with the school because they watched it all happen and didn't do anything about it, and they blamed me for everything. I dropped out and got my GED. I got a lot of shit for it, too. I was harassed by bitches. I had so much anxiety that it made me drop out of high school.

—Meghan, 17

> There's tons of harassment at this school. For God's sake, if you don't wear your hair the right way, they act as if you're diseased.
> If you're gay, of course, you're harassed. It seems as if the school gives us rules, but they don't enforce them. Everyone teases everyone. No one does anything to stop other students from teasing. It really affects self-esteem and confidence and grades and the students' decisions to show up for class.*

Another f***ing day of high school. God, I hate it! It's only homeroom and three kids have already called me a Jew and let me know that they are going to be waiting for me after school and I *better* be there. It's not even 8:00 in the morning, and I am trying to make my survival plan for today, avoid the problem spots in the halls.

> What I remember best at the last two high schools I attended is the nightmare of the abuse I endured, the fear that wherever I went the same thing would happen, and the guarded relief I felt every time it didn't. I wish I'd gotten some support from my parents, friends, relatives, teachers, nuns, priests, anyone. The ones who knew what was going on were not supportive, and I never felt I could talk to those who didn't know.
>
> —Jan

Shit, it's dodgeball again in gym. I better cut out on that class. Well, at least I have a couple of joints with me today so I know I can go out with the guys at lunch time. (They don't give a shit about me, but at least for the moment, as the old saying goes, a friend with weed is a friend indeed.) I can drive away for a couple of periods and get stoned. That will keep me "safe" for a while, but shit, I will have to come back to school later. How am I going to get the things I need from my locker and not get humiliated or punched out? How? How? Why the hell does this happen to me every f***ing day! Why doesn't *anyone* stop it? The teachers hear the teasing and taunting. They, along with the principal, know I am spending as much time as possible stoned. Hell, in chemistry the teacher is telling the class a story about two kids who were caught wasted out in the parking lot. Well, shit, one of those kids was me, and as I am here in class today listening, I'm tripping on acid. I am in PAIN, and I need HELP, and THEY KNOW! What is going on? Hey you, counting the days until you retire or you chatting with the popular cute student in your class, HELP! I am in pain! HELP! In trig class, right after getting back from my two periods of liquid lunch, the teacher sadistically says, "It smells like alcohol in here." He goes up to the preppie kid sitting in front of me and sniffs around for a while, looks right at me, makes some comment to let me know he knows, and then goes on with the class. My life really hurts, and all I can do now is try to smoke enough

FACT

Students who thought hazing was a problem felt isolated from adults.

40 percent of the students said they wouldn't report hazing.

When asked why they would not report hazing, 36 percent replied: "There's no one to tell. Who could I tell?"

27 percent said, "Adults would not know how to handle it." [70]

pot to pretend it is bearable. At home at night I am silent, entrenched so deep in my own head. Partly still stoned, deeply depressed, my anger turns to its only available victim: me. I don't know how to say to my parents: "Help me. I'm really messed up." I can't admit I am desperate, sad, alone, an outcast in high school. I have come to live believing every cruel thing that has been said to me or about me is real and true. I wish I could fade away. I am frightened, but even harder to show is the fear and anger. I no longer wait until reaching school before contemplating my plan of avoidance. My weekends become planning sessions. My only consultant is my marijuana-affected mind. What are my options? I know my thinking gets more desperate day by day.

—RICKY, 17

How can you absorb new information when you have to be in fear of your life every day? When you can't trust the other kids in the hallway? In the cafeteria?

—Erika

FACT

More than 160,000 students skip school daily to avoid harassment from other students.

ADVICE

How do schools handle bullying, harassment and intimidation? Some are very active and attentive in discouraging it. They have teachers who notice how kids treat one another and who intervene when they see trouble brewing. They encourage kids to report incidents and take them seriously when they do. They have "safe rooms" throughout the schools—places kids can go when they feel threatened that offer more protection than, say, the bathrooms or stairwells.

Unfortunately, most kids (and many teachers) report that this is not the case in their schools. Many kids report being blamed for the abuse they receive, being promised attention the situation never receives, or being encouraged to somehow disappear—either to eat lunch alone in the office or library to avoid harassment in the cafeteria, drop or change a class, or in some cases, leave school or transfer out.

Describe the bullying, harassment or hazing at your school.

_____

_____

_____

_____

Are there places in your school that feel safer than others? If so, where are they?

_____

_____

_____

_____

IF WORDS COULD KILL

As I sit in class, I think to myself, *How could people be so cruel to others and not even care how it makes others feel? What did these innocent people do to deserve all this humiliation?* Nothing, but just try to make it in this difficult but wondrous part of life. High school is supposed to be filled with humorous and shocking moments, not ones of regret and misery. The sad part about all of this is that nobody knows about it. These victims of bullying are scared of telling because of being labeled as a NARK. So what can we, the people witnessing this, do? Confront people when you see them bullying someone and ask them how they would feel if they were in that person's shoes. So think about this: If our school walls could talk, what would they say about our behavior?

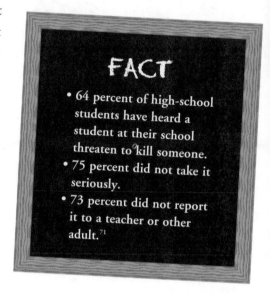

FACT

• 64 percent of high-school students have heard a student at their school threaten to kill someone.
• 75 percent did not take it seriously.
• 73 percent did not report it to a teacher or other adult.[71]

—Carey, 17

I've only been out of high school for two years, so I can remember a lot of the feelings I had. I don't remember ever feeling as if my life was threatened, although we knew some students carried weapons. In fact, I had a few friends who did so strictly for self-defense. They never bragged about them or showed them around.

Walking toward the building, you could always tell when the school was using the metal detectors. There were massive lines outside the doors. My classmates thought these security measures are a joke. If they wanted to bring a gun into school, they could do it, easily.

—Joanna, 20

It was a dark and stormy night, the night before I started the ninth grade. Well, actually, I can't remember what the weather was like, but I was anxious about starting high school because of things I heard from others who had already been there. The seniors had the "right" to demand that the freshmen wear certain articles of clothing and make them perform strange and unnatural acts. I believe this is called hazing. We freshmen were told we all had to wear white socks. I would occasionally see seniors torturing my fellow freshmen by making them stand on one foot while doing strange things with their fingers, hands and faces. Fortunately, I was not harassed in that fashion. Unfortunately, the maturity of these people would not change for my entire high-school experience.

The first year was a real drag. (Well, all four years were!) I wanted to rebel against the hazing, but I was afraid to, so I compromised with myself. I wore white socks, but I put on a pair of black socks over those. They weren't gonna make me do anything I didn't want to!

—Jon

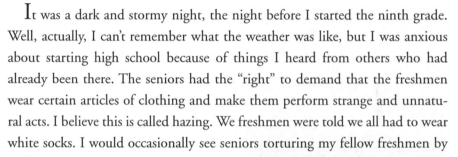

THE FACTS

Hazing is any humiliating or dangerous activity expected of you so that you can join a group (sports team, club, gang, etc.).[72]

- 48 percent of students who belong to groups reported being subjected to hazing activities
- 43 percent reported being subjected to humiliating activities
- 30 percent reported performing potentially illegal acts as part of their initiation

THE FACTS

Nearly three-quarters of the high-school students who reported they were hazed said they had one or more negative consequences.

- 24 percent got into a fight
- 23 percent were injured
- 20 percent hurt someone else
- 18 percent had difficulty eating, sleeping, concentrating
- 16 percent committed a crime
- 15 percent considered suicide
- 10 percent got in trouble with the police[73]

Daily, more and more people would use those words—fag, homo, queer, sissy. Eventually, things moved from not only words, but also to violence and pranks. The word "faggot" was written on the locker next to mine because they made a mistake about which locker was mine. People put gum in my hair, stuck papers on my back and threw things at me. There was physical violence, death threats. The school did "the best they could do," as they put it. In my mind, little was done.

—Robert[74]

Aside from the usual disagreements that erupt into fights, we have groups of powerful kids in our school who have fiercely loyal followings that would really go after anyone who disagreed or reported them.*

Girls punish other girls for failing to achieve the same impossible goals that they are failing to achieve. Girls who are smart, assertive, confident, too pretty or not pretty enough are likely to be scapegoated.

—Mary Pipher

Calling somebody else fat doesn't make you any skinnier. Calling someone stupid doesn't make you any smarter.

— "Cady"[75]

THE FACTS

HARASSMENT OF GAY TEENS

- High-school students hear an average of twenty-six anti-gay comments every day: 97 percent of them hearing derogatory remarks from peers, while 53 percent hear homophobic comments made by school staff
- 65 percent of GLBTQ students reported being sexually harassed, 42 percent reported physical harassment, and 21 percent reported physical assault
- 83 percent of the GLBTQ teens had been called names or threatened
- 65 percent had been sexually harassed with sexual comments or inappropriate touching
- Nearly all gay teens are repeatedly harassed at school and are three times more likely to drop out or commit suicide than other youths.[76]

You can't stop conflict between students. You can have monitors ten feet from each other throughout the school, and there will still be fights. I was in a fight in the cafeteria, and my anger and adrenaline totally blocked out the teachers and monitors and every single authority figure around me.

The only thing you can do to prevent fighting is to set harsh punishments. Let it be known that fighting will result in expulsion and enforce it. I think the school spends too much time worrying about cell phones and not enough time on the students who are getting teased ALL DAY and going home crying—the kids who are getting constantly teased because they are overweight or their family doesn't have enough money for designer clothes. These are the kids who get guns or make bombs and come to school. Instead of arresting or expelling them, talk to them and find out why they brought the gun to school. Expel the kids who tortured them relentlessly for the past ten years. The verbal harassment should be taken a lot more seriously. If a student comes in the office and says, "A bunch of girls were calling me fat," suspend them. Most of the fights in this school are caused by teasing.*

ADVICE

PROTECT YOURSELF: REPORT HARASSMENT

You do not need to take it, and you don't need to handle it alone. Here are a few steps you can take to reduce the risk of harassment, bullying and abuse:

- Keep track of what went on. Write down what was said, what was done, who was involved, and where and when (date and time) it happened.

> You always had to be careful who you bumped into in the halls or who you looked at.
> —Joanna, 20

- If you have identified a safe adult (see page 226) talk to him or her about what's going on. You're more likely to get the help you need if you can get an adult involved.
- As much as possible, approach the authorities in your school in a calm and rational manner. State the facts and share a *copy* of your documentation. Request support or intervention without threatening anyone. Make it clear that you feel your safety is in jeopardy.
- If adult intervention does not seem to have any impact, or actually makes things worse, do not give up. Adults don't always have all the answers. Some adults might blow you off because they don't know what to do. If you get a blank look, a brick wall or a response that you don't like, tell somebody else. There *is* a caring adult out there. Keep trying, keep trying, keep trying.
- If necessary, look for support outside your school. Call a local or national help-line that can advise you of where to go for help. (In some areas, dialing 211 will connect you with a local Infoline.)[77]

Adults would not be subjected to racial taunting in the workplace or be expected to endure insults directed at body size, clothing or accent. It would be rare in the adult world for an individual to be shoved up against a wall, knocked to the ground, spat upon, groped, attacked by a group of colleagues for coffee money or denied access to the bathroom until they forfeited their ball caps.

—*Irene McDonald*[78]

High school sucks with every senior calling me a stupid freshman. That's not cool. Sometimes I feel like saying something, but I won't because they might beat me up.

—Marc, 14

STICKS AND STONES

FACT

Teens are victims of violence more than any other age group.

—William Goodwin[79]

THE FACTS

GIRLS' TOP 10 SAFETY WORRIES (AGES 13–17)[80]

Being attacked with a weapon	35%
Being forced to do something sexual	34%
Getting a disease such as AIDS or cancer	32%
Getting into a car accident	29%
Being called names	27%
Being gossiped about	25%
Being teased or made fun of	22%
Being kidnapped	20%
Terrorist attacks	15%
Natural disasters	13%

It's a Crisis . . . Now What?

I was repeatedly pushed and beaten on the school bus. One time I actually blacked out from a blow to the head. The bus driver just laughed, and the other students yelled out, "Cool! Do it again!" And it wasn't just me. I saw kids shut in lockers, put up on the flagpole, beaten up, and verbally and physically harassed—all in the presence of the teachers.*

High school is where you realize the unpredictability of your own journey in life. You realize that good things happen to bad people, and bad things happen to good people. An event may happen, and you may not have an immediate protector. You may have to experience this event and make decisions by yourself.

—*Peter Volkmann*

Crises come in all shapes and sizes. 9/11, the shootings at Columbine High School or the death of a loved one are all examples of obvious and extreme crises. Sometimes the cause of a crisis can be less extreme. Divorce, moving to a new school or losing one's home can all throw a person into a state of crisis.

—*Peter Volkmann*

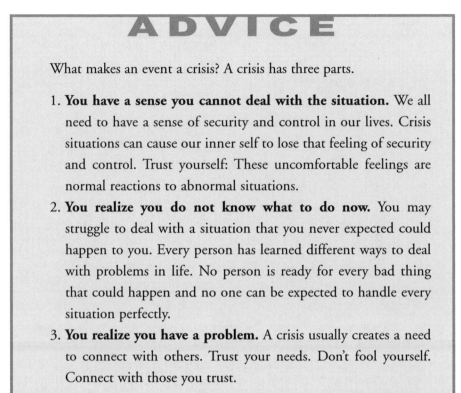

ADVICE

What makes an event a crisis? A crisis has three parts.

1. **You have a sense you cannot deal with the situation.** We all need to have a sense of security and control in our lives. Crisis situations can cause our inner self to lose that feeling of security and control. Trust yourself: These uncomfortable feelings are normal reactions to abnormal situations.
2. **You realize you do not know what to do now.** You may struggle to deal with a situation that you never expected could happen to you. Every person has learned different ways to deal with problems in life. No person is ready for every bad thing that could happen and no one can be expected to handle every situation perfectly.
3. **You realize you have a problem.** A crisis usually creates a need to connect with others. Trust your needs. Don't fool yourself. Connect with those you trust.

—PETER VOLKMANN[81]

What are some things that can be done to deal with a personal crisis?

_____

_____

_____

_____

_____

ADVICE

It is not what happens to you in life that really matters; it is how you deal with what life gives you. High school is the time we realize how much we cannot control. Pretending that things will get better or "not understanding" the reality of an event no longer works. Welcome to adulthood. Here are some "crisis-buster skills" that work for adults; they just might work for you as well.

1. **Talk to someone you can trust.** It would be best if this person is a well-grounded adult who you respect. Every time you talk about what happened, you give your brain an opportunity to process the event. Processing events includes sifting through the emotions caused by your experience and realizing your skills in dealing with the event. By connecting with others, you do not feel you are alone.

2. **Watch what you eat.** You may find yourself craving comfort foods that are not nutritious. Examples are chocolate, doughnuts, chips and French fries. Try to stay away from caffeine. Your body has been stressed, and caffeine stimulation will only add to the stress. Drink a lot of water to allow your system to flush out stress chemicals. Eat nutritious foods such as fruits and vegetables. Be careful in using alcohol and recreational drugs to numb yourself and make you feel artificially better. These chemicals have short-term effectiveness with long-term negative ramifications.

3. **Do something relaxing.** Take time to laugh with others. Watch a funny movie. It is important to laugh and have fun. You laughed and had fun before the crisis; allow yourself to have fun again.

4. **Practice deep breathing.** Deep breaths have an immediate effect in lowering stress in your system. Give it a try when you are not stressed out. It is relaxing. No kidding.

5. **Get back to your normal routine.** If your life has changed where you will never have the past version of normalcy, such as with the death of a loved one, create new normal routines. Humans find comfort as creatures of habit.

6. **Buddy up.** Make an agreement with someone that each of you will keep an eye on the other. Spend time with a trusted friend or family member. If you care about their life, they in turn will care about your life. Find a safe adult you can contact if you are struggling with life. Add new safe adults as life takes you on your journey.

—Peter Volkmann[82]

Most of my class was going to the public high school. I told my parents that I wanted to go to the Catholic high school instead. They were surprised and not particularly happy about my decision. My grades had fallen dramatically in the last two years; the teachers had told them that I had not been "applying myself." Tuition would be high, there were no buses to the school from where I lived so I'd have to be driven both ways, and they'd have to buy uniforms for me. It didn't matter. I had to go to that school. I got hysterical over my decision, and my mother finally sided with me. I took the entry tests, passed, and it was a done deal. I was so relieved. At last I could escape the hell that was my life.

Or so I thought.

Because of the distance to the school, my mother arranged to pay a boy who was a junior to transport me to and from the high school. Another junior friend of his would also ride, as well as two of my former classmates from junior high. I didn't know which two until the first day of school.

More bad luck: The other two were boys who had been part of the gang of my junior-high tormentors, although they had been minor players. At first I thought that everything would be all right; summer had given us all some space. I had blossomed over the last three months, and I no longer looked like a little girl. The braces I'd been wearing for the last three years had come off, too. But none of that mattered to them. I was still the same girl, the one to be jeered at. Once my former classmates had settled in and made new friends, they were quick to start in on me again.

The major difference in this school was that all of the abuse on school property was strictly verbal, and most, but not all of it, was concealed from any adult or faculty member. And I was no longer "Dogface" or "The Dog." I was

You really *can* help stop bullying and aggression. Making it cool to be nice rather than cool to fight is a great place to start. If you believe that standing up to a bully will put you at risk—and in some situations it can do just that— you can still help by becoming an ally of the person being picked on. Simply being nice to kids who are the targets of aggression or teasing, being accepting of them or acknowledging them, can make a tremendous difference. And anything you can do to help validate their experience ("Wow, that was pretty harsh!" "He had no right to say/do that to you." "Boy, you didn't deserve that!") can provide more support than you can imagine.[83]

christened with a new name—now I was "Tweety Bird," or just plain "Tweety." I had no idea who came up with that or why. Maybe it was because of my diminutive size or my nervous demeanor, just like Tweety always on the look-out for Sylvester. Being called any name not of my choosing was humiliating, but it was nothing compared to the previous two years.

Where it got ugly was in the car.

Every once in a while, on the way home from school, the driver would stop at a bookstore or some other shop. On these occasions, his friend would go with him, and our instructions would be to stay in the car. As soon as they were out of sight, I would get jumped. My classmates were too mature to beat me anymore; instead, I would be held down and groped, their hands and fingers squeezing here, pinching there, their hands crawling up my legs. Once in the fracas, a button was ripped off my blouse and the blouse was torn. None of these encounters lasted very long or progressed very far. To them, it was just fun, but the effect on me was devastating.

During this time I did a pen-and-ink drawing. In the middle of the paper is a

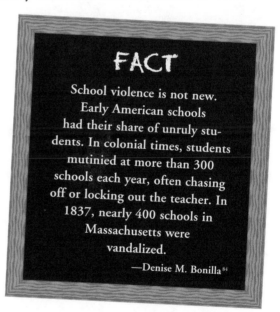

FACT

School violence is not new. Early American schools had their share of unruly students. In colonial times, students mutinied at more than 300 schools each year, often chasing off or locking out the teacher. In 1837, nearly 400 schools in Massachusetts were vandalized.

—Denise M. Bonilla[84]

naked woman. She is crouched, her legs drawn up against her belly. Her arms are clutching her head, which is bowed tightly down. There is no ground or foundation beneath her; she is simply there. She looks defeated, as if she is trying to protect herself from a bomb blast. Beneath her and to the right are the words, written in my old microscopic script, "There is no mercy." For me this drawing expressed perfectly the depth of my misery, and I felt some release after finishing it.

But release soon turned to panic and fear. What if someone saw it? They would know. They would know what was happening to me, and I couldn't, I wouldn't let that happen. I modified the drawing to make it more benign—to disguise the truth it told. I drew beautiful flowers all around the figure. I filled the page with flowers and made it almost impossible to read the message I had written. There, that was better. The secret was still safe with me.

I know that I came to blame myself, for if no one would speak up and come to my defense, didn't that mean that I deserved what I was getting? Didn't it prove that the boys were right about me, and I really was the ugliest, stupidest and most hideous freak on the face of the planet?

FACT

Surveys show that GLBTQ teens are more likely to get involved in fights at school that require them to receive medical attention, more likely to be threatened or injured with a weapon, and more likely to skip school because of concerns for their safety than their heterosexual peers.[85]

All those tortured years, I never told. To tell would be to admit that they all had hurt me and that I was a damaged person, the biggest failure of all. But what had been done to me for those four years continued to hurt me and to poison every "normal" relationship I tried to have.

Counseling was brutal, painful and frightening, but it saved my life. It gave me back the life I had lost. It let me see myself for the first time as I really was, rather than what I thought I was. It gave me the courage and confidence to accomplish whatever I set my mind to.

—*Jan*

I used to be a punching bag. Steve Urkel, Mark Foster, Ralph Whiggam, you name them—they could all look down at me and laugh. Glasses, braces, bad asthma and allergies, big-boned, very reserved—the whole nine yards—I was an irresistible target to anyone looking to establish his own "don't-mess-with-me" reputation. I didn't like where I stood in the after-school hierarchy, but I was young (and they were young). So, not wanting to cause any trouble, I took the jabs, the uppercuts and the sidearms. I listened to them say, "You're not like us. Be like us." That, to me, seemed counterproductive in and of itself: Would I like to be the kind of person who mistreats another this way? The more I didn't want to be like them, the more they attacked, the more I didn't want to be like them, and so on. It had taken me a long time to get this far in defining who I was and to believe in it enough not to change. I wasn't about to give in now. As long as I did not cry "Uncle," I was winning. I was stronger than they were.

> An "eye for an eye" leaves everyone blind.
> —Martin Luther King, Jr.

But one day, I lost. A punching bag will only swing in silence for so long. Eventually, if you hit it hard and often enough, it will swing back at you . . . hard and uncontrollable. The day I swung back—the day I lost—was the day Casey-plus-three jumped me. In the end, I was not hurt physically, but I felt a peculiar mix of nausea, fear and degradation. I felt brutal, knowing that I was capable of doing what I had done to another—four other—human beings. I instantly became haunted by a vision of my future, transformed into a ruthless monster controlled by his own anger. I had never, nor have I ever since, been so afraid. I cried louder and deeper than the four on the ground before me. For the next several days, I sent myself into near exile. I wouldn't talk to or interact with anyone. I had let loose Mr. Hyde, and I couldn't be certain how easily he could break free again.

—Adam, 18

A D V I C E

YO . . . CHILL-OUT

What do you do when a fight starts in your school? It takes courage to do the right thing. This isn't easy, but here are some things you can do.

- Refuse to watch, join in or encourage incidents. (Standing by passively is not going to help.)
- Speak out: "Don't treat him that way." "Stop hitting her." "Hey, cut it out." "Don't call him that name." "This isn't right."
- GO GET HELP!
- Make a joke to try to diffuse the tension or distract the aggressor in a neutral, nonthreatening way. (This can be risky, even if you inject some humor or tell a joke.)
- Bear witness and report incidents. There is no dishonor in telling if your sole intention is to prevent a problem, stop a problem or help somebody else. (See page 102 on how to report incidents.)
- If the adults you approach do not seem helpful or supportive, it may be because they just don't know what to do. Whether you are the target of aggression, or if you're speaking up on behalf of someone else, if the adult's response does not feel supportive, *do not give up*. Go to other adults until you get the response you want.
- Be a friend to the person being bullied. Make an effort to include students who are normally left out or rejected.
- Realize that the bully may also need help or a friend.
- Learn to recognize mob mentality. Kids will do things together that they will not do on their own. Take a breath. Are you getting caught up in the emotion of the group? Ask yourself: Is what you are doing or saying hurting somebody?

Any of these strategies can make a significant difference in the quality of the school climate. *It's okay to do the right thing.*[86]

How do students at your school encourage fighting?

_____

_____

_____

What could you do to prevent fighting in your school?

_____

_____

_____

What could the adults do to prevent fighting?

_____

_____

_____

What are you willing to do the next time a fight breaks out, either to avoid being involved or to actively help de-escalate the conflict?

_____

_____

_____

What needs to happen in a school so that students will not need to fight?

_____

_____

_____

HOLDING ON, HANGING IN AND STEPPING UP

There was a gym instructor, Mr. Boyle, who was an okay kind of guy. He was short and stocky, and someone to be respected. Hard to believe, I know, but true! He was a nice, friendly, nonjudgmental kind of guy. As long as you tried, he was happy. Unfortunately, I never had him as an instructor. I knew about him because there were several gym classes going on simultaneously in the gymnasium.

> Students won't stop fighting until they see that there are other ways to handle it. Telling them won't be enough. They have to see results.*

One day, one of the thugs that I had the misfortune of having classes with, Dan, was harassing one of the other students, Dave. Like me, Dave was a bit overweight and lacking in self-confidence. Dan enjoyed preying on people like us for fun. He was pushing Dave around, poking him with his finger and just generally saying nasty things to him.

I saw a red streak fly through the air. It was super Mr. Boyle, flying through the air with the greatest of ease. He did a mid-air tackle, and he and Danny were on the floor! Danny was totally freaked out. Super Mr. Boyle was more pissed than I have ever seen. He had a hold on old Danny boy and was yelling in his ear, trying to get his attention and pointing out that that type of behavior was not acceptable in school or society in general.

> New high-school students will be able to recognize the trouble areas after the first week of school. Just look out for the kids who are obviously causing trouble and never make contact with them. Don't pick fights with them; just leave them be and let them destroy their own lives.
>
> —Paul, 19

All of us were ecstatic! Finally, justice had been done to one of the bullies in school! They usually got away with murder, or at most a slap on the wrist. We were hoping Mr. Boyle would kill Danny, but, alas, no such luck. Danny had detention for several days and that was about it. But I never saw him hassling Dave again. And he was always quite sheepish when around Mr. Boyle.

There were fights . . . from the first day of school. Where the staff was, I do not know. I myself was not a fighter. So my way of dealing with the violence was to become a joker and to be invisible.

—Andy

It's unfortunate that not all bullies were disciplined, and the ones who were, only a few times. I used to puzzle over this, and I think that most of the teachers enjoyed watching this happen. I think quite a few teachers in high school dislike the majority of the students.

—Jon

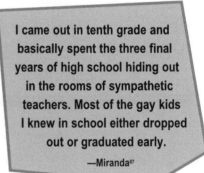

Being "out" in school is really tough. Once a boy who didn't like me began yelling comments at me in the hallways. I ignored it, as usual. (You learn to after a while; it's just OLD!) He took it far enough to come to the window of one of my classrooms and do it. He was suspended. It's just not worth trying to "catch" everyone, though.

I came out in tenth grade and basically spent the three final years of high school hiding out in the rooms of sympathetic teachers. Most of the gay kids I knew in school either dropped out or graduated early.

—Miranda[87]

Once (while I was coming out), I decided I would test the world and count how many comments I got. I was called a "faggot" *thirteen times*. Within what, five minutes? There's just no point in trying to stop it all. If you truly love yourself, that should be enough.

Plus, the homosexual community in general is beginning to take back the word "faggot." Think about it. If WE use it, we demonstrate that it really doesn't have the effect it used to; we can show strength and confidence against opposition.

Again, if you need to, *talk to somebody!* It's not fair to go through anything alone.

—Alex, 17

Expressing your angry feelings in an assertive—not aggressive—manner is the healthiest way to express anger. To do this, you have to learn how to make clear what your needs are and how to get them met without hurting others. Being assertive doesn't mean being pushy or demanding; it means being respectful of yourself and others.

—*American Psychological Association* [88]

There are too many kids on the buses. Kids need their space. People come into less conflict when they're not so crowded. We should probably have cameras on the buses, and people should actually look at them. I witness a lot of harassment on the bus.*

ADVICE

STICK UP FOR YOURSELF

Let's say that someone in your life is doing something that really bothers you. You want them to stop what they're doing. What can you do? If you can't simply *avoid* the other person, you can do things that can make it more likely you will get what you want. Regardless of the relationship you have with the other person, you need to be strong and assertive in dealing with the behavior.

Here are some alternatives:

- Respond to a confrontation or criticism by "agreeing" and changing the subject. For example, someone says something critical or nasty, and you simply say, "Yeah, no kidding," and start talking about something else—or just walk away.
- Request a different behavior (or ask that a certain behavior stop): "I don't like that word. Please don't use it around me." "Please quit asking me if I want to get high with you."

- State your preference: "I don't care to discuss that." (And then cheerfully change the subject, redirect discussion.) Or "Please don't touch the stuff on my desk." (No need to justify or explain why.) Or simply, "No, thanks."
- Use a "promise:" "You can borrow my CD as soon as you return the last one you borrowed." "We can continue this discussion when you can stop yelling at me." (And walk away.)

If the person continues to mistreat you, you may want to re-evaluate your attachment to that person, or consider spending your time and energy on people who value you and treat you more respectfully, as you deserve. Certainly, if the behavior escalates, or starts feeling like harassment or abuse, *tell someone!* (See page 102 for practical tips on reporting harassment.)

CHAPTER SIX

Too Big, Too Small and Not the Right Look at All: Body Image and Health

ARE YOU OBSESSED with six-pack abs or the size of your butt? How much time and energy do you put into trying to look a certain way in order to feel happy? What does it cost you physically, emotionally and spiritually trying to attain the perfect look? Here are some of the challenges you can face when trying to get your body through the high-school experience.

DO I LOOK FAT?

Obesity. Doesn't that word sound horrible when you speak it? A few years, and more than one hundred pounds, ago that word never fazed me as much as it does now. I have had firsthand experience with this extremely contagious "disease." I have stared it in the face, buckled down and conquered it.

My weekends consisted of lying on the couch eating bags of candy, bowls of ice cream and cereal. I would eat fast food daily. When

119

I came home from school, I sat and ate until dinner. This disturbing trend followed me throughout my early teenage years. Eating was my passion; it consumed my life.

> I find it impossible to ever be satisfied with my body. After each pound slips away, I still find the need to be thinner.
>
> —Sarah [89]

I lacked self-confidence, avoided social situations and stayed home. Every day in class I would be called names, most of them extremely harsh. I was an easy target! Since I was afraid to fight back, the verbal abuse would be spewed from all directions. Did I realize there was something wrong? No, but soon I received a rude awakening.

In ninth grade, applying for working papers was more than I had bargained for. A compulsory physical was needed, and I was afraid to have this performed. I acquiesced and had the district doctor perform the procedure. I stepped on the scale, closing my eyes. Descending, I saw the number: 297. My heart sank! A few days later an envelope from the school health office arrived in the mail. Apparently, my blood pressure was way off the charts and my cholesterol level was through the roof. Something needed to be done, and soon. Eager to reform my ways, I vowed to lose at least fifty pounds over the summer.

I began the weight-loss process. I dreaded the treadmill, the StairMaster, the recumbent bike and the dumbbells, but I got accustomed quickly. Initially, I would burn about 300 calories via cardiovascular work and then eat triple that when I got home as a reward for my hard work. However, those little "pat on the back" sessions quickly came to a halt. By the end of the summer, I had trimmed roughly forty pounds. That was such a confidence booster; I could not wait for school to begin!

I am presently 110 pounds lighter and teeming with self-confidence. I am now my family's inspiration. The "new" me, as cliché as it sounds, is ready to pursue an exciting future. Losing such a large amount of weight was an amazing experience. Although my battle with obesity has been both a physical and emotional roller coaster, I am now a believer that anything is possible.

—*Andrew, 17*

ADVICE

WHERE IS THE PROOF?

I am too fat, thin, short, tall; my muscles or my breasts are just not big enough; I'm ugly. These thoughts plague us all from time to time, and if we choose to focus on believing them, they can really drag us down.

So what can you do about these thoughts? Try putting your thoughts on trial, just like you see on TV or in the movies. Ask yourself: Where is the proof that any of these characteristics about myself are not good enough? Sure, you might believe it, but believing it does not make it true. If you were to believe that you are seventeen feet tall and green, would that really be accurate? If you can change your thoughts, your feelings will change as well.

I knew I shouldn't have gone. For the past few weeks, it was all anybody talked about: Senior Day at the lake. Big picnic, minimal supervision, celebrating our upcoming graduation. But I should have known better. (Anything involving *this* body and a bathing suit could not have turned out well.)

God, what was I thinking? Down by the lake, people saw me coming, but even the people who are supposed to be my friends acted like they didn't know me, mortified that this enormous blob would come near them. Nobody talked to me all day.

There was plenty of food, but I don't feel comfortable eating in front of other people, and to be honest, I didn't have much of an appetite *for once.* Swimming was nice—the contrast of the warm sun and the cool water was strangely comforting. I don't need companions to swim and besides, in the water, nobody can see your thighs, right?

I figured things would be better that night at the dance. I had this really cute outfit and put a lot of time into my hair and makeup. I actually thought I looked pretty good, all things considered. I walked out to where the dance was and saw these two friends coming over to me. Cool. We were gonna hang out and dance and talk and everything was gonna be okay.

But no.

They just came over, picked me up and threw me into the lake. I could hear people laughing hysterically as I broke the water, went under, went down, praying desperately that I could just die down there and never have to come up, ever. But I did come up. By then, seconds later, the show was over, and everyone's attention had drifted elsewhere.

It was the worst moment of my life. Worse than that day in gym class when I couldn't climb up the rope. Worse than when that guy "mooed" at me when I walked down the hall. Worse than that party when a well-meaning neighbor took the snack out of my hand and said, "You really don't need that."

I was a liability to my friends, a joke to the others. I'd never felt so alone, so isolated, so disliked in my entire life. I spent the evening alone, waiting on the bus, dripping and shivering, counting the seconds until I could go home and get away from these people.

No one came out to check on me or see if I was okay. I doubt that anyone even noticed I wasn't there. I never even went in to hear the music, something I normally love. I couldn't bear to be around any of them. I hated them—almost as much as I hated myself. I wanted to hurt them. I wanted them to feel the pain I was feeling. Don't they know that there's a person in here? Yes, even under all this fat.

—Carrie, 18

Food was carefully monitored in my household. My mother was either "on" a diet or "off" a diet. Since I was overweight, I was only allowed to eat certain foods that were low in calories. More enticing foods were "off limits." Of course, the more forbidden something is, the more you want it. Those cookies and other treats would call my name. I would sneak food upstairs. My mother kept a watchful eye on the sweets. We would go through a ritual to determine who had eaten the two missing cookies. It was okay if my brother or sister had eaten them, but not if I had. This led to a tremendous amount of guilt. It got to the point that I would walk to the store to get my "fix." I also remember walking to the store to replace the forbidden foods I had eaten. Needless to say, guilt was associated with eating anything that wasn't considered a "diet" food. The kids at school and my siblings constantly made fun of my weight. In gym class I was usually one of the last two people picked for team sports.

> High school has done a number on my body image. Ironically, it's the biggest problem in my life, and no one really knows about it. I am not the least bit overweight, but it's hard to see such an emphasis placed on "that perfect body" every day at school and not think I'm fat.
>
> —Krystal, 17

When I hit high school, I was tired of the constant teasing. I also became interested in boys. At the age of sixteen, I decided to essentially stop eating. Over a three-month period, I ate a bite or two of my dinner, and that was my food intake for the day. I cooked dinner and cleaned up, so it was easy to hide what I had not eaten.

Out of desperation, I started purging, making myself throw up. That started a whole cycle of eating, feeling guilty about it, feeling desperate to get rid of it, and then feeling relieved after purging. The more I did it, the harder it got to purge.

I had major dental problems from all of the purging. In addition, I had no energy and had trouble getting out of bed in the morning. At one point my potassium was dangerously low, and I had to take potassium supplements to keep my heart functioning normally. During the school day all I could focus on was what I was going to eat when I got home. I got good grades in school, but my major goal was getting home to eat. My mother was at work, so I knew that I had time to eat and vomit before she got home. I had a sore on my hand and broken blood vessels around my eyes. I also had recurrent throat infections.

The constant thoughts about food and the isolation I put myself into because of my eating disorders kept me from living my life. My mother even warned me not to tell the extended family about my eating disorder.

I found a support group. It was helpful, but I had a need to get beyond hearing about what people ate, how many times they purged and how many laxatives they took. I was never very good at speaking in big groups of people. I decided to find a private counselor to help me with my individual issues. To this day, I still have issues with food. At times of any intense stress or sadness, I want to eat.

I know now that purging only makes me feel worse, and it does not keep me from gaining weight. I was at my heaviest when I was purging regularly. I am not saying that I do not have occasional slips, but my life is more balanced than in the past.

—*Sharon*

ADVICE

WHEN REAL ISN'T REAL

The "perfect women" you see on TV and in movies, or in magazines and catalogs, have an image that's simply unattainable for about 99 percent of the female population. That perfect body you want to achieve does not generally exist. Even the most perfect-looking models have a lot of help to look the way they do. Makeovers, surgery, full-time trainers and the miracles of photo retouching, which can eliminate zits, elongate torsos, lengthen legs, enhance cleavage and hide a multitude of flaws, account for much of what we see in the media. (Oh yeah, by the way, that guy with the six-pack abs and the rippling muscles? He just might be a creation of Photoshop, too!) Work with what you've got, but learn to love what you see in the mirror!

My high-school years were spent very differently from those of the average teenager. While most of my classmates were thinking about getting their drivers' licenses, who to go to the prom with, the football game on Friday night or where they were going to go to college, I was battling my own demons. I don't remember a single time that I was more concerned with the average high-school things than I was about food, working out or losing weight. I was completely uncomfortable with myself, and I hated the whole "Oh, my God, did you see her outfit today?" scene. I despised how completely fake everyone was, but I totally gave into it—I never went to school without my hair done, my makeup on, and a cute pair of shoes on my feet. Sweats were not an option. Neither was leaving the house without makeup—I had to make sure that I looked good for everyone so that they wouldn't talk about how crappy I looked. But no matter how cool my clothes were or how many "friends" I had, it was never enough to make me feel secure about myself. Even though I had one awesome best friend and a boyfriend I adored, I just couldn't deal with those insecurities like everyone else seems to. I found an alternative that made me feel powerful, and in control and good about myself.

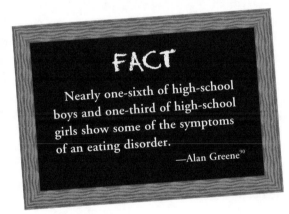

FACT

Nearly one-sixth of high-school boys and one-third of high-school girls show some of the symptoms of an eating disorder.

—Alan Greene[90]

Years of not being true to who I was were catching up with me—I was miserable. I started bingeing and purging as a way to block out how much I was hurting. When I was in the middle of a binge, nothing else mattered. I was totally focused on the food—how it tasted, how much I just wanted to be full. I wasn't thinking about anything else. I eventually stopped bingeing, and I got to the point where I was throwing up everything that I ate.

An eating disorder seems like it's about food and being thin on the surface, but it is really about emotional issues and feeling in control. After I came back from treatment, nobody really understood how uncomfortable I was. Going back to school was terrifying—I was scared that everyone would treat me differently and think I looked fat. I didn't want people telling me that I looked healthy because to me that meant they were pointing out that I had gained a lot of weight. But nobody understood that logic. So a lot of people told me I looked great, which was really hard for me to hear. Even though the symptoms weren't there, the thinking was still there. It was really hard because most people thought that I was cured. They had no idea how much I was struggling. Nobody really understood how uncomfortable I was. I had one teacher look at me when I came back and ask me what he was supposed to do with me. I was mortified—like I had to have a babysitter or I couldn't handle going to health class. It was awful, but I tried as hard as I could to be normal even though I had no idea what had been going on at school. What was even more difficult was that no one knew what to talk to me about, and I had no idea what to bring up, so conversation was awkward. I didn't want to talk about my fear foods, my group therapy session from the day before or how I was having gastrointestinal problems.

Needless to say, I spent a lot of Friday and Saturday nights at home with my family.

Eating disorders don't just go away, and no matter how good they can make you feel, eventually that good feeling will wear off. Eventually the hair on your head starts falling out, you're cold all the time, you grow hair all over your body (the body's attempt to stay warm), and you have no energy for anything. I realize that people need to get help when they're ready. But I also know how an eating disorder can destroy your life.

—Arianna, 22

HUGE AND RIPPED

I noticed in my senior year of high school that my fellow athletes were gaining on me in terms of strength and size. This was not all that surprising as I was athletically gifted, but not dedicated enough to stay atop the heap forever. Interestingly, a few fellow sportsmen made incredible gains in very short times. One guy wrestled 135 pounds our junior year and benched 185. Come senior year, he was benching 300-plus pounds and weighed upwards of 185 pounds. Another friend gained similar weight and strength the same summer.

> Guys are in competition, especially in the weight room. One will say, "I can bench 215 pounds," and the other guy says, "Well, I can bench 230 pounds." If you're stronger, you're better.
> —Jon Maxwell[91]

I didn't really know what steroids were until that year. I saw changes in others' facial structure and in their moods. They, of course, did not. The scary thing about the steroids—which were offered to me after we talked about them—is that there is no doctor's exam or any kind of testing before you take them. My friends bought them on the black market through their friends, and the cycle began. We tend not to think of the lifelong consequences, such as liver damage, reproductive system damage, etc. We just want to get big *now!* Life for high schoolers *is* high school. It's hard to imagine what comes afterwards because high school is so all-encompassing to us when we're there.

> In some cases, part of the motivation for using steroids is to improve athletic performance. But for many others, it's simply a matter of vanity, the desire to look good in a hunkified world . . . as buff as they can.
> —Bill Hewitt[92]

I was never pressured into taking steroids by my coaches, but I know people who were—indirectly at least. In the case of my buddies, their parental pressure to succeed and get that scholarship was so great that they took the easy way. Who knows how it is affecting their lives now?

—Bryan

THE FACTS

HEALTH HAZARDS[93]

The major side effects from abusing anabolic steroids can include:

- jaundice (yellowish pigmentation of skin, tissues, and body fluids)
- high blood pressure, cholesterol problems
- kidney or liver tumors, increased risk for prostate cancer
- severe acne (often on back)
- chest pains, overexerted heart, trembling
- shrinking of the testicles, reduced sperm count, infertility
- baldness (both men and women)
- development of breasts in men
- not growing, staying short
- risk of HIV/AIDS or hepatitis when injected
- extreme irritability, aggression, extreme mood swings, paranoia, jealousy, delusions and violence
- depression
- dependence
- impaired judgment stemming from feelings of invincibility
- use of other drugs to alleviate side effects

I probably felt most trapped in gym class. High-school gym class consisted of the coach throwing out three basketballs, and the classes of boys forming the "tall & talented" team, the "short-but-tries-hard" team, and the "we-don't-even-remotely-care" team. The latter I barely fit into. Most of the time I spent sitting on the sidelines waiting for the period to end.

—Joel, 21

There was always PE and showers. Because of the comparisons being made within, locker rooms are torture chambers in the memory.

—Ralph Keyes[94]

NO SWEAT

Ah, yes, gym class! Almost every fat person in the entire universe hates gym class. It's where you go to be laughed at and ridiculed, judged incompetent and unworthy by your peers and mostly by the gym instructor. You get to go there and change into your jock strap and shorts and T-shirt, revealing your body, which you yourself dislike intensely and all the other "normal" guys hate, and they let you know it.

I hated teams because I was always last or next to last to be picked by the team "captain." You know, you get that last-name-to-be-called thing going. No fun. And I really hated the "shirts" and "skins" teams. I hated having to run around with my obese chest and abdomen exposed. Very embarrassing! And usually the girls' gym class was on the other side of the

> When I would change in gym, I thought everyone was looking at me and judging the size of my breasts or thighs. But then I realized other girls were just as self-conscious about their bodies as I was. They were checking everyone else out because they felt weird about how they looked.
>
> In the locker room the other day, everyone was complaining. I mean everyone. One girl said her nose is too big. Another kept talking about her thighs being huge. A third moaned that her legs are too short and her ankles too big. They all looked fine to me.
>
> —Laura Potash Fruitman[95]

> Our gym classes are set up for kids who are already good in gym. The rest of us hate it. I hate being forced to play games I can't play, climb ropes I can't climb and run farther than I can run. I hate being picked last for teams. I spend a lot of time looking for ways to get out of class, and PE is the only class I've ever cut. I know I need more exercise, but I wouldn't be so wigged out if they would give us stuff I could actually do.
>
> —Cookie, 16

Work out.
Everyone, without exception,
should exercise. Find some athletic
activity that you enjoy and do it.
Football not your thing? Fine. Swim,
run marathons, weight train. You'll look
better, handle stress better, and it's
a great way to meet people.

—Joel, 21

gymnasium. Ah, yes, stared at and judged by everyone! Bummer!

So we're running around in gym class, playing fun things like dodgeball, climbing ropes, running miles and miles, doing calisthenics, all sorts of fun, fun things. I am a loner by nature, and I do not love teams or group activities in the first place. But when added to the competitive nature of some of those young, testosteroned, gotta-win guys, the stress levels increase drastically. Supposedly, sports and physical activity are fun and enjoyable. But they surely aren't when in close contact with instructors and peers who take these activities far too seriously.

—Jon

FACT

The average high-school graduate will have spent 15,000 to 18,000 hours in front of a television, but only 12,000 hours in school—and a lot fewer with their families. Young people who watched four or more hours of TV per day had greater body fat and body mass than those who watched less than two hours per day.[97]

Several experts contend that music, math and sports can help structure the brain faster and better than simply hanging out or watching television.

—Tim Wendel [96]

It Might Be Your Brain . . .
Ever wonder why you act the way you do? The part of your brain that helps you make good decisions and have good judgment is still developing. However, the part of your brain that loves excitement and risk and wants to have a lot of fun is already developed and working overtime!

My body is not perfect, but I don't let that fact take over my life.
—Sienna, 17

WHAT ARE YOU LOOKING AT?

FACT

EATING FOR SUCCESS

Students who receive higher grades eat breakfast more frequently and are not as distracted by hunger during class. Many students do not eat breakfast regularly or have lunch periods at the right time for them, and many believe that students are often too hungry to be able to concentrate in class.[98]

I am unique and special. There is only one of me in the world, so I have no reason to alter myself to fit the world's view of the perfect person.
—Katie, 18

Stop eating junk food. Eat healthy. If it means that you have to learn how to cook, good! It'll be just another skill that you have.
—Joel, 21

ADVICE

BUILDING A
BETTER BODY IMAGE

- Accept the fact that your body's changing. In the teen years, your body is a work in progress. Don't let every new inch or curve throw you off the deep end.
- Decide which of the cultural pressures—glamour, fitness, thinness, media, peer group—prevent you from feeling good about yourself. Then do something to counteract this (like not buying magazines that promote unhealthy body images).
- Exercise. It helps improve the your appearance, health and mood.
- Emphasize your assets. You have many.
- Make friends with the person you see in the mirror. Say, "I like what I see. I like me." Do it until you believe it.
- Question ads. Instead of saying, "What's wrong with me?" say "What's wrong with this ad?" Write the company. Set your own standards instead of letting the media set them for you.
- Ditch dieting and the scale.
- Challenge size-bigotry and fight size discrimination whenever you can. Don't speak of yourself or others with phrases like "fat slob" or "thunder thighs."
- Be an example to others by taking people seriously for what they say, feel and do, rather than how they look.[99]

Nearly 40 percent of teens who responded to a nationwide survey said they would feel better about themselves if they lost weight or bulked up.[100]

DYING FOR FUN

FACT

More kids worry about their weight than about getting in a car accident, getting cancer, being beaten up or attacked at school, or having a problem with drugs or alcohol.[101]

FACT

Water:

- allows the body and brain to communicate.
- gives the brain an instant boost and improves brain functioning.
- strengthens the immune system.
- gets rid of toxins in the body.
- increases alertness, coordination.
- improves concentration and ability to focus.
- improves academic performance and behavior.
- can suppress appetite.

Here's the deal: When each of us is born, we receive a body. You can love it or hate it, accept it or abuse it, ignore it or dress it up, but regardless, your body is the only one you will receive. The relationship you have with your body is the only one that lasts from birth to death—longer than your relationships with family, friends or boy/girlfriends.

—*Chérie Carter-Scott*[102]

THE FACTS

Here are the most common ways high-school students put themselves at risk:[103]

- had sexual intercourse (46.7%)
- had one or more drinks of alcohol in the past month (44.9%)
- did not use a condom at last sexual intercourse (37%)
- were in a physical fight in the past twelve months (33%)
- rode with a driver who had been drinking alcohol (30.2%)
- used marijuana in the past month (22.4%)
- smoked cigarettes in the past month (21.9%)
- rarely or never wore seatbelts (18.2%)
- carried a weapon in the past month (17.1%)
- were overweight (13.5%)
- went without eating for twenty-four or more hours to lose weight or to keep from gaining weight in the past month (13.3%)
- attempted suicide one or more times in the past twelve months (8.5%)
- vomited or took laxatives to lose weight or keep from gaining weight in the past month (6%)
- used cocaine in the past month (4.1%)
- injected an illegal drug (3.2%)

THE FACTS

SMOKING AND TOBACCO

Tobacco poses a unique health hazard because it is the only product that kills when used exactly as the manufacturer intends.

—Campaign for Tobacco-Free Kids[104]

The tobacco industry has intentionally designed and marketed addictive, lethal products and deliberately hidden their well-known risks.

—*Journal of the American Medical Association* editorial[105]

Tobacco is more harmful to teens than to any other age group, partly because their bodies are still growing and developing tissue is more easily damaged than mature tissue in adult bodies. Nicotine is at least as addictive as heroine or cocaine. A young person is thirteen times more apt to smoke if his or her best friend does.

—Eleanor H. Ayer[106]

Cigarettes kill more Americans than AIDS, alcohol, car accidents, murders, suicides, drugs and fires combined.

—Institute of Medicine[107]

THE FACTS

ALCOHOL: DRINKING AND DRIVING

I think it is important for parents to show their kids
that they can have fun without drinking alcohol. Many of my
friends who drank had parents who drank, and that opened
the door for abuse and experimentation with drugs,
which lead to more reckless behavior.

—Sarah, 23

There are a great number of people addicted to
illegal drugs and cigarettes. Nothing is ever done about this.
Just trying to punish kids is ineffective and doesn't
address the real problems.*

When teens drink, they increase their chances of becoming
involved in crimes, suicides and violent encounters with others.
They are also more likely to engage in risky sexual behavior.

—Haley R. Mitchell[108]

Young people who drink and drive are at a higher risk
of being involved in a crash than adult drivers who have
had the same amount of alcohol.[109]

20 percent of young people drove a car or other vehicle
after drinking alcohol. Significantly more males at 23 percent
than females at 16 percent reported this risky behavior.[110]

CHAPTER SEVEN

Oh, the Things That This Life Brings: Coping, Change and Loss

WHAT WOULD the high-school experience be without a little stress, anxiety and depression? (Fun?) Chances are, you're having to deal with a lot more than just homework and tests. Jobs, family problems and emotions can complicate even the best high-school experience. The question is not *if* you're gonna have to face these things, but *when* and *how*. Here's what other teens are going through. Maybe they have some clues you can use.

SADNESS AND DEPRESSION

Why do I cry in the shower? Because it is the only place where I am alone, the only place I can express all of the thoughts I feel. I cry because I don't like to hold my feelings inside so then that's all I think about. I don't like that I cry more than I smile, and I don't like that I always feel like this life isn't for me.

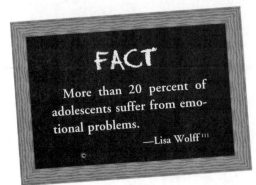

FACT

More than 20 percent of adolescents suffer from emotional problems.

—Lisa Wolff[111]

But I do like living in this world, and I love my family. That's the reason for my existence. I hate that I always feel down and that I never feel like going on. But I know that tomorrow is another day. I just always think about this quote that I heard in a movie: "This day, too, shall pass," and to me it means a lot. The worst day of your life will be a memory later on, and that's why I try to live. I think a lot about my life, and I know that now it may seem like my days will never get any brighter, but I still try. I try because I don't want to regret anything when I am older. I just want to accomplish a lot of things before I die.

—Princess, 15

Maybe I could have talked to somebody, but at the time, it didn't seem like I could. I felt invisible. I mean, everybody around me was busy with their own stuff, and I didn't think anybody really cared about my problems. My mom and dad were fighting all the time, my sister was working constantly, and my best friend spent all his time with his girlfriend. It was weird—I kept hoping that somebody would notice how bad I felt, but I just couldn't say anything to anyone. I wanted to, but I was convinced that nobody had ever felt the way I was feeling, so nobody could understand. I was scared, too.

—Steve[112]

Cultivate a support system, either in or out of school, or both, so that you can talk about problems as they occur. Get help! Don't keep problems to yourself; it will only make things much worse.

—Jan

When I feel sad or depressed, I go crazy trying to cheer myself up or I just call a friend and have a very long conversation. Other times, I make my mood worse by listening to the saddest song I can find and crying.
—Ana, 17

FACT

7 to 14 percent of kids will experience an episode of major depression before age fifteen.
—Lisa Wolff[113]

ADVICE

Signs and symptoms that can accompany depression:

- Feeling anxious, "empty" or "numb"
- Feeling hopeless, like there's nothing to look forward to
- Feeling guilty or worthless
- Feeling lonely or unloved
- Loss of interest in regular activities—things are not fun anymore
- Difficulty concentrating in school and doing homework—sometimes school grades fall
- Difficulty concentrating on other activities, like reading or watching TV—not remembering what a book or TV show was about
- Having less energy and feeling tired all the time
- Sleeping too much or not enough
- Not eating enough (smaller appetite) and weight loss, or eating too much (bigger appetite) and weight gain
- Thoughts about death—sometimes attempts at suicide
- Spending less time with friends and more time alone
- Frequent crying, often for no obvious reason
- Feeling irritable (every little thing gets on your nerves)

- Feeling restless (being unable to sit still or relax)
- Physical complaints, such as dry mouth, dry skin, difficulty having bowel movements, headaches, stomach or chest pain, vomiting, dizziness[114]

If you recognize these feelings in yourself or in a friend, it's time for you or your friends to share these feelings with a safe adult. See page 226 for tips on finding a safe adult.

SLASHED

The summer before tenth grade, I started to hang with the wrong crowd. I thought they were cool because they drank, smoked and did other deviant things. Tenth grade was huge because I was in a new school with new people, and I wanted to be cool and skinny.

I never smoked, but I stole money for the cheap beers I drank. I started to act promiscuous. By the end of the summer, I got into a physical fight with this one girl over her boyfriend and whether he liked me instead of her.

The following day, she asked me if her boyfriend had f***ed me with a pickle. My reply was "no," and she told me everyone had been saying it. I didn't think about it much because I looked good in a bikini and she didn't.

The first day of tenth grade (and high school) was probably the worst day of my life. I had to face eight hundred new faces. I took a deep breath, held my head high and walked in. There were so many people I didn't know, but they knew me. Not by Manda or Mandy, but by "Pickle."

I walked to class, but pickle-talk was all around. People I'd never seen in my life were saying I was nasty and had sex with a pickle. That's when I figured out who my real friends were and weren't.

In every class there were people taunting me. I wanted to cry so bad. I went home and cried myself to sleep. I would wake up, go to school, come home, cry myself to sleep and wake up the next morning to do it again.

I begged my parents to send me to another school or get me home-schooled. I prayed every night to just be normal. I wished all those mean people would be nice and that they knew how I felt. I swore I wouldn't be mad if the subject just dropped and I could enjoy school again.

Just a "Hey Manda, what's new?" is so much better than getting pickles thrown at you. I was afraid to go to my junior prom because I heard they were going to re-enact *Carrie,* but with pickle juice instead of blood.

I was anorexic, only ninety-three pounds and debating what's worse: being fat or being made fun of. I shrank three inches due to calcium deficiency. I was very, very unhappy. I tried to reach out and put a "signs of depression" poster on the fridge. I always slept, and I withdrew from all my friends and family. I often thought I couldn't take it anymore.

Finally, one day I locked myself in my room with a knife. I cut myself. There is still a scar there to this day. It felt like an escape. I went to do it again, but my older brother had seen me go into my room with the knife and got suspicious. He kicked my door down and grabbed me, then he sat me down and watched me until my parents got home.

I have never been more scared in my life. When they finally got home, my brother said I needed to be checked out. My parents laughed at me and said nothing was wrong, that I was just looking for attention. My brother finally told my parents what I had done. They transformed before my eyes. We were in the car heading to a hospital with a psych eval unit in the blink of an eye.

While the doctors were observing me, my father paced back and forth, screaming, "No child of mine is a nutcase!" and "She's fine. There's nothing wrong with her!" My mother was crying; I think that's when she finally got it. The next morning I was released, and my mom got numbers of doctors who take our insurance.

We went to the first doctor we could get into, which was about a week's wait. It was the longest week ever. My mom followed me everywhere. She camped out in my room at night. She sat on the toilet when I show-ered—forget the curtain, she had to monitor me—and I couldn't cook dinner or use sharp tools.

I couldn't talk on the telephone without an eavesdrop-per. They wanted to make sure I wasn't getting any more ideas. Eventually, I got to see a counselor and a psychiatrist. Every Monday I chatted with the counselor for an hour and with Dr. K whenever I ran out of pills.

My counselor, Mark, convinced me that food was my friend and reassured me that everything was okay. I liked spending time with Mark. Dr. K would growl and pick his nose a lot. He would ask me irrelevant questions. I seriously think he got me confused with other patients.

Part of Mark's "food is good" program was for me to get a part-time job at McDonald's. I only worked there for six months, but between the anti-anorexia therapy, the side effects of the medication, and McDonald's being my favorite food, I blew up to 180 pounds.

After I quit McDonald's, my family and I went on a mini-vacation. We went to the shore, but I refused to wear a bathing suit. I wore turtlenecks and jeans to cover up my fat thighs and turkey neck.

It was 90 degrees, and I was hot and once again unhappy. I had to see Dr. K, and he asked me how I was doing. I said some bad words, and he rustled around some papers and told me he couldn't see me anymore. I was actually glad. I hated the pills I was on. I walked around like a zombie, and if I forgot to take them or was two hours late, I had a panic attack. Believe me, they aren't fun. I was so embarrassed that I would go in my room to be by myself.

After being fired by Dr. K, I didn't go back to another shrink. I didn't want to explain everything all over again. I stopped going to Mark, too. I thought it was a waste to be "half-cured." And it wasn't good enough.

After that, I didn't care. I had a real F-you attitude. I got loud and bitchy, and if anyone started with the pickle, I gave them a piece of my mind. Even to this day, with less than one month to graduation, I still hear it and wonder, *Why?!*

In a few short months, we are going to be out on our own in a college somewhere. I had expected teasing and name-calling in junior high, but not high school (especially my senior year).

I quit McDonald's about thirteen months ago. I haven't exercised greatly, but I portioned my foods and didn't eat so much fast food. I'm down to about 150, and I'm comfortable in my skin. So what if don't wear a size zero

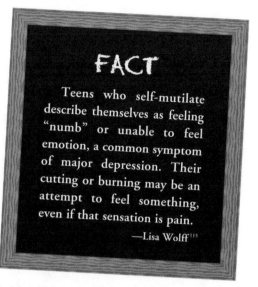

FACT

Teens who self-mutilate describe themselves as feeling "numb" or unable to feel emotion, a common symptom of major depression. Their cutting or burning may be an attempt to feel something, even if that sensation is pain.

—Lisa Wolff[115]

anymore? I think I look good and feel confident, and you can't convince me otherwise.

To this day, my father is in denial and swears I'm a drama queen. I ask my mom to talk to me, but she softly replies, "Okay, honey," and then changes the subject.

—Amanda, 17

I didn't want to tell anyone. I was extremely ashamed of what I was doing to myself, although at times when I did cut myself, I felt an amazing sense of power, of control. But afterwards I felt ashamed, guilty and always alone. So scared, too frightened to talk. I became uncommunicative and reverted into my shell.

—Jae Chesson, 15[116]

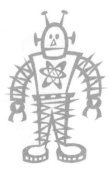

THE LESSON LEARNED

"Times are tough, and times are hard,"
I said as I picked up the shard
And placed it against my wrist,
And began to turn and began to twist.
Then the blood began to flow
Out of my arm and I watched it go,
The shard of glass fell from my hand . . .
I couldn't stand.
Like the glass,
I fell down.
Too stressed-out and all tight wound
On the edge don't topple over.
I'd have died if I'd been sober.
All the drugs and all the drinking damn near killed me,
So start thinking—is it worth the risks you take?
Is it worth the sacrifices you make?

—Melissa, 16

I see so many kids
hanging out, smoking [marijuana],
drinking and all. It's the stress: They've got to
help pay the bills, there's no father in the house
or mom's out doing her thing. They don't know
any other way to handle the stress, so there
they are getting high.

—Delisa, 18

WASTED DAYS
AND WASTED NIGHTS

High school was one of the worst times of my life. Frankly, I think there were times I just stayed as busy as I could so I wouldn't notice how much pain I was in. Drugs, alcohol, cigarettes and food were alternate ways to numb out when they were available. No, I'm not gonna recommend them, but I can certainly understand their appeal. I guess the workaholism, which is kind of a drug in its own way, ended up paying off for me because it turned into a diploma that was also my ticket out of that nightmare and a way to escape my family and the town we were in, which I also hated. I might have dealt with what I was going through, socially and emotionally, if I had a shred of evidence

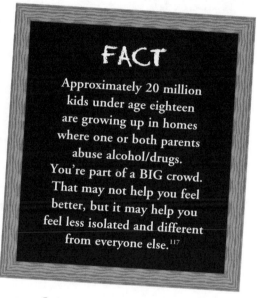

FACT

Approximately 20 million kids under age eighteen are growing up in homes where one or both parents abuse alcohol/drugs. You're part of a BIG crowd. That may not help you feel better, but it may help you feel less isolated and different from everyone else.[117]

that there was anyone I could really trust. I eventually found the support I needed—a good thing, because after a while, nothing could keep me numb for long.

—Beverly

When I wasn't wasted, I felt bored, lonely and depressed. I thought I was ugly. I didn't fit in with anyone. When I drank, I felt more mature. I'd dress in revealing clothes and wear lots of makeup. Eventually, I got to the point where I didn't care what happened to me. Guys that I'd go out with would treat me really bad, and I'd let them. After a while, I couldn't have a good time unless I was wasted.

—Leah[118]

Drugs really affected one of my good friends during sophomore year. He was a completely different person when he was on drugs, which was nearly every day. When I talked to him, it was like I was talking to a stranger. I could have told his parents or guidance counselor or someone, but I didn't because I knew he would get mad. I now regret not having told anyone. He left for college, and for all I know he is failing out.

—Elizabeth, 17

I'm a huffer. I know I'm addicted. I used to pretend that I wasn't, that I could quit anytime I wanted. But it's too hard to stop. Getting high is what I like best of all; it's all I ever think about.

—Marty, 16[119]

I tried every mood-altering substance to which I had access, anything to take me out of where I was, to make the feelings go away. I was looking for something that would make me normal.

—Kathy Cronkite[120]

I know I'll always be an alcoholic. I mean, you can stay sober a long time, but if you start drinking again, you're going to get the exact same stuff happening in your life again. That's a given, you know? You won't suddenly be able to handle it, I guess. It just won't happen for you. Maybe if you're like a normal person, you can. But for me, and for other kids like me? Never. I should never drink.

—Miranda, 16[121]

ADVICE

Along the journey through high school, many students face the issues of addiction and recovery. If you are abusing anything (drugs, alcohol, sex, gambling, etc.) and want to change your life, here are some things to consider.

- Change is hard. You will need to ask for help.
- Some people may not want you to change. You might have to say good-bye to them.
- Others may not understand why you seem different. Be patient with them.
- If you hang around the same people you were with while using, chances are strong you will use again.
- Using occupied a part of your life. Find something healthy to fill that time (exercise, volunteer, go to a 12-step meeting, etc.).
- Learn from others who have gone through a similar experience. Ask your doctor, teacher, counselor or any other safe adult about finding a support group in your community.

Suddenly, there was pressure from all sides. I couldn't find enough hours in the day to study, go to classes, work, eat, socialize and sleep. So sleep was the first thing I cut out. Being tired made the stress even greater. I found myself lighting up at least once an hour. I smoked to relax after classes and at night, and in the morning I smoked to get stimulated and focused before I went to class. Smoking really helps your concentration. Pretty soon—like within the first month—I had nailed down a pack-a-day habit.

—Will, 18[122]

ADVICE

DRUG-FREE STRESS RELIEF

- Take a warm bath/shower.
- Walk, run or swim (great ways to release endorphins, your body's natural feel-good drugs).
- Talk it out (sharing lets out some of the intensity).
- Learn relaxation breathing and muscle relaxation exercises. (See page 157.)
- Practice and rehearse situations that stress you out.
- Challenge your negative thoughts. Change "I can't do chemistry" to "I have had little success with it so far, but I could improve in chemistry with extra help, more study time, asking the teacher more questions, finding a partner(s) to study with, etc." (See page 268 for more on changing unhealthy thoughts to healthy thoughts.)
- Take a break from the situation that is stressing you out. Listen to music, draw, write, hang out with your pet. Try moving to another spot or room.
- Break it down. You don't have to learn the whole chapter at once. Get the first main idea down and feel good about that, then move on to the next.
- Eat spicy food . . . another good source of endorphin release.
- Drink water to ensure that you are hydrated. A hydrated brain handles stress better.
- Stay away from nicotine and caffeine, which can increase anxiety.
- Help another person. Sometimes the best way to get past our stress is by doing something for others.

THE FACTS

In a survey of one thousand high school students, the following were identified as the most difficult part of being in school. Note that some students checked more than one item.

Getting good grades......70%

Pressure from parents ...45%

Pressure from teachers ..39%

The rules.....................33%

Knowing what to do
   after high school.......33%

The social scene............31%

Too many kids..............25%

No one knows me.........13%

Stress reactions vary from person to person: What's challenging and curiosity-provoking to one individual can trigger paralyzing fear in another. Just because a subject or activity is easy and pleasurable for you does not mean it will be for everybody else.

WOUND-UP AND WIRED

After about a week of what was supposed to be the "best years of my life," I came to my mom, crying. I told her that I hated school and wanted to drop out, even if that meant I would work at a terrible job for the rest of my life. Patiently, my mom explained that I was *not* going to drop out of high school, and that it takes a few weeks to adjust. I listened, but I still wasn't so sure. After all, my friends seemed to have no problem with this adjustment. I was just a loser. So I went to my dad. My dad told me the same thing my mom had, and added that I probably felt like a loser because according to upperclassmen, I was one. And so were all the other freshmen.

I started to think that maybe my parents were right, but I still wasn't 100 percent sure. So I called my grandmother. After all, she had taught high school for several decades, so she ought to know something. My grandmother, just like my parents, said that I just needed some time to adjust.

The most difficult part of being in school is the pressure I put upon myself to succeed. I'm a perfectionist in all I do, and I worry and get stressed about just about anything.*

With this knowledge in mind, I set out to school that Monday. I still hated school, but I knew that it would get better. And it did.

—Morgan, 14

Stress is the general feeling you get as a result of a lot of different kinds of problems and challenges. Imagine that every word, relationship problem, tough homework assignment and issue with a parent is a separate rubber band around your head. As your life gets more complicated, more rubber bands are layered on until your head is completely covered. Stress is the pressure you feel on the inside.

—Earl Hipp [123]

A Day in the Life of a Teen Mom: It's 6:00 in the morning, and I am waking up as my boyfriend and my baby's dad, Saul, is getting ready to go to work. I really don't want to get up, but I have to. I take a bath, and it's now 6:20. Time to do my hair. Now it's 6:38, and I have to get my two-year-old daughter ready for daycare. I finish getting her ready, and now I have to pick up my room so it won't be so messy. It's now 7:15, and I am running out the door, getting in my car and driving to the daycare. I talk to my daughter to let her know she's going to daycare. I am worried that she's gonna cry. (I feel horrible when she cries, like I am a bad mom.) It's now 7:30, and I am leaving her in the room at daycare. She's doing okay, and I am running out the door, going to school. I get to school, sit down and the late bell rings. We start class. I am so sleepy. On to second, third, fourth, fifth, sixth, seventh, and finally eighth period, the last class. I am doing well in school, but I am so tired now. Time to go to the daycare to pick up my baby. I missed her so much. It's 2:30, and I am driving to pick up my boyfriend from work. I pick him up, and now he's driving me to work. I have to be at work by 4:30. While he's driving me to work, this is when we get a chance to catch up on what happened in our day. He drops me off at work and goes home with our baby. I usually work four hours on school days. At work, we get a fifteen-minute break. I usually use that time to do some of my homework. It's finally 8:30. Saul comes to pick me up. When I get home, he has already given the baby a bath and picked out her clothes for daycare. That's a big help. She always waits up for me. Saul's mom leaves food so that I can eat when I get home. I eat and finish my homework while Saul puts Kari to bed. I am just so sleepy. It's now about 10:00, and I am so, so tired and sleepy, and so is Saul. We go to bed to start again tomorrow.

—Cristal, 17

> What would make school more supportive of what I need would be just for people to realize we are teens who have other things going on in our lives that can affect schoolwork, like jobs, family and relationships. The teachers push and push and don't know when it's enough.*

> We get way too much homework. I don't think we need so much. I saw this TV show that said kids do better in school if they don't have so much homework because they have more free time to do other stuff and don't have so much stress. Also, the books are too heavy. Some of the girls are having back problems from carrying their books around all day.
>
> —Matt, 17

ADVICE

SEVEN SLEEP-SMART TIPS FOR TEENS[124]

1. Sleep is food for the brain: Get enough of it, and get it when you need it. Even mild sleepiness can hurt your performance—from taking school exams to playing sports or video games. Lack of sleep can make you look tired and feel depressed, irritable and angry.

2. Keep consistency in mind: Establish a regular bedtime and wake-time schedule, and maintain it during weekends and school (or work) vacations.

3. Learn how much sleep you need to function at your best. You should awaken refreshed, not tired. Calculate when you need to go to sleep to get at least 8.5 hours of sleep a night.

4. Get into bright light as soon as possible in the morning, but avoid it in the evening.

5. Get to know your internal clock (your circadian rhythm). Then, you can try to maximize your schedule throughout the day. For example, to compensate for your "slump (sleepy) times," participate in stimulating activities or classes that are interactive, and avoid lecture classes or potentially unsafe activities, including driving.

6. After lunch (or after noon), stay away from coffee, colas with caffeine and nicotine, which are all stimulants. Also avoid alcohol, which disrupts sleep.

7. Relax before going to bed. Avoid heavy reading, studying and computer games within one hour of going to bed. Don't fall asleep with the television on—flickering light and stimulating content can inhibit restful sleep. If you work during the week, try to avoid working night hours. If you work until 9:30 P.M., for example, you will need to plan time to "chill out" before going to sleep.

The National Sleep Foundation recommends that teens get 8.5 hours of sleep on a school night. Teens typically sleep seven hours, and 12 percent of teens sleep less than six hours. Sleep-deprived students are more likely than others to feel tired, daydream, have difficulty paying attention or fall asleep in class. Students who feel they do not get enough sleep are more likely than those who feel they get enough sleep to skip class.

ADVICE

DON'T LET YOUR BACKPACK GET YOU DOWN

Toting all your books, notebooks, calculators, snacks and water bottles can be a real pain in the back. Here are a few tips to help you prevent injuries that can become long-term back problems:

- Watch the weight. If your backpack forces you to lean forward to carry it, it's too heavy! If you can't avoid carrying more, consider getting a backpack that has wheels and a telescoping handle.
- Pack smart. Load the heaviest items closest to your back.
- Use both straps. Carrying your backpack over one shoulder can cause neck and back pain, headaches and posture misalignment.
- Get a quality backpack, one that's not too big and comes with well-padded or air-filled straps and cushions for your lower back to help distribute the weight properly.
- Learn how to lift. Face the pack, bend at the knee, use both hands and lift with your legs.

—Nancy Tipton[125]

WHAT CAUSES THE
MOST STRESS FOR YOU?

✓ When a teacher is in a bad mood and takes it out on me

✓ Stupid school drama

✓ Smarter kids in the class and the teachers favoring them

✓ When teachers and parents put extreme expectations on me that
  I feel like I have to meet

✓ When there is a conflict between schoolwork, sports and my job

✓ When I have all these expectations and goals to meet

✓ Standardized tests

✓ When teachers think their class is the only class I care about

✓ A class that is chaotic

✓ A room that is too small or has too many students, without proper
  ventilation

✓ A classroom without windows

✓ Having multiple exams in one week

✓ When adults want me to be a genius (I am a regular person who excels
  in certain areas, not unlike my peers.)

✓ The verbal and physical abuse of my peers

✓ Adults who are afraid to give me a compliment

✓ Adults who constantly focus on what I do wrong and never notice what
  I do right

✓ Competition for grades; competition for college admissions

✓ Finding a social niche

Anxiety for me came in the form of panic attacks, general anxiety about performing well on exams, and embarrassing myself in front of others. The panic-attack problem stems from general anxiety, so coping with this part was the first task. I went to a psychiatrist and was given a medication that helps resolve the chemical imbalance inside the brain. This helps, but it isn't the entire solution.

The first way of coping with a panic attack is to break the cycle of thinking about the same fear over and over. To accomplish this is actually quite simple and, when mastered, can be done at almost any time. There are many different techniques for coping with anxiety, but one stood out and worked very well for me. Doing relaxation breathing for as little as a few minutes can drastically reduce a person's anxiety and can be done as much as necessary. It never loses its effectiveness.

Another great way to reduce anxiety is to put cold water on your wrist or the back of your neck. The cool water simply diverts your attention to something else, breaking the cycle of thinking of the same thing over and over. Finally, it is important to remember that "this too shall pass" means that just because anxiety is present now doesn't mean it will be forever—all bad things come to an end.

The fear of not performing well on exams is a problem that feeds on anxiety, but can easily be stopped. My father put a large amount of pressure on me to do well in sports, school or anything I tried to do. If someone is putting pressure on you to do well in school, confront them on it; it is best for the relationship. Even after my father stopped putting pressure on me, I still found the need to put the pressure on myself to do well on exams even when no one was forcing me to do well. This made high school very rough because of the pressure of getting into college. Finally, I asked myself, *What does this test really matter in the scheme of things?* It is only one test; it doesn't make or break me.

In my case, anxiety caused me to have to use the bathroom if I got too nervous, which took time away from the exam. To resolve this, simply ask a doctor to write a note for you to be able to have more time. A note for more time is very common for a plethora of different reasons. Having extra time to take my tests enabled me to overcome my anxiety about testing situations.

The most annoying problem is worrying about how I am perceived by others. If I do something, will I look stupid? I didn't want anyone to see I was nervous. What if I had to use the bathroom on a long car trip? These were all sources for anxiety. You need to ask yourself: *If nobody was around, would I feel embarrassed?* Most of the time, people aren't even paying attention to what you are doing, so they won't notice. And what if they do notice? Well, if they are anal enough to point it out, they probably don't feel good about themselves and do things just as stupid, if not more stupid. Finally, most of the time you are nervous, you think people can tell very easily. Most people can't tell at all. There is no sign that says "Hi, I am nervous" on your back. Do whatever you need to do to calm down and forget about it.

And don't sweat the small stuff. There are way too many problems in life to focus on one simple thing. Have I been limited by my anxiety in high school? Only if I let it. Do I care what others think about me? Yes, but only to the extent they know I am not a jerk, nothing more. Is taking medication a bad thing? No. (Would you say to a person with high blood pressure or a hyperactive thyroid, "Don't take medication"?) Anxiety is a chemical imbalance. To this day, I still take medication for it. In college, I look back now and realize high school was pretty short, and to get worked up over three or four years is not worth it. Take high school for what it is worth, make friends, try your best and have fun.

—*Peter, 19*

ADVICE

RELAXATION BREATHING

L earning how to breathe can really help. You can relax your mind and your body by doing this simple exercise.

1. Place your hand just above your belly button. You will notice that as you breathe in, your diaphragm pushes outward, and as you exhale it moves back inward.

2. For relaxation breathing, we need to reverse this. As you inhale, try to pull your stomach inward; as you exhale, push it outward. Keep practicing this with your hand above your stomach until it becomes clear.

3. Inhale slowly through your nose for a five-second count, hold that breath for five seconds, and then slowly let it out through your lips for five seconds. Try to make a slight hissing sound as the air passes out of your lips.

4. Imagine your lungs are like pear-shaped balloons. Picture them filling up with air slowly from the bottom to the top.

5. Continue to breathe like this until you feel your mind and body relax.

6. Setting aside a few minutes a day to practice relaxation breathing can help prevent stress from sneaking up on you.

ADVICE

PROGRESSIVE MUSCLE RELAXATION

Tensing, holding and then relaxing your muscles can help you release the tension that gets stored in your body. Here is another simple exercise to try.

1. Find a comfortable place to sit or lie down.

2. Close your eyes.

3. Tense your facial muscles (squeeze your forehead, clench your jaw, purse your lips), hold for five seconds and then release.

4. Move on to your neck and shoulder muscles—tensing, holding for five seconds and then releasing.

5. Slowly continue to work down your body, tensing, holding and then relaxing the muscles in your arms, back, stomach, hips, legs and feet.

6. Once you have mastered relaxation breathing, combine it with these muscle exercises.

ADVICE

ANXIETY ATTACK TOOL KIT FOR HIGH-SCHOOL STUDENTS

Everybody feels nervous and tense sometimes, but when this makes it almost impossible to pay attention, think straight, sit still or just feel comfortable in your own skin, you may be experiencing anxiety or a panic attack. If this ever happens to you, here are some tools that you can have with you in school at all times. Using these tools can help you relieve anxiety and regain your focus.

Touch tools (things you can carry in a pocket or purse):

- Loose change: Feel and count it in your pocket. Try to tell if it is heads or tails
- Rubber bands: Wear them around your wrist and snap them to feel the sting
- Moist towelettes: Feel the cooling on your skin . . . try it on your inner wrist or neck
- A pebble: Place in your shoe and concentrate on the discomfort

Smell tools:

- Essential oils: Lavender and mint are calming
- Perfume
- Smelling salts: Can break the intensity of a strong panic attack

Taste tools (any of these strong flavors can break the intensity of an attack):

- Sour candy

- Chili peppers

- Gum

- Mints

- Cloves

Visual tools:

- Count the number of ceiling tiles, or people wearing red, or the number of floor tiles

- Look around for things that start with the letter "B" (or any other letter of the alphabet)

Mental tools:

- Count backward from 100 by threes, twos, etc.: This shifts your mind from panic to focus

- Talk back to yourself: Reassure yourself this has happened before and that the feeling *will* pass this time also

- Take a word and see how many smaller words you can make out of it

- Memorize the words to a favorite song or poem

FACT

Suicide is one of the three leading causes of death for young people 15–24 years old. In a given year, more teenagers and young adults die of suicide than from cancer, heart disease, AIDS, birth defects, stroke, pneumonia and influenza, and chronic lung disease combined.[126]

SUICIDE TUESDAYS

We had moved from the city to suburbia. New school, different environment, different people. My family was quite miserable as my father was totally stressed-out from working two jobs to pay for our house, which was above his means. Both my parents were stressed-out trying to take care of a new home and a multitude of ungrateful children. I was very unhappy, very depressed and very miserable.

I had liked and was used to city life. There was quite a lot to do, and I was never bored. To me, suburbia might just as well have been another planet. It was strange, and I had no idea what to do there. I did not like it. At school, I was the new kid and fat as well, and they disliked me very much. (I didn't know that I was fat until I started at the new school. They let me know real quick!) I was miserable.

I was so unhappy that I decided to kill myself. I don't mean I was just toying with the idea. I decided that I was going take this course of action, and it would be my final action. I would be miserable and unhappy no longer.

I remember clearly that I was standing in my bedroom, leaning against my dresser, when I made this decision. In the next few moments, I saw, in my mind's eye, a "vision" of myself, dead from my suicide, my body lying in a casket. My family was all around the casket. They were extremely distressed and upset, crying and unhappy. And I realized that they were totally shocked and horrified that I had killed myself. They could not understand why I had done such a

thing. They wished that they had had some idea of how miserable I had been so they could've done something to prevent my death. And my parents also had great feelings of guilt.

I was very surprised at this revelation. I had thought that my family did not care about me at all. And I was amazed at how very badly they felt, and at how much they were suffering. I did not want to cause anyone that amount of pain.

—Jon

I spent a good part of the summer before high school getting to know someone. We had summer school together, and I spent about four solid hours with
him each day, really bonding and building a beautiful friendship. By the end of
our month and a half together, he had become one of my best friends. He was
one of the reasons I had the best summer of my life.

When school finally started, though, we didn't hang out. I never saw him on
the weekends, but our friendship was still as strong as ever. I talked to him in
classes, and despite our lack of hanging out, I felt a real bond between us that
would never be broken. I had found someone who thought about the same
things I did, and in fact was smarter and much more well-rounded than me.

About a month into school, he killed himself during first period on campus.
He jumped in front of the train that runs next to the history and foreign-
language buildings. I suppose it would have been less shocking and disturbing
if anyone had seen it coming, but they didn't. It was a complete surprise.
Everyone who knew him—his parents, his closest friends, everyone—was
stunned. He seemed so happy. He was always smiling and kidding around.
A completely normal, well-adjusted, popular, happy kid. He was one of us—
a regular guy. He was on the football team, in a band, and in all the upper-level
classes. Everyone adored him.

It was the first time I had ever really "lost a loved one." Knowing someone
who commits suicide is different from having a grandparent or another close
relative die. Although you love your grandparents (presumably), they don't
really know you. When you are around them, you show the side of you that
you believe they want to see—the good student, the responsible young adult,
etc. Your grandparents, and even your parents, don't really know the side of you
that your friends do. In some sense, your peers know the true you better than
your family does.

Fifteen-year-olds feel immortal; old age and death are (seemingly) so incred-
ibly far away. Thoughts of death aren't even in the back of one's mind. Steven's
death brought thoughts and feelings to the surface that I had never had
before—emotions I wasn't ready to experience. One of my fifteen-year-old
friends is *dead;* he's not coming back. Someone my age. It was very sobering.

That whole experience changed me, and I think that is ultimately why my girlfriend left me. After Steven's death, I became much more introspective and quiet. I paid less attention to the people and things around me; I became less outgoing, less charming, less funny. It kind of stripped away the bullshit. But that was who I became, and no matter how hard I tried to change back and to seem like the old Isaac, no one bought it. I became alarmingly good at expressing my feelings. It was too much; my girlfriend was frightened by my devotion and love toward her. Anyway, she left me, and that's all that matters. That was when I really unplugged from the world.

Between that and Steven's suicide, my year could not have been salvaged in any way. I became really, really depressed and spent all my weekends alone in my room, watching TV. Thankfully, I was able to find something that I could obsess over—the *X-Files*. I bought all seven seasons on DVD from China (at very affordable prices) and watched them all day, every day.

I sincerely believe that if it hadn't been for the *X-Files*, I might have killed myself. I could think about something besides my losses and focus on something other than my pathetic situation.

—*Isaac, 16*

ADVICE

Suicide. There are few other words that can generate as much fear, anxiety or panic. It is a sad fact that many high-school students consider committing suicide. If you have ever had these thoughts, you are not alone. If you are currently thinking of harming yourself, please tell a safe adult (see page 226 for details on how to find a safe adult) or, better yet, several safe adults.

Responding to suicidal people is hard; many adults are not prepared. Telling a few adults how you are feeling increases the chances that one of these adults will know how to get you the help you deserve. If no adult is available, please call a suicide prevention hotline. (See the list of resources in this book or look in your local phone book.) If you cannot focus on finding the information here, call 911.

What should you do if you know a friend is possibly suicidal? The answer is very clear; you need to tell a safe adult. We know you are concerned about your friend getting angry at you if you tell. No one likes feeling like they have ratted out a friend; no one likes having a friend get angry at them. However, none of these concerns will matter if a friend commits suicide. The guilt can be overwhelming. Do not keep this a secret; tell a safe adult. Your friend's life could depend on you doing so.

ADVICE

5 REASONS
WHY HONESTY PAYS

1. It's easier. You don't have to keep coming up with new lies to cover up the old ones.

2. Innocent people will not get into trouble.

3. The truth may not always be fun to face, but facing it now could mean avoiding much larger problems later.

4. Most people can forgive a mistake and respect those who admit having made one.

5. It just feels better!

DEATH, LOSS AND GRIEF

Sometimes things happen for a reason even though we do not understand or accept that reason. I had a great, happy life with all of my family, but now since my brother died, it is not the same anymore. My brother's death changed everything.

I remember when I used to see people in the news had died. I really didn't feel any pain for those people or for their families. I did not know what it felt like to lose a loved one. Now, I feel the pain.

When you lose a loved one who meant something really special in your life, it is the worst type of pain. This feeling is so hard to let go of because it is still difficult to accept that my brother is gone. There are times when I just want to quit. I feel like there is no point for me being here. I just want to leave and be with my brother forever, but then I get up and think about my parents. I cannot fail them or my brother. I want to accomplish the goal that I promised my brother, the one I was going to fulfill to make him and my family proud. Oh God, why is it so hard to be strong? It is so hard to make believe that I'm happy in front of other people, when deep inside I am breaking slowly into pieces every day. It is so painful to know that my brother is gone.

Everybody out there in the world needs to know something: Don't waste your life doing the wrong things. Take advantage of what's left of your life to become closer and spend time with that special person you love so much. You never

> There's no "correct" way to mourn a death. Some people cry; others don't. Some people become depressed for a long time; others snap out of it quickly. Some people go through periods of anger and guilt for having done (or not done) something to or for the deceased. Some people may even be angry at the person who died—for dying. What you see on the surface may bear little resemblance to what a person feels inside.
>
> —Alex J. Packer[127]

know when you could lose him and then you will regret not having spent more time together.

Since my brother's death, our lives have not been the same. Abraham was everything for us. He was the main reason we were here in the United States. My brother Abraham was my inspiration to go on with my schooling and to become someone in life. He was going to be my teacher. He was deaf, and he was going to teach me sign language so I could become an interpreter.

I want to make myself, my brother Abraham, and my family proud by fulfilling my dream. I hope that my brother is listening to me right now. If he is, I want him to know that my family and I will always love him. He was the best brother, son and friend one could ever have. He was unique and special, and we miss the beautiful smile that was always on his face.

—Vianey, 16

When I was in sixth grade, my family was given the horrific news that my father had breast cancer. After a couple of years doing chemotherapy and radiation, my dad went into remission. It appeared that he had finally defeated his cancer, but this joyous defeat was short-lived.

A few years later, when I was a fifteen, his cancer returned with even greater force. This time around, I went on with my life like nothing was wrong. I indulged in the very things that my father, in his authoritarian way, had done everything in his power to prevent me from doing. I drank excessively, smoked, used drugs and, worst of all in my father's eyes, became promiscuous. It was as if I had set out to do the complete opposite of what morals my father had tried to instill in me over the years.

In December of my sixteenth year, my father passed away. After his death, my drinking, drug use and sexual issues just worsened. It was only when I turned nineteen that I started to settle down a little and really confront the loss of my father. I was always in denial, and it seems that the denial carried over a

> When I lost my grandfather in 2003, I felt like I could not make it without him in my life. But after his death, I realized that he had only made me a stronger man, and that he would want me to keep his legacy alive and growing. So I always feel that any time of death, hurt or sorrow is always made to strengthen your soul and make you a soldier for the journey of life.
>
> —Jordan, 17

few years after he had actually died. I finally had to come to terms with the fact that my dad was dead and that I would never see him again. This evoked a very helpless feeling.

When I was able to accept the fact that he was dead, the next step of my grieving was regret and guilt. Why hadn't I spent more time with him when he was alive? Why did I do all of those things that my dad had tried so hard to protect me from? In my mind, I began to think of myself as some sort of monster. Now, at the age of twenty-two, I am happy to say that I am closer to conquering this self-destructive phase and moving on to acceptance. But this is a stage that I have not yet conquered, and I believe it will take me a good deal of time to do so.

I now acknowledge the fact that I was angry with my father. I was angry that he was leaving me and would never see me graduate, or walk me down the aisle, or be a grandfather to my children. I know this sounds selfish, but it is in our human nature to have these selfish thoughts on a subconscious level. I know that I avoided him during his final stage of life because to me that sickly body and weak soul were just a shell of my father. I realize now that he himself needed to be disconnected, to prepare himself in some way for moving on to his next life.

It is also more obvious to me now why the drugs and alcohol were so appealing. They were effective in numbing the pain I carried inside. My sexual issues were more difficult for me to understand. I do, however, see that the guys were just a poor substitute for a love I so badly needed. It is strange, but at the time, I knew most of these guys didn't love me, but it was almost like I set out to make them love me. Sex was just one way that I held the power.

If you should find yourself in a similar situation, I cannot say that you will ever forget, but life does get better. I found one thing that has really helped is not to hide memories of my father. I used to keep pictures tucked away because I thought it would be too painful to see them on a daily basis. Now I keep framed collages of my father on my walls and talk about him frequently to people—not about his dying, but rather his living.

—*Danielle, 22*

ADVICE

A ttending a funeral is a way of supporting the bereaved, consoling yourself and honoring the dearly departed. You never get a second chance to go to someone's funeral. Here's what to do:

- Dress conservatively. You don't have to wear black, but loud, attention-getting outfits are out of place.
- Sign the registry.
- Respect the rites. You aren't required to participate in activities that are foreign or objectionable to your culture, language, religion or relationship to the deceased. Be observant and respectful. Try to blend in with the tone and traditions of the occasion.
- Feel free to decline speaking or participating in rituals with which you are uncomfortable. It is not considered proper, however, to decline if you are asked to be a pallbearer.
- Don't be too jolly. You don't have to put on fake grief, but do maintain a subdued decorum to show your empathy.
- Express your sympathy. A simple "I'm sorry" is appropriate.
- If you can, send flowers or donate to the deceased's favorite charity.

• Write a letter of condolence—a short, warm note that acknowledges the death, includes a fond recollection and closes with an expression of sympathy.

• Let it out. Somebody's death, even if you didn't know the person, can set off all sorts of feelings. Don't keep them bottled up inside. Write them down in a journal. Talk to people about how you feel, about the person who died. If you don't find the comfort or support you need from your family or friends, talk to a teacher, counselor or member of the clergy.[128]

CHAPTER EIGHT

Overachieving, Overextended and Overloaded: Responsibilities and Balance

HIGH SCHOOL IS the best time of your life. Relax and enjoy it! Oh, by the way, only taking three AP courses this year? What do you mean you are not going out for varsity? You don't have a date for the prom? What do you mean you're cutting your hours at work? Hey, three As, two Bs and a C! What the heck is wrong with you this semester?

Got the point yet? High school can be a time of great joy, and it can also be filled with stress. A lot depends on you and your attitude toward these four years. High school is often the first time that you will have to balance your time between schoolwork, a job or community service, dating and perhaps a sport or other extracurricular activity.

Learning how to manage your time is essential for surviving all these possibilities. How much is too much, academically, socially, or in terms of extracurricular activities? Knowing when and how to ask for help, and learning when to say, "I would love to get more involved, but I have too much on my plate already," are important skills for you to develop. High school is a time when you will have to deal with stress; how you deal with it can make all the difference.

> At my high school, the pressure to receive good grades is almost unbearable. Nowadays, it is not good enough to just get decent grades or even good grades. To get into a good college and remain competitive, you must earn a grade point average often in excess of a 4.0. This can be done by taking honors and advanced classes such as AP courses. This pressure often causes students to take nearly impossible schedules, which leaves them with a never-ending barrage of homework. It makes a social life nearly impossible! Also, it takes away from what I believe to be a good high-school experience.
>
> —Matt, 15 [129]

MAKING THE GRADE

For someone who is used to getting "As," it's pretty hard to adjust to being behind and struggling to catch up and understand things. I had a really hard time with keeping up in school when I was in the hospital, partly because I didn't have the teachers and partly because my concentration was terrible. I was scared of going back to school because I didn't think I was going to pass any of my finals, and I would have to repeat my junior year. Luckily, my guidance counselor was there; without his help, I don't think I would have passed my classes like I did. He talked to the teachers and found out what my options were, and with his help I made it through the year.

—Arianna, 22

> I wonder if my parents ever had to deal with the pressures of being perfect in high school. It seems that they expect me to be perfect at *everything* I do. I am expected to do everything, and when I can't, I feel I have let everyone down.
>
> —Kimberly, 18

THE FACTS

PROBLEMS WITH PERFECTIONISM

If you are still thinking that, in the overall scheme of things, striving to be the best at everything you do and, in the process, pushing yourself and others a little too hard isn't such a big deal, consider the following problems you may encounter:

• Stress and stress-related illness

• Burnout

• Anxiety and panic attacks

• Obsessions and compulsions

• Alcohol, drug and food addictions

• Other addictions (for example, exercise, spending)

• Eating disorders

• Workaholism (being hooked on work, staying busy)

• Unnecessary sacrifices (for example, social life, vacations)

• Loneliness and isolation

• Impaired personal relationships

• The tendency to simply give up when you can't get it perfect

—Miriam Elliott and Susan Meltsner[131]

WHAT A PERFECTIONIST SAYS

✓ "If I can't do it perfectly, what's the point?"

✓ "I should excel at everything I do."

✓ "I always have to stay ahead of others."

✓ "Things should be done right the first time."

✓ "There is only one right way to do things."

✓ "I'm a wonderful person if I do well; I'm a lousy person if I do poorly."

✓ "People shouldn't criticize me."

✓ "Everything should be clearly black or white. Grays are a sign of confused thinking."

—Jim Delisle and Judy Galbraith[130]

I think that instead of all teachers giving tests on the same day, there should be restrictions for different departments.
For example:
Math tests only on Mondays, Science only on Tuesdays. Instead of having all the tests on one day, usually Friday, they can be evened out to give the students more time to study.*

Most of my classes . . . I just don't care; I'll just sit through them and not listen to a single thing anyone says. Because of this I have a low GPA, and my mom is really unhappy about it. I know it's just because she cares, but I hate how every time I'm around her she brings school up. And that's the last thing I ever want to talk about. So, yeah, mostly high school sucks. I can't wait until next year when I'm finally done with it.

—Sammi, 17

If you can, schedule your hardest classes for when your brain works best.

—Marlin S. Potash and Laura Potash Fruitman[132]

Group projects were awful. The work never was divided evenly, and then trying to work out when you could get together with someone was a pain. And, of course, the formation of the groups was also stressful, as you never wanted to be the last person left without being in a group.

—Josh, 20

I wish I had taken college classes at my local community college while still in high school. This would have given me a positive academic environment to contrast against the structure and stress of high school. I was enrolled in classes that I felt under-challenged in. Subsequently, I never studied, didn't care and lost interest in my work—opting to just kill time by drawing pictures in my notebook and passing notes. Because of my lack of interest, I got mediocre grades when I could have been excelling. In college I've learned how to succeed academically. I've learned to love learning.

—Joel, 21

There is support
for the resource kids,
the ones who are having
a hard time in school.
There's support for the
smart kids, who have lots of
opportunities. How about
some help for kids in
the middle?*

THE FACTS

"D" and "F" students are
more likely than "A" students
to:

- Skip breakfast
- Get less than seven hours
  of sleep
- Fall asleep in class
- Not exercise
- Report that their parents
  do not know about impor-
  tant areas of their lives
- Experience problems with
  their family
- Not visit a library
- Not participate in activities
  such as sports, art or
  music. [134]

The dictionary
is the only place where
success comes
before work.
—*Arthur Brisbane*[133]

By the time I graduated from high school,
I had taken a total of seven classes from my community technical
college and a nearby liberal arts university. When I entered college as
a full-time student, I wasn't nervous about the work or the expectations.
I had already gotten comfortable with the way institutions of higher learning
function. I had experience with public computer labs, research papers,
college bookstores and the registrar's office. All of this reduced the
element of the unknown as I started my four years at college.

—Wendy[135]

ADVICE

THRIVE VS. SURVIVE

You are going through high school in a time of major change. Almost every state in the country now requires its students to pass an exit exam, or series of exams, in order to graduate. Getting through high school academically is a significant challenge for many students.

Here is the big question: Do you want to just get through high school, or do you want to get the most out of these four years?

It is in your best interest to get as much out of your high-school years as possible. Be active in extracurricular activities, volunteer in the community, take challenging courses and strive for high grades without damaging your physical, emotional or spiritual health.

If your goal is just to survive high school, we will let you in on the two steps that almost always will lead to graduation.

1. Go to class **EVERY DAY.**

2. Do your homework **EVERY NIGHT.**

That is all that it takes if graduating is your only goal. We have never seen a student fail to graduate who practiced these two steps.

If your goal is to excel and get more out of your high-school years, then you will have to put more into the experience. In addition to the two steps mentioned above, you will need to:

- Take a wide range of challenging courses. (Speak to your school counselor at the VERY START of high school and ask which Advanced Placement, International Baccalaureate or Honors courses are available at your school. If you are really willing to put in the extra time and effort that these courses require, don't take "no" for an answer when requesting to be placed in these courses.)
- Study. (See pages 178–182 for details on how to study.)

- Ask your teachers for extra help. (See page 188 for information on how and when to ask.)
- Get involved in your school and/or community. (See chapter 10 for information on anchors and outlets.)
- Organize and prioritize your time.
- Take a leap of faith and believe that the effort and sacrifices you make now can lead to lifelong rewards!

LEARNING TO LEARN

I try to write neatly, even when I'm writing fast. You might think you'll remember what all your notes mean, but if they're too messy, you never will. Also, anytime teachers ask a question while talking, I write that down. Sometimes those same questions turn up on tests. And I put a star by things the teacher says more than once—that means it's pretty important. Sometimes I re-copy my notes that evening if there is a lot of material. It helps me remember things, and if something isn't clear, I can ask about it or look it up before we go on to something else.
—Tanya, 14[136]

My parents were right when they said high school would be something you need to work hard at to be successful. At fourteen, you don't always realize how important getting good grades is until it's senior year and college is staring you right in the face.
—Ashley, 19

I try to answer multiple-choice questions in my head before I look at the answer choices. Sometimes one of the answers is the same as what I came up with.
—Michael, 17[137]

ADVICE

WHY WON'T YOU JUST "STUDY HARDER"?

E ver been told, or had it told to your parents, that you need to
STUDY harder? Here's the PROBLEM. . . . Many students have
never been shown HOW to study. Think about it. If we ask you to
BAKE a cake but never tell you what ingredients are needed, where it
needs to be cooked, for how long, or how to combine the ingredients,
chances are the cake is going to be a failure no matter how many times
we say that you need to BAKE harder!

ADVICE

STUDY TIPS

In an ideal world you will have:

- A desk of your own with room to work and keep supplies. (Yes,
  some people do work better sprawled out on the bed or floor, but
  most of us will do best at a desk, especially for writing.)
- An adjustable chair for comfort, support and posture.
- Good lighting, both overhead and task lights. You might find it
  helpful to come home to full-spectrum light bulbs in your study
  area.
- Paper, pens, pencils, calculator and, if possible, a
  computer all located within arm's length.
- A thesaurus and dictionary.
- A clock to manage your time.

- A distraction-free location, as in no TV, music or PlayStation. (Okay, before you say it, YES, some people do study better with background sound like music and some even with TV. However, be HONEST with yourself. If you just like having it on, that is NOT the same thing!)

If home offers few of these opportunities, check out your local library, community college, boys' or girls' club, or any other community-based after-school educational program as a necessary home-away-from-home study center.

I come from a big family: two parents and five kids, of which I am the oldest. The normal fight for the bathroom is nothing like that seen on the Brady Bunch show, if anybody seriously watches that anymore. And forget about having a quiet place to read and do your homework; it's not gonna happen. My best advice is to stay as late at school as possible to finish up your reading or serious subjects like chemistry or physics. Check to see what buses run from your school to close to home; there might be an alternative program or night school that goes on after normal school hours with transportation. Or catch a cab if you can spare the money for a fare.

—Michael, 18

My parents respected my study habits. I chose to study in front of the TV because I needed a minor distraction to really concentrate on what I was studying. My grades were an indication that this worked for me. However, my sister needs a very quiet environment to study in. My sister and I liked to plan ahead with our studies, whereas my brother crams.

—Sarah, 23

ADVICE

READ THE TEXTBOOK

Look for what the teacher and/or author think are important.

- Read the ENTIRE assignment.
- Then reread the introduction and/or summary. Focus on the author's statement of most important points.
- Notice each boldface heading and subheading.
- Notice any graphics—charts, maps, diagrams, etc. They are there to make a point. Don't miss them.
- Italics, bold-face print, chapter objective and end-of-chapter questions are all included to help you. Pay attention.
- Have a dictionary within reach so you can quickly look up any word when you are not sure of its meaning.
- If your eyes get tired or you have a hard time reading, you can cut down the glare by putting a sheet of colored acetate (an inexpensive, thin, flexible plastic sheet, available at most office-supply or art-supply stores) over the page you're reading.

Your notes are a key, but the key only opens the door if you take good notes to begin with. (For a highly effective notetaking system, go to our Web site at *www.highschoolsnotforever.com* and click on tips.)

ADVICE

HOW TO STUDY

- **Find a study partner.** For subjects like math and science, it really pays. If you can explain a process, formula or define vocabulary to another person (your partner), then you don't have to rely totally on memorization as you truly now understand the concept.
- **Do your toughest subject first.** If you have homework in biology and algebra, which you love, and history, which you hate, do the history homework first. Your mind will be fresher, and you'll get through it quicker.
- **Prepare a snack before you start studying.** You would be amazed at how much time you can waste going back and forth to the fridge.
- **Use acronyms to remember a specific item.** You form acronyms by using each first letter from a group of words to form a new word. This is particularly useful when remembering words in a specified order. Two examples of common acronyms are: SCUBA (Self Contained Underwater Breathing Apparatus) and LASER (Light Amplification by Stimulated Emission of Radiation).

ADVICE

WHEN TO STUDY

- For most people, finding and keeping to a routine time for studying works best.
- Some work most efficiently if they begin right after getting home from school. Others may need an hour or so to de-stress and just chill before moving on to study.

- Some work best before eating dinner; some are only ready once their tummies are full.
- You may have events after school, such as practice, games, performances, etc. Those days will require flexibility in terms of when and where you study.
- Be creative: A cross-country runner memorized his biology vocabulary on his daily run. Another student put Post-it notes with vocabulary terms on his bathroom medicine cabinet so that he could learn new words every day while brushing his teeth.
- Read your material and notes again shortly before bed. Many feel that the mind will subconsciously try to sort and make sense of new information.

FIND WHAT WORKS FOR YOU! Everyone is different and needs to find his or her own way that works. Don't think you have to study exactly the way that is described above, but you do need to find a way that will truly work for you. If you need to sing, dance or draw a word, idea or concept in order to make it your own, then DO IT!

MY STUDY PLAN

Where do I study best? _____

_____

_____

_____

What supplies do I need? _____

_____

_____

_____

What are the best time(s) for me to study? (Be aware that you may have to experiment a bit to find your most effective study hours.)

_____

_____

_____

_____

TESTING, TESTING, OH GOD, PLEASE, NO MORE TESTING

I do excellent with reviewing for tests, but when I take them, I panic.

—Clara, 15

[My high school] had an interesting take on education. The plan, it seemed, was to cram a student's head full of information, test the student repeatedly, and then move on to an unrelated subject with frightening speed. . . . Everything was either meaningless or on the test.

—Ned Vizzini, 19[138]

What really angers me is how the state tests determine if we graduate. If I complete all my required classes, I can graduate, but if I failed my tenth-grade test, I can't graduate. That burns me up inside. I believe students should not have to worry about a test that determines if they graduate high school.

—Damitra, 15

ADVICE

TEST-TAKING TIPS

For a lot of people, "test" is the nastiest of four-letter words. If you feel nervous about taking a test, here are a few things to try that just might help you relax and perform better:

- Drink water before the test, even if it is only a few sips from the water fountain. Your brain works better when you are hydrated.

- Breathe! When people get stressed, they do not take deep and calm breaths. (Try the relaxation breathing techniques described on page 157.) Controlling your breathing can help you relax and perform your best.

- Don't psych yourself out. Telling yourself that you can't do well on tests only makes it harder. Try writing a little note to yourself on the top of your test, such as, "Yes, I can do this" or "I know this stuff." Look back at this note frequently.

- If you memorized formulas or certain facts for a test (see the information on acronyms on page 181), write them on top of the test as soon as you get the test. You might want to tell your teacher *before* the exam that you will be doing this so he or she will know you are not trying to cheat.

- Some people can sit still and do well on a test. Others need to fidget or chew on something to stay focused. If you are one of these students, bring gum to chew or hard candy to suck. If your teacher will not allow that, try wearing a soft cord or leather necklace that you can subtly chew on. A rubber band on the wrist to pull on or a stress ball to squeeze may also help you focus.

ADVICE

EATING FOR THE SAT,
ACT OR ANY OTHER
LONG EXAM

Taking the SAT or the ACT exam is the mental equivalent of running a marathon. It makes sense to prepare for them in a way that is similar to how marathon runners prepare for a race.

- The night before, eat a large pasta dinner. The complex carbohydrates in the pasta, which take time to break down into energy, provide pep for the next day's event.
- The day of the test, have a breakfast of protein (meat, eggs, tofu, beans). Proteins are quickly converted by the body into energy that you can use that day.
- It is always a plus to be well-hydrated for a test. Drink lots of water or fruit juice. Avoid caffeine as it can dehydrate you. Even if you feel more alert at first, there is a rebound effect that will leave you feeling sluggish later, perhaps while you are still taking the exam.

KNOW YOUR TEACHERS

The quality of your relationship with your teachers can influence your academic success, especially in classes that are graded subjectively. (If you've made a positive impression, it might influence your teacher when he or she has to decide between a borderline A– or B+.) A good relationship can also help when you need letters of recommendation for college or a job.

—Roarke O'Leary[139]

THE FACT

What do students (ages 16–18) do when they don't understand what their teacher is teaching in class?[140]

- 46 percent raise their hand and ask the teacher
- 34 percent ask a friend for help
- 10 percent do nothing and hope it won't matter
- 6 percent remain quiet so no one knows they don't understand
- 1 percent ask mom or dad for help

ADVICE

TEACHER TACTICS

Y ou're going to spend four years dealing with your high school teachers. Why not make the relationships work for you? Here are some suggestions:

- Sit in the front of the classroom so you will be more familiar to the teacher. The center rows of seats are also good choices.
- Make a positive impression. Ask questions and participate in the discussions and activities.
- Show that you are paying attention. Many teachers are looking for things like eye contact, good posture and note-taking.
- Even if your grades are not as high as you'd like, making an effort and working to your potential can put you in line for more favorable reviews and comments on letters of reference.
- Take advantage of opportunities to meet with your teacher to discuss any lengthy questions about class material or assignments.
- Be positive and take responsibility for your studies, especially when discussing a grade you believe is too low or trying to improve your overall standing in class.[141]

ADVICE

HOW AND WHEN TO ASK FOR HELP

- Don't be afraid to ask a question during class.
- If that's not enough, see your teacher after class and ask when he or she will be available for extra help.
- You may have to give up something else you planned to do to meet with the teacher. The teacher may not be available right away or at a time that's particularly convenient for you.
- If possible, bring specific examples of where you're stuck or what you don't understand.
- If you still don't understand, or are not getting what you need, talk with a safe adult who can help. (See page 226 for tips on finding a safe adult.)

COLLEGE

Stuff that stressed me out the most was making sure I was ready for college. I was freaked about not really being in control, not knowing what to expect. And I was nervous about being more independent and stuff. I think that was the main stress. What am I gonna do for college? I have all these tests. All the stress from your parents about college, like which schools to apply to, which scholarships to apply for and having enough money.

—Matthew, 18

It is not necessary to go to an Ivy League school to be successful in life. Also, you do not need to know what you want to be or do when you first get there. Don't worry about a major your first year. Use the time to explore your interests.

—Danielle, 22

THE FACTS

How Do Colleges Decide If They Are Going to Admit You?

Every college has its own specific way of choosing who it will let in. However, the following four topics will almost always be examined.

1. **Grades:** Not everyone is a straight-A student, and not every college requires an A average for admission. However, a college is more likely to admit a student with higher grades.

2. **SAT or ACT Scores:** These exams are given throughout the country several times a year. Ask your counselor when you can take the ACT or SAT. Also ask about the need to take any SAT II exams and how to prepare. Most four-year colleges require you to take one or more of these tests.

3. **Extracurricular Activities:** Here is where you can really shine if you don't have the highest grades and/or test scores. Colleges like seeing that you are involved in your school and/or community. You do not have to have a long list of activities. Most colleges would rather see you involved in a few things, for a long period of time, than see a list of twenty different activities, knowing that you cannot possibly be spending quality time in all of them. Taking a leadership role can really help get you noticed.

   Here are some ideas on what you can do: join a club (if you can't find one you like, start one); join a team; join the band or chorus; become a class officer; become involved in school plays; volunteer your time to help others.

4. **Challenging Classes:** College work is harder than most high-school work. Colleges like knowing that you are willing to work hard and grow as a student. Ask your school counselor which Honors, Advanced Placement or International Baccalaureate courses are available in your school.

Volunteer work is generally regarded with as much respect as paid work. Employers consider volunteering to be as valuable as job experience because they know that volunteers have a range of duties and are highly motivated. College admissions officers are also impressed by teens who volunteer. Donating your time shows you're a dedicated and compassionate person, a characteristic that can set you apart from other applicants.

—Rebecca Greene[142]

When you are choosing a college, consider how well the college matches your career choice(s), whether it provides the extracurricular activities you wish to participate in, whether they offer the type of degree you want, the student population, the location (in a city or the middle of nowhere), and whether you have friends or family nearby (if you think you'll need to have them close).

—Danielle, 22

FAMILY AND WORK

I don't know what I'm good at. I know it's not school. I'm busy taking care of my stepdad's house. He's in jail, so I had to fix the roof and the electrical. Then I have to go over to help take care of my grandpa. He's got cancer, and my mom has to work. I don't want him to die. He's one of the only people in my life who ever really cared about me. I do stuff at his house, too. All kinds of stuff I have to fix over there. The door's broken, and there's something wrong with the plumbing. Then my teachers act like their assignments are the only things I have to do or think about. I've got so much other stuff going on that I can't concentrate on school. They hassle me, and then I lose it and get another detention for acting out. I'm failing everything. I get sent to these alternative programs, and everybody thinks I'm so stupid.

—Alex, 16

Some teachers don't realize that some students need to work forty hours or more just to get by.*

> I was different.
> I LIKED, even ENJOYED
> school. Unlike most kids, I signed
> up for summer school EVERY year.
> I never admitted it to my friends,
> because who in their right mind signs
> up for summer school? (I did.) But I
> loved the freedom from the many
> responsibilities I had at home.
> —Christine

BALANCE

Clubs, academics and the balancing act: This can be a problem. Your work should come first and foremost. Clubs are usually after school and can be a great place to relax. But don't go if your five-paragraph essay is due in less than twenty-four hours! You can hang out at the club almost anytime; your grade is important! I'm telling you from firsthand experience, it can be sheer murder if you miss too many assignments! With assignments, do the hardest stuff first and work toward the easy stuff.

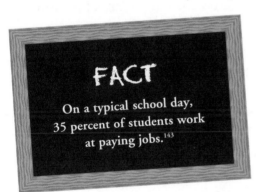

FACT

On a typical school day, 35 percent of students work at paying jobs.[143]

As for the clubs, find something you like. If the school doesn't offer it, then try and find a sponsor for the club. This is where good teacher-student relationships come in handy. Once you've found a sponsor, get the word out on the daily announcements, put up posters, tell everyone you know! You should get some people there. The only creative writers I knew were in my class, but once I started the Creative Writing Club, several more people began to show up.

The balancing act is a challenge. You shouldn't break promises to the club unless you really have to! But don't leave the hard stuff to the last minute. There is no shame in asking a peer or teacher, for that matter, for extra help!

—James, 17

> If you need to work full time to help your family make enough to live on—not just to buy snacks and extras—it may be right to leave school. But don't drop out until you find a good job and have talked to your counselor about going to night school. If night school won't work, ask your school counselor about Saturday school or about taking the GED (General Educational Development) exam. Many employers and some colleges will accept this in place of a high-school diploma.
>
> —Victoria Sherrow [144]

The greatest challenge that I have ever faced in high school was stress. Stress is a part of your daily life. Over time, it can really mess you up. The buildup of my stress occurred as a result of time constraints. There are only twenty-four hours in a day, but it always seemed like I needed thirty hours to get everything done. I went to school all day (7:00 A.M.–2:00 P.M.), JROTC after that (2:00 P.M.–4:00 P.M.), work (5:00 P.M.–11:00 P.M.), homework (12:00 A.M.–1:00 A.M.) and then sleep (1:00 A.M.–6:00 A.M.).

To deal with this overwhelming problem, I made myself more personal time and did things in order to condense my schedule. Instead of doing my homework at home, I did it during my lunch period or in a class that I didn't need to pay attention in. This increase in personal time helped me to relieve my stress through either relaxing to music or physical activity.

When my stress wasn't a problem anymore, I became more personable and did better academically.

—Anthony, 18

Throughout my high-school experience, I have been a very involved student. When I started secondary school, I realized that my school district had many extracurricular activities available, like sports and clubs. I also go to school in a very diverse area, so there are many opportunities to volunteer, fundraise and participate in community projects. When I first started junior-high school, my mom told me that I could get involved in anything I wanted to as long as I could keep up with my schoolwork. I chose rowing. I had tried the rowing machines and found out that I liked it and I was good at it. That experience made me realize that I wanted to try new things. I liked feeling good about what I could do and wanted to learn to do better.

> When I was playing volleyball and basketball, my grades were actually higher because I was forced to schedule my time wisely.
>
> —Sarah, 23

I wanted to take advantage of as much as I could because my school had so much to offer. I used my beginning rowing skills to go onto the crew team, and I realized how much fun it was working as a team. I went on to become very involved in many sports. I joined the ski club and learned how to ski. I had been on a community swim team when I was younger, so I eventually went on the varsity swim team. I started doing one varsity sport a year, then two, and eventually participated in three varsity sports a year. I was on the swim team in fall, the ski team in winter, and the crew team in spring. When I graduate, I will have earned nine varsity letters.

It is not just the value of hard work that I have learned. Being involved in extracurricular activities has been a big help to keep me on schedule and organize my schoolwork. Knowing that I have so many hours of practice or meets, I have to do homework and complete assignments whenever I have the time. I can't put off schoolwork until later because I may have to go to practice and will be too tired to do it afterward. If I have a lot of homework, I will have to do some before and some after practice. I also have learned to prioritize and become really good at time management. I always have work with me and take advantage of any time I have to keep working on assignments. Waiting in a restaurant, in a doctor's office, etc., are good times to get some work done. I am also very careful to try to do something right the first time because I may not have the time to try to do it over. I always have schedules to follow, and that makes me stay more organized and productive.

By being so involved, I always had some place to be, and I always had a schedule to follow. It kept me focused and on track. These activities have a big social benefit, too. They always kept me feeling like I was a part of something, a group or a team. It gives you the feeling of belonging, and it is great to have friends involved in activities with you. It really makes you feel good.

—*Caitlin, 17*

> We need a required break during the day, either lunch or a study hall. Full schedules catch up with you.*

> At least once a week, chill with your friends, but make sure you leave yourself "me" time.
> —Melissa, 16

PERSISTENCE

I have struggled many times in high school, mostly because I never went to class. I was constantly cutting classes to hang out with my friends and try to make the day go by faster. The people who I thought were my friends really turned out to be my enemies. I was pressured so many times to cut class with them, and I never wanted to let them down. Instead, I let myself down.

I repeated tenth grade three times because I was so far behind in everything.

> There is enough stress in your life without adding to it by promising to do more than you can do. So think before you say you will head the committee to hold a frog-jumping contest. Or that you will spend the weekend passing out flyers to warn people that spaceships will land in their city on the Fourth of July. The word "no" is a perfectly good word. Use it, and you will cut down on your stress.
> —Terry Dunnahoo[145]

> I've missed more than nine thousand shots in my career. Twenty-six times I've been trusted to take the game winning shot and missed. I've failed over and over and over again in my life. And that is why I succeed.
>
> —Michael Jordan[146]

I even went to summer school and failed. I was so confused and didn't know what the hell my problem was. I hated myself for making the wrong decisions. I believed I would never succeed and graduate. Everybody around me made jokes and said stupid things like, "You'll be twenty-five by the time you are out of high school" or "Your brother's going to graduate before you, and he is only fifteen!" Even the kids in my classes insulted me because of my age.

As time went by, I became fed up with the whole situation I'd gotten myself into. The only thing for me to do was to go to class and do my work. I stopped being friends with all the people who pressured me from the start. They had all dropped out and gotten hooked on drugs. I didn't want to be a part of that world. Sure, it was all fun and games at the time, but I knew for a fact that I did not want to be a lowlife for the rest of my life.

Currently, I am a senior, and I am going to graduate this June. I finally made it, and I don't give a shit what people think about my age. As long as I have my diploma in hand, that's all I care about. I plan to go to a community college for two years, study business management and then transfer to a four-year college.

For anyone who is in the same situation as I was, get out while you still can, before it's too late. Don't let anyone tell you differently. I wish I had listened back then.

—Kristen, 20

> Destiny is done one day at a time.
>
> —D. Trinidad Hunt

Being a full-time student from 8:00 A.M. to 3:00 P.M. and going home with a load of homework every night, then trying to study for a test, making bottles, changing diapers and living on my daughter's sleep schedule, not to mention keeping her occupied or happy at the same time, is exhausting. Sometimes I have no time for myself to do anything. I find myself depressed or confused half the time. I try to make sense of my life and stay on track, but with the everyday ups and downs of getting good grades, keeping friends and family happy, and being a good mother, I am very tired! But in the end, it is all worth it. I just have to give a little more effort than most.

—Amber, 18

> Courage means doing the right thing, even when it's scary or difficult. It means that you try your best to succeed, even when success isn't guaranteed. In fact, the greatest courage often follows failure. You pick yourself up and get back on the horse. Courage means facing the monsters in your closet and under your bed—things you're afraid of, whether real or imagined.
>
> —Barbara Lewis[147]

> All it takes is just one person telling me I can't do it, and I'll use the fear of failure as fuel. I might get knocked out, but I'm going to fail swinging.
>
> —Will Smith[148]

> Finish school. Somewhere. Anywhere. Do an apprenticeship, an internship, early admission, a GED. Get your diploma. That little piece of paper will give you more leverage than you can imagine.
>
> —Beverly

CHAPTER NINE

Safe and Secure or Just Been There Before: Parents, Teachers and Other Adults

WHETHER THEY DRIVE YOU to school, to soccer practice or just plain drive you crazy, for better or for worse, adults are a part of the high-school experience. Parents, teachers, counselors and other adults can be sources of inspiration, support and comfort, or the causes of stress, fear and anxiety.

In this chapter you will find examples of healthy and helpful adults, as well as stories of adults who made life harder for students. You will also find detailed information on how to find a "safe" adult to help you through your high-school years.

TEACHING
THE WRONG LESSON

When I became the Youth & College Division President of the New York State National Association for the Advancement of Colored People, the

> High school is the first school where I realized that if I was having trouble with a class, the reason could actually be the teacher.
>
> —Paul, 19

overwhelming attention from my school was a dream as far as exposure. However, when the pressures of the NAACP position started to negatively affect my academic achievement, the principal and certain teachers in my school had a much less supportive attitude toward me and the time and work that my leadership role required. I was raised with a profound respect for adults and their opinions. However, when adults start talking about you and showing negative connotations toward you, that does not help you learn how to balance your extracurricular involvements with your academic responsibilities.

—Jordan, 17

> I don't like how teachers say that we can't have food or drink in class, but the teachers are allowed to eat and drink in class. I don't like how they are allowed to be late to class and don't get in trouble.
>
> —Allen, 15

> Why bother being a math teacher if you don't have the patience for the students who don't know math?
>
> —Marla, 14

> What I remember best is feeling frustrated at not learning anything new. I felt frustrated with teachers who knew less about a given subject than some of the students, and the teachers being unwilling to admit they did not know.
>
> —Lisa

> I had to work after school until 9:00 tonight. My boss has been giving me grief. But I figure I can either sit home and get yelled at for nothing, or get yelled at and get paid for it, with the extra bonus of getting out of the house.
>
> —Darlene, 17

I had a teacher who made me rewrite a research paper when he, in fact, lost it.
—Stephen, 22

It bothered me when my teachers acted like they thought we were not as smart or mature as we were—or at least as we felt. By high school, I was ready to be treated as an intellectual peer, and I resented being talked down to or told to complete tasks that I felt required less brainpower than I had.
—Philissa, 19

In my math class I had three different teachers all year long, and in biology I had many different substitutes. I believe that during this time I learned to be more patient, knowing some of my teachers didn't know all about the subject they were teaching.
—Chelsey, 14

Sometimes it's not the kids who are making the school bad. Sometimes it's the faculty that can unknowingly affect the moods of the students.*

Go to an adult in this school for help or support? You're kidding, right? There's no one here I trust. I'm sure they'd tell my parents anything I said or would spread it around with the other teachers. I think the worst thing would be to confide in someone here and later have it thrown up in your face. I've seen that happen, too. It's humiliating, even if you're not the one they're talking to. I'll keep things to myself, thank you very much.
—Carlos, 16

It is very difficult to form any kind of relationship with your teachers because they have so many students, and therefore have no time for you. Many of them also don't seem to care if you pass or fail their class.
—Rachel, 15

WHAT BUGS YOU MOST ABOUT YOUR TEACHERS?

✓ I don't like being marked late when I've already arrived in my home-room but I'm not in my seat.

✓ Teachers aggravate me when they have the attitude of, "Oh, I get paid whether you learn or not." They should go the distance to teach what needs to be taught.

✓ Taking notes in school is annoying, especially when the teacher reads them out loud and goes too fast.

✓ Some students learn things slower than others, but teachers expect you to learn like every other student. It's annoying!

✓ How they act like your best friends and insist they are your age.

✓ Their indifference to my excuses, no matter how valid they are.

✓ Some are very hypocritical.

✓ When you tell them something and they think it's a lie.

✓ They pressure you too hard to be perfect.

✓ When they take our deviance personally and don't look at it as just a part of growing up.

✓ When they hate their jobs and that is reflected in their attitudes.

✓ When they don't care if you pass or fail, and when you ask for help they say you should have paid attention more during the lesson.

✓ That they can be inconsiderate and do not understand what students are going through.

✓ Critical and judgmental teachers.

✓ Teachers who deliver in a monotone voice. "Book teachers" who teach strictly out of the book.

✓ Favoritism. Teachers who let certain kids get away with coming in late or turning stuff in a day after it's due, but who give other kids zeroes or detentions for doing the same things.

✓ When they hate you for no reason or if they prejudge you.

✓ Teachers who don't give you clear directions and then jump all over you when you ask them what they mean.

✓ We need teachers who can actually teach well. For some of my classes, I have to teach myself when I come home. If a lot of students complain about a teacher, there's probably a reason for it.

Something to remember about your teachers: Most of them got into this profession because they care about kids. Most want to help and want you to learn and succeed. Most want to do a good job and want to make a difference. All teachers have feelings. And sometimes their feelings show.

SHAME ON YOU

Back when I was in ninth grade, I had a teacher who put a hex on me. We'll call her Mrs. Sugar Cookie. Yeah, I know, Mrs.? Can you believe this lady is married? Well if you had her as a teacher, the answer would be no. She proved that anybody, and I mean anybody, can catch a hubby.

It wasn't enough that Mr. Warren gave me detention. Oh no. He had to chew me out in front of the whole class. I don't see what he was so pissed off about. So I chew gum in there all the time. I'm doing okay in class. I'm quiet and don't bother anybody. Why'd he have to call me names? "Problem child." "Immature." "Inconsiderate." "Self-centered." God, I hate this place more every day.

—Darlene, 17

I had her for an interior design class. One day we were showing her the finished product of a book we had made, and she got mad at me so she "hexed" me. We were supposed to cut out shapes to make the pictures in the book, but since I hated the time-consuming cutting, I drew and colored them instead. In my opinion, it looked better, too, because it was more detailed. But when she saw what I did, whew, she blew up and said, "Shame on you, Emily. You weren't supposed to draw. I hex you!" I was dumbfounded and in shock.

The whole class heard, and I was so embarrassed. My classmates offered their condolences afterward, saying how sorry they felt for me and how weird Mrs. Sugar Cookie was. I was at a point of hating her so much I just laughed. But this was just ridiculous. I was forced to do the project over, too.

She was so odd. She didn't know how to play a VCR. She always talked about boobs. She put a lot of info on tests we didn't even learn about. She called us "hoes" and yelled at us for absolutely nothing. How can I hold a grudge against someone like this nutcase?

> I have a physics teacher who loves to call my low grade out to the whole class at least three times a week and tells my status on how I am doing in the class as well. It is not the embarrassing part that gets me, but the fact that I am the student and he is a grown man who acts with this type of behavior. I feel that my status in any class is really between me and the teacher, and when teachers come out of the code I follow, well, let's just say we don't see eye to eye.
>
> —Jordan, 17

I can now look back and laugh at this memory that I'm sure not a lot of teens, or anyone in fact, experienced. To this day, I remain hexed because she never lifted it. Only the one who did it can lift it, and I hope I never see Mrs. Sugar Cookie again. Beware my fellow readers. It's a cruel world out there.

—Emily, 17

> I was on the cross-country team, but I wasn't any good. I was primarily doing it to keep involved, and it was a great way to keep in shape. I was running a race, and I was almost always last. I prided myself on finishing every time without walking. The coach ended up pulling me out of the race so he could get home early. I was so embarrassed and offended.
>
> —Lynsey

> Question authority, but first raise your hand.*

I got busted for shoplifting. It was just a matter of time, I guess. My father came to get me. God, what a holy mess. He kept saying I did it as a "cry for attention." That's insane. With everybody constantly watching me, criticizing me, telling me how I should wear my hair or when to go to bed, watching what I eat, this was one place where I felt like I could gamble for a little control. The last freakin' thing I want is attention.

—Sharyn, 16

Being my dad's first child, there tends to be jealousy issues with my stepmom and me. She always makes me break up with my boyfriends and tells their parents horrible things about me to where they lose interest in me. I don't blame her for not letting them in my room, but still, he has to sit downstairs all alone when everyone is upstairs. It sucks! My boyfriend and I have been together for a long time. She has never liked him, and he is a very likeable person. She threatens to tell his parents things, even though nothing ever happens and he doesn't even go in my room. It's really stupid. I can only talk on the phone once a day for ten minutes. He lives thirty miles away, and I barely see him. It's really hard in the house I live in.

—Toni, 17

There is one teacher in my school who constantly yells at me for no reason! I had a note saying I could carry my backpack since I have a major back problem due to a sickness. We're not supposed to have backpacks. And she sent me to the office saying I wasn't working with her when all I did was hand her the note!

—Kelly, 17

Most of the teachers are on a power trip. They always have to be in control, like this one teacher I have. He gets mad if another student asks you a question about what he just said, even though he talks too fast and uses too many big words. He thinks he is the only one allowed to talk.

—Nicole, 15

WHERE WERE YOU WHEN I NEEDED YOU?

I've always thought that it all would have been so much better if someone had just *listened* to me, and not just *watched* me. If they had taken the time to actually *get* me, see and hear where I was at that time. I often wonder what might have happened if one person—just one person—had taken the time to acknowledge that I was in a crappy situation, that stressful things had happened in my life and that it wouldn't always be like that, instead of trying to paint some artificially cheerful picture of all the stuff I was supposed to be grateful for and happy about. If one person had told me that it was probably the *worst* time of my life, I might have actually believed it, and I think that might have made me feel a little less crazy.

—Clare

Gym class: Hated by most obese children, a place to be harassed and embarrassed by some of our fellow students and by the Nazi gym teacher. I had the same rude, condescending gym teacher I first encountered in the seventh grade. It was in the spring, and we were outside playing some inane sport, which I have never been good at and never have been interested in. I missed the ball or something like that, and this teacher remarked that I had had too much chocolate Easter bunny. Most of my fellows thought this quite funny, and I heard it over and over again for years. Ha ha ha. So funny!

—Jon

I wish my parents had been more interested in my scholastic studies and supported my life interests. At times I felt very alone knowing that it was entirely up to me to make it. Ultimately this reinforced my strong sense of self, but back then I felt stranded.

—Nancy

Home life and the parents who control it are a huge part of life for a teen. Relationships with parents through this age of disarray vary. I have friends who don't speak with their parents; I have friends who smoke with their parents. Both of these are extremes. What I've come to realize is this: I am (and perhaps you are, too) angry, and that's okay. Why shouldn't I be? I live in a world where the cops (who I pay with my miniscule check) who are supposed to protect and serve me instead hassle me, where the administration at my school harasses me, and where teens, who are just like me, sometimes pick on me because we sit at different tables and wear different clothes. I read about the misery and poverty in different parts of the world as I watch my elders turn cold shoulders, and I watch immoral men make immoral laws in the name of

> What I really hated was when one of my fellow students, known to be a major asshole by most of the other prisoners, would act up and the authority figures would punish all of my fellow inmates. Now, we all knew who the assholes were. Why didn't the teachers? Didn't they know we had no influence over the assholes? Usually these unruly assholes were also bullies, whose actions against us were usually not noticed by the instructors.
>
> —Jon

morality, and the sum of these things makes me livid. However, just because I am infuriated is no reason to take this out on the people who love me most but don't feel my rage. You (and I) have to understand that they won't understand.

—Kyle, 17

I started at a new junior-high school in eighth grade. Despite peer taunt-ings, a lack of friends and teachers who saw my talents as more trouble than I was worth, I managed to limp to ninth grade in the same district. In ninth grade I fared a little better in the friends department and buried myself in my schoolwork. I also struggled with profound depression. That summer I attempted suicide twice and gave up believing there might be any kind forces in the world—if God, or some such being existed, surely I would be allowed to die.

> Some teachers are so dense sometimes. I swear, you could come in wearing a sign that says, "I want to kill myself," and they'd just look at you and say, "Open your book to page 83."
>
> —Dotti, 18

In tenth grade, a new history teacher started at the high school. At first he seemed exciting and outrageous, tattooed, loud, ask-ing for our opinions and ideas. I felt com-fortable enough to talk with him before lunch and walk down the hall. I finally felt that I had found someone I could understand and who might just like me. I didn't need him to think I was smart or special—I just wanted anyone who would listen and maybe commiserate. One day just after class began, when a student was complaining about homework and parents to a friend, my history teacher paused and listened. I can still hear his laughter and see his ponytail shaking. He almost doubled over in laughter and, trying to control himself, declared, "You will find later in life that these years are the best four years of your life. Someday you will experience real stress, real pain, and you will wish you were back here."

I felt like I had been hit by a bus. I wished I had been. I spent weeks miser-able, trying to comprehend the idea that I was living the best part of my life now. That what I felt was the best I would ever feel. I remember thinking, "If this is the best time of my life, I'm screwed."

—Emily, 23

HOME-GROWN HURT

I had a very privileged childhood. My parents gave me everything I ever wanted. I went to camp as a child and continue to go now as a riding instructor. My brother and I had four-wheelers, go-carts, cell phones, you name it, but as I look back I realize that what I did not have was attention from my parents. I never had one-on-one time with them; instead I got *stuff*.

It was a major upset to my life when my parents were separating. I was going to have to live alone. This transition was not easy at first, and I hated my parents for a while. With time, I have realized I cannot change people, but I can change myself and become a better person. The things others do cannot determine my happiness. I do.

—Kate, 20

High school was really hard for me. I did ninth grade in New Jersey, tenth grade in South Jersey, eleventh grade in Chicago and twelfth grade in New York. These changes were even harder as I wasn't with my parents. They remained in India, where we are from. My family thought that by sending me to the United States to study I would have a better future. Everywhere I went I had to stay with a relative. It was very hard to keep up my grades and get along with the family. They would always complain about something. I tried to keep everyone happy, doing things for them. At the same time I had to study, do my homework, help cook and clean up.

It was very difficult; it took months before I could connect with my parents by phone. It was, and still is, very hard to be successful in school without my parents. During the last week of ninth grade, my uncle decided that he didn't want to keep me. I failed my first final exam ever. In tenth grade I moved in with another uncle who claimed to have trouble with the rent, but just did not want to spend any money on supporting me. Then it was on to

Chicago to live with yet another uncle who always lectured me about getting married. After living with him I then moved back in with the uncle from ninth grade, and we moved to New York.

I still deal with all of these problems. I guess I have learned to work my way around them and to be strong. I know how hard I must work to achieve my goals.

—*Komal, 18*

My parents were divorced when I was four, but the fights were ongoing. They'd be on the phone yelling at each other, taking each other to court every year. When they say they're doing this in the best interest of the kids, f*** that. When the kid is screaming in their face that *this is not in my best interest,* when they don't hear that, it really makes you feel like you're not important at all. I threatened suicide just to get them to stop fighting.

I felt like I meant nothing to my parents. All the unique things about myself that I was proud of were not valued at all. If they had pushed me, I could've really gone far. But they just didn't care. You don't ignore kids or shut kids down when they're passionate about something. It got to the point where I just didn't have it in me to fight anymore. When no one responds, you just quit trying.

I would sleep in school with a blanket on a bench in the locker room at lunchtime. I was too stressed-out to sleep at home. There was no gentleness anywhere. It's always lonely when it feels like you try to do good things in life and keep getting shut down. It's like an extra hard backhand.

—*Simone, 21*

How do you stay sane when everyone else around you is going crazy? How do you stay sane when your family is going crazy? You check out, one way or another. I get a lot of practice. I should know. I wrote the following words a year ago:

FACT

One out of every eight Americans is a child of an alcoholic. [149]

My mom's drinking again—a lot. When my mom drinks, she gets drunk and mean. She drinks because she's miserable. She drinks because she's lonely. She drinks because she wants to kill my dad. So it seems.

My mom always gets violent when she gets drunk. She usually breaks the dishes, the pictures, the lamps—whatever she can throw. Last night was the scariest, though. My mom got drunk and threw not only lamps and dishes, but knives as well. She was mad about money, mad about having kids, mad about being married to my dad. She was just mad.

She got so out of control that my dad had to hit her to knock her out—just to stop her, so we could leave. This was the first time I'd ever seen him hit her. You don't know what fear is until you walk over your mother's unconscious body. We had to walk over her to get out the front door. We had to leave to let her calm down, so my dad said. As I was walking over her, though, I stopped to make sure she was still breathing. She was, but I was too scared to stay and too scared to go. I feared that she would die there on the cold floor, all alone.

Every time my parents have a drunken fight, I go home the next day, after school, to find my mom asleep on the couch—sleeping it off—and to find my dad cleaning up the mess. He's always home putting things back together, hugging us and promising it will never happen again. I usually can't wait to get home to see him and to see that everything will be okay. Today when I got home, my mom was sleeping on the couch. The glass was gone, and so was my dad. He left a note for me on my pillow. It read simply, "I can't take it any-more. I'm sorry I have to leave, but your mom has pushed it too far this time.

Please know that I will always love you. Love, Dad." Dad, how could you leave without me?

I wrote those words a year ago. I was heartbroken, confused and scared. Since then, my mom has gotten sober. My dad has come home. Life is a little saner. But most important, I am stronger. My parents

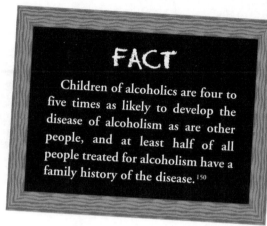

FACT

Children of alcoholics are four to five times as likely to develop the disease of alcoholism as are other people, and at least half of all people treated for alcoholism have a family history of the disease. 150

still fight, but without the violence and alcohol. I am stronger because I somehow learned to be stronger and saner all by myself—by checking out and leaving the fighting to them. I have a friend I talk to, actually, an older woman. I guess you can call her a surrogate mother. She's my 4-H leader. We ride horses together each week and talk about my family. She helps me to see that my mother is an alcoholic and that my family is just a family living with an alcoholic. When I'm not able to ride with my friend, I ride by myself.

I get out of the house, away from family issues, and think about my future. I like to ride by myself and imagine what life will be like when I have a career and a life apart from my family.

I think "checking out" this way is the only way I've come to stay sane amid some pretty hefty family insanity.

What can you do if your parents are abusive? Avoid getting into arguments with them. Don't let them trick you into fighting with them. Don't believe them when they call you names or say terrible things about you. And if it looks as though one of them could hurt you, LEAVE THE HOUSE AND CALL FOR HELP.

—*Evelyn Leite and Pamela Espeland*¹⁵¹

—Lori, 18

> I would probably do anything for a teacher I liked.
> —tenth-grade student, gang member

THANK YOU FOR BEING THERE

When I had a problem in a class, I asked the teacher for help. I got as much extra help as I could until I understood the topic. I would advise others in high school with a similar case to know their teachers, even if they hate them. It helps, first of all, when you want recommendations in the future. Mainly, however, it helps with the class you're having difficulty with. Make sure the teacher knows you're struggling and need help. Set appointments (early in the morning, before first period worked best for me) to get extra help. Ask them as many questions as you want because they are paid to help you. Most teachers will be glad to help anyway, although some won't.

—Paul, 19

> I love many adults in my life because they give me a positive mind-set and ambition to carry on in whatever direction life desires to take me. Adults are not perfect, but they do have the answers to life and they are a source of strength that helps me endure in this world. I am proud of the adults that I encounter because they all have a life lesson to teach me and a drive that helps shape me into the man I am today and toward the man that I will eventually become.
> —Jordan, 17

> As teenagers, we need to have an adult that we admire. We need an adult who knows what teenage students want and is willing to help us get what we need. Someone who can help us overcome the crises we encounter daily and give us a start in the right direction. Someone who is willing to help us believe that we can do anything if we put our minds to it.
> —Dorraine, 20

I have no memory of my high-school guidance counselor. I never met her during my four years of high school. I honestly do not remember how I came to be accepted into a college. As I try to piece together how my education came about, I have come to the conclusion that it happened through my participation in an organization called ASPIRA.

ASPIRA, not my guidance counselor, helped me and my mother put together whatever was needed to become a prospective college student. There was never any action on the part of my high school or the guidance counselor in making my college education a reality. All she did was send in my high-school transcript.

> I wish the administrators would just listen to us. Most of the time, when there is a problem, they just jump in and start handing out punishments. They need to hear both sides of the story, or at least listen and try to understand what happened.*

Approximately three years ago, I found my old high-school yearbook, and I searched through it and discovered who my high school counselor was for the first time in my life. I knew her face but *never,* while I was a student, did I ever meet with her or speak to her.

—Nydia

> Have the teachers take two minutes to get to know us and ask about how our day was or what we did over the weekend, instead of only asking about our homework.*

In my first year of high school, I messed up pretty bad. Fifty-fives all down the line for all my classes. At the end of that year, I met my guidance counselor. At first I used to go to his office to spend less time in class. He actually talked to me, didn't put me down and believed in me regardless of the stupid mistakes I've made.

We discussed a way for me to take eleventh- and twelfth-grade classes to see if I could graduate with my class. I didn't set my hopes too high because I felt

I could fail. My attitude began to tone down, and when I started bringing home those summer-school report cards, my parents' attitudes changed, too. They finally believed in me, my face no longer had a frown, and I began to believe in myself one hundred and ten percent!

—Sonia, 19

I had a science teacher in high school who gave us a test that we all flunked! Instead of blaming us, he apologized! It amazed me that he took responsibility for our failing the exam. Over the next two weeks, he went over all the material more slowly and made sure that we understood it. We even had a mock test before the real

> The thing I liked above all was that if you needed help, you got it. It's amazing how much the teachers care about you.
>
> —Bobby, 14

test to ensure that all the students succeeded. He was more concerned about the fact that we had all failed the test than he was about placing blame. I learned that when something goes wrong, sometimes "authority" can be in error. I mean, I grew up in a household where the adults were never in error, so this gave me a taste of an adult owning the problem, taking responsibility for a situation that didn't turn out right, and doing something about it.

—Roshael

> I don't like when teachers take their anger out on students. When I have a nice teacher, I learn more.
>
> —Jason, 15

The teachers who treated their students with respect were definitely the best ones I had. I enjoyed being given challenging assignments and getting the opportunity to work closely with my teachers on them. I also had several teachers who were able to pull off the "friends with their students" pose that many others just embarrassed themselves attempting. I appreciate the time I got to spend with these teachers in their classrooms and homes, the personal advice and support I got from them, and the fun my classmates and I had with them.

—Philissa, 19

I have to feel like I'm gonna be taken care of. If you do like me or if you don't like me, I need to know you're gonna be there. Don't try to help me; don't "therapize" me. I just need somebody to listen because when I talk I figure things out really well. I just want somebody who can love me no matter what, that I can be the most important person to somebody. I want to know that I can f*** up and you're still gonna give me a hug.

—Simone, 21

Probably the most significant and maturing event of my school life was when I got caught cheating on my Spanish final in eleventh grade. There were so many of us taking this test that they had us all in the cafeteria. I was sitting in the back of the room, but somehow my teacher saw my crib sheet. I remember him tapping me on the shoulder and marching me out of the room, all the way through the cafeteria. It was embarrassing from beginning to end.

Now this teacher's mother had gone to school with my mother, and I thought that their lifelong friendship would have some influence on the outcome of this event. I was sure he'd let me off the hook, but he nailed me. He didn't give an inch.

After school let out, I had to go back and spend the first week of summer vacation moving books from one end of the school to the other for several hours a day, cleaning up and getting the school ready for summer break and the following year. He eventually let me take the test over, but he made me work for the opportunity.

The amazing thing was that he managed to maintain a personal relationship with me. I even went to Spain with him for six weeks that summer and stayed friends with him throughout high school. He made me see that my cheating had not been a betrayal of our friendship, but a betrayal of myself. He held me responsible for my behavior, but he never held it against me personally. (I did pass the test!)

—*Steve*

Telling my dad I was pregnant wasn't easy. He screamed at the top of his lungs. His face was as red as a maraschino cherry. "You'll get an abortion. You have no choice but to get an abortion," he said.

I told him I was keeping the baby with or without his consent. It was my mistake, and I was going to take responsibility for my choice. Dad was furious. I had to move in with my mom after he kicked me out.

One thing that truly annoys me about high school is when teachers don't know how to discipline their students. In one of my classes, my teacher will give you a gazillion chances before she finally does something about it. It's really distracting for me because there are many students in my class who are extremely disruptive, and all she would do is tell them to stop but they would continue. She just lets these students walk all over her.

—Aleesa, 15

Mom put down her foot and flat-out told me, "You're going to graduate even if kills you. You will live your dream. Things may be complicated, but I will do everything to help you." Any hard feelings I had toward my mother vanished.

Not only did my mom have faith in me, so did my teachers. I strove to graduate and make my dream come true. I went through most of the year uncomfortable, grumpy and sick. I never told anyone, but one day my teacher pulled me aside and told me that she was proud of me for not wimping out and for sticking with school. I cried because I never knew how much people could care like that.

I do *not* regret defying my father. Whenever I look at my daughter, it only makes me more determined to graduate. I will live my dream that I've had since as long as I can remember, just like my mother said. I'm almost there, and nothing will stop me.

—Monica, 17

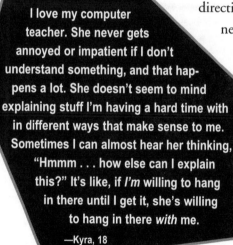

I love my computer teacher. She never gets annoyed or impatient if I don't understand something, and that happens a lot. She doesn't seem to mind explaining stuff I'm having a hard time with in different ways that make sense to me. Sometimes I can almost hear her thinking, "Hmmm . . . how else can I explain this?" It's like, if *I'm* willing to hang in there until I get it, she's willing to hang in there *with* me.

—Kyra, 18

What got me through high school was the direction provided by the school's one business education teacher. Looking back, she tended to spot students who had an aptitude for business. I took every business course the school had to offer. I even enrolled for shorthand, but I decided to withdraw because I was the only male in the class and I already had a "nerd" image. As a result she gave me special attention and actually provided two years of instruction in accounting where I was the only student. Her efforts inspired several students to go on to college and join the business world, including a few, like myself, becoming CPAs.

—David

I was a very negative, quiet, "into myself" kind of person. I had few friends at school. I didn't get along with a lot of people. I got good marks, but I lived my own life. By grade ten or so, I got into such a state of depression that I couldn't cope anymore. I started skipping school, spending my time alone, walking around just trying to get away from life and things that were happening.

My math teacher never mentioned my skipping. He just let it go. One day, I was sitting in this math class, and I started doodling on the back of the assignment paper. I had "insanity" written over all these scribbles and squiggles. I ended up spending my entire eighty-minute math class drawing this picture, coloring and sketching and drawing more and more until the whole sheet was covered.

> My eleventh-grade social-studies teacher was very sharp-minded, and he was the first person who taught me that you didn't necessarily have to believe what people in positions of authority were telling you. This was an incredible revelation to me. He made me realize that you didn't have to take on faith what anyone was saying, including him. In terms of my intellectual development, I owe this man a great debt.
>
> —David

The next day when I came back to class, my teacher handed back my assignment. Of course, I had gotten a zero on it because I hadn't done any of the work, but on the back of my drawing he wrote, "Life is trouble. My door is open. You are more than welcome to come anytime."

I went later that day. He'd been sitting back and watching me for a long time, knowing that I had problems. I guess he knew that if he'd have come to me, I would not have responded and would have blocked him out instead. But because he left it up to me to make this decision and I wanted to talk to somebody, I chose to go to him. He never questioned me about my picture, my marks, my skipping or anything else. I didn't really want to talk, so I just sat there for about forty minutes. I never really came up with anything to say, and he just sat there and let me sit alone and be quiet.

> Some teachers have this, like, built-in radar. They really pay attention to their students and notice when something is going on. I love the ones who listen and let you know they're there if you need them.
> —Dotti, 18

At the lowest point in my life, this teacher offered me a sanctuary by allowing me to go into his office anytime I got stressed-out in class. I could leave class and go and sit in his office, whether he was there or not. I went often. He gave me the guidance to be able to make decisions on my own, and he made it possible for me to sit in a room quietly and be able to think through my problems.

He taught me something very important that year. I still have that paper, and now and then I take it out and look at it. I remember that there was somebody out there who cared, who would just sit and listen, and who wouldn't judge. I don't know where he is anymore, but he had a tremendous influence on my life.

—Deanna

WHAT DO YOU APPRECIATE MOST ABOUT YOUR TEACHERS?

✓ Even if they're tough, the ones who treat you like an adult.

✓ The ones who are interesting and teach you things you haven't learned before.

✓ A teacher who cares and values students' opinions and values.

✓ Some never give up and help you regardless.

✓ The way they try to understand your problems.

✓ When they give you freedom and let you learn for yourself.

✓ The ones who actually care if you make it in life, who actually sit down with you when you have a problem.

✓ A teacher who goes that extra length to teach as well as be open enough to learn.

✓ Their sense of humor and their ability to try to have students understand the curriculum.

✓ When they adjust to student needs.

✓ A teacher who is open to new ideas and concepts. One who seeks self-improvement and being up-to-date with their skills.

✓ The teachers who do a good job supporting students, giving them encouragement if they don't fit in.

✓ The ones who love their jobs and really enjoy being with kids. You can tell who they are.

✓ The ones who make their classes entertaining and who care about the kids.

✓ Teachers who care are wonderful to talk to, especially the ones you've known for a long time.

✓ Teachers who can relate to students, joke around during class, and make learning fun, instead of dreadful, boring, sleepy classes.

ADVICE

GETTING HELP

If you don't understand why you got a certain grade, it's okay to talk to your teacher. This will work much better if you:

- Ask when the teacher will have time to discuss the grade.
- Don't do it in the middle of class.
- Don't put the teacher on the defensive by accusing him or her of being unfair.
- Keep the conversation focused on why the teacher gave you that grade and not on the negative consequences the grade will have for you.

- Politely ask the teacher to explain how the assignment would need to be different to get a higher grade (and if redoing it would be an option).
- Thank the teacher for taking the time to explain or clarify the situation.

CONNECTING
WITH SAFE ADULTS

©Zits Partnership. Reprinted with special permission of King Features Syndicate.

My parents gave us a lot of freedom. They allowed us to make a lot of choices, and we had to deal with the consequences. They were extremely supportive of our academics, lives, sports and general well-being. They did not impose themselves; they mainly listened and gave us advice when we asked for it. All through high school I did not have a curfew, which was a result of earning my parents' respect and trust. In the end, it was more important to not lose my parents' trust than to gain acceptance from my peers, mainly because my parents had done so much for me.

—Sarah, 23

Remember that your parents sometimes forget that you are not just their little boy or girl anymore. Sometimes it takes them quite some time to realize this. I'm still trying to get my parents to see this with me.

—Michael, 18

Teachers were always there for me in ways that my parents may not have been. I always felt that I could talk to at least one of my teachers about my concerns.

—Sandy

The needs of parents and the needs of teenagers are at odds with one another. If you can get out of your roles and begin to relate as people, if you can say you're both right and take it from there, you'll stand the best chance of liking each other and, most importantly, liking yourselves. And people who like themselves are remarkably easier to get along with.

—Alex J. Packer[152]

Students may feel that they don't have anyone to talk to. Myself, I won't see administrators or counselors because there's no relationship there. But I could very easily talk to my teachers or coaches.*

Although your parents rarely make sense and you wonder if they are completely screwy, they'll be there even when your friends leave you.

—Melissa, 16

Find somebody you can trust—one decent, caring, accepting adult who won't have some big agenda about the choices you're supposed to make. You do not have to go through anything alone.

—Beverly

ADVICE

MY PARENTS DON'T TRUST ME!

Do your parents trust you and appreciate how mature and level-headed you are? Or do you sometimes think they see you as a ten-year-old? Or worse, do they mistrust you, assuming that any minute they're not watching you, you're up to no good?

Gaining—and keeping—your parents' trust is a great way to increase your freedom and privileges. Even if you have a history of sneaking around or disregarding their rules and requests, you *can* change things with your parents so that you're not competing for power or constantly at odds with one another. Here are a few suggestions:

- Reliability builds trust. Follow through on your commitments. Do what you say you'll do. Come in on time—or better yet, come in early.
- When you blow it, avoid blaming or making excuses. Take responsibility for underestimating how long you thought something might take, forgetting an agreement or getting distracted—and make specific, definite and committed plans to make it right.
- Really, REALLY avoid doing things they specifically asked you not to do, even if you probably won't get caught.
- Respect their space and their stuff. If you break something, fix it or replace it—without being asked.
- Pitch in unexpectedly. Act more mature than they expect you to.
- Keep them informed if you're running late—before they start to worry.
- Involve them in your life. Let them meet your friends. Tell them things you're doing. Let them know where you're going.

- Ask for definite and clear instructions or expectations. Make sure your picture of what they want is the same as their picture.
- Don't leave out important information your parents will care about (and freak out about) if they find out later.
- Look for ways to create win-win solutions to problems and disagreements with your parents. Think: "How can we *both* (or all) get what we want?" Parents may be more cooperative when they see you making a sincere effort to consider their needs and their feelings.
- In some situations where they're resistant to letting you do something, ask what you could do to make them more comfortable or agreeable to your doing what you've asked them to allow. Even if the answer is usually "Nothing," there may be times, especially if you've been behaving reliably and maturely, when they'll be willing to deal.
- Even if you've never really given them a reason to mistrust you, understand that they may be having a hard time letting go or allowing certain things for reasons that have nothing to do with you—like their own fears and experiences, or worries about your safety, for example.
- If your parents say they trust *you* but they're concerned about the people you hang out with, build up a history of resistance to peer pressure and "bad influences." Again, let them get to know your friends. Let your parents see you as accountable for your behavior regardless of how others are behaving, and not likely to just go along with the crowd.
- Use mistakes and errors of judgment as learning opportunities. Make a plan. Think in terms of how you'll handle (or avoid) similar situations more positively, maturely or constructively in the future.

If you have violated their trust in the past:

- Understand that it may take some time before they can let go of their suspicions and fears.
- Realize that it's up to you to build up a new and more trust-worthy track record.
- Be willing to invest time, patience and persistence in rebuilding their trust.
- Validate their concerns and remind them of how you've improved: "I know I haven't been all that reliable in the past, but I've really been trying, and I want to get this right. I've been home on time every night I've gone out for the past three months."
- Ask for new opportunities to regain their trust in you, and do whatever you can to give them evidence that their faith was well-placed.

Describe an area in which your parents really seem to trust you: _____

_____

_____

_____

Describe an area in which your parents seem to trust you less than you might like: _____

_____

_____

_____

What events or experiences have contributed to this lack of trust? _____

_____

_____

_____

What type of commitment or behavior do you think it would take for your parents to trust you in a similar situation again? _____

_____

_____

_____

_____

What are you willing to do or offer in order to give your parents a good reason to trust you? _____

_____

_____

_____

_____

> Parents are more likely to really listen if you aren't angry or hysterical and don't have a chip on your shoulder. The more your behavior resembles a tantrum, the more likely your parents are to reject your pleas. The more rational, logical and reasonable your approach, the more likely your parents are to consider your request.
>
> —Chérie Carter-Scott[153]

ADVICE

PARENT MAINTENANCE

Things you can do to get on good terms with your parents:

- Acknowledge their presence
- Notice and be sensitive to their moods
- Watch your timing (adjusting requests and behavior to the emotions and needs of others)
- Talk to them, volunteering information about things that might interest them, and asking about what's going on in their world
- Bring things up before they become problems (and avoid ever volunteering your parents before checking with them first)
- Let your parents know where you are
- Smile on occasion
- Pick up after yourself
- Do things without being asked

—Alex J. Packer[154]

ADVICE

FINDING A SAFE ADULT

Of all the factors necessary for a student to succeed in high school, none has been proven to be more important than having at least one adult who is there for you and supports you unconditionally. Sometimes these people are easy to find and may be as close as right there in your home. Other times that special adult may work in your school. If you have not already found a supportive adult, here's how to seek one out.

Some of us are fortunate enough to have parents, extended family members, teachers, clergy or other adults in our lives that we can turn to for support and guidance. However, many students do not have safe and supportive adults in their lives. Hundreds of books have been authored on how to best help teens succeed in school and in life, and yet the most important factor seems to be having at least one adult in your life you can count on for support no matter what.

So what does a safe adult look like, and how do you go about finding one? The good news is that there are many adults who are willing and able to support you as you move through your high-school years. It does take some effort on your part to identify these adults and to connect with them.

Here are some of the characteristics of safe adults:

- Safe adults tend to lead balanced lives. They are not always in a state of crisis.
- Safe adults are consistent. Although they, like all of us, have good and bad days, they do not listen to you patiently one moment and then yell at you the next.
- Safe adults do not make you feel uncomfortable. They are not sexually or emotionally inappropriate with you.
- Safe adults are not looking to be seen as cool by teens. They understand that they are adults and are not looking to be a part of your peer group.
- Safe adults can clearly tell you that they do not like something that you may have done while still letting you know that they like you as a person.
- Safe adults do not always tell you what you should do. They give you choices and help you think through the possible consequences of each choice.

• Safe adults do not gossip or bad-mouth others. Here is a good rule of thumb: If a person tells you secrets about others or really says a lot of bad things about them to you, there is a very good chance that he or she will also talk about you in this way to others.

• Safe adults are also human. They do not always know the answer to a particular question, but they honestly admit when they do not know. They make mistakes like the rest of us, and it is important not to put anyone on too high of a pedestal.

How to find safe adults:

• Talk to adults. Safe adults are not likely to just come looking for you. You will need to interact with a number of adults in order to determine which ones you feel comfortable with.

• Ask the adults if they are willing to listen to you when you have questions or problems. Ask when it would be okay to call, or stop into their office or e-mail them. Ask them to clarify their boundaries: Can you call them at home or at work or after 10 P.M.? What is an emergency, and what can wait until tomorrow?

• Start by sharing little things about yourself and see how the adult reacts. Do not just sit down and tell all of your deepest secrets and fears the first time you chat.

• Don't fall into the trap of looking for the "cool" teacher, neighbor, etc. Many safe adults are more laid back and are not looking to be the center of attention.

• Listen to your instincts. Just as you can tell which teachers really care about kids and which are counting the days until they retire, you can get a good feel for which adults are sincere and which really are not to be counted upon.

It is important to have
more than one safe adult to count on.
Even the most dependable person may not
be available all of the time. People go on vacation,
have crises of their own or even leave the area.
It is a good idea to have a back-up person or even a
couple of people you can turn to in a time of crisis.
In the back of this book you will find blank Safe Adult
Cards. Once you have identified safe adults, fill out the
information on these cards listing the adults' names,
phone numbers, e-mail and other contact information.
If possible, take the card to a local copy center
and have it laminated so that it will last.
Carry it with you at all times.

Who can you go to for career
guidance? Relationship advice?
Academic help? Health, body or
addiction issues?

_____

_____

_____

_____

_____

FACT

According to research
by the Search Institute in
Minneapolis, teens need at
least three adults in their
lives (besides their parents)
who they can go to for
advice and support.

—Rebecca Greene[155]

_____

_____

_____

_____

What other areas of your life might benefit from the counsel of a trusted adult?

_____

_____

_____

_____

_____

Where else could you find an adult you can trust who would be available for you?

CHAPTER TEN

_____

_____

_____

_____

Saving Graces and Positive Places: Anchors, Outlets and Attachments

IF YOU KNEW you were going to be stranded on a deserted island for four years, you would immediately start thinking about what you would need to survive during those four years. Well, high school can be very much like that deserted island. What will you need to get you through these four years?

High school is a time when a sense of belonging, support and being a part of something can really help students succeed academically, stay out of trouble and ease some of the feelings of loneliness and not fitting in. Whether you're drawn to the football team, the band, the chess club or stage crew, or an internship, community service or a part-time job, the important thing is to have *something*. Here are some of the survival tools that helped get students safely through their four-year journey.

LIFELINES

✓ My four years in ROTC

✓ My friends and my f*** you attitude

✓ Sticking to people who meet my test of friendship

✓ Knowing that I have so many people who love and appreciate me that it doesn't matter who hates me

✓ Knowing that anything is possible and to always think optimistically

✓ Working hard

✓ Keeping a sharp tongue and a quick wit

✓ Without sports I'd be on the streets right now

✓ Doing my work and staying true to my friends

✓ Finding a clique or a group of people I could relate to

✓ Definitely keeping involved!

✓ A few good friends I could rely on and a supportive family (even if I didn't recognize it at the time)

✓ With high-school crew team, I was able to get through senior year

FACT

On a typical school day, seven in ten students spend time participating in activities such as clubs, sports, music, art or other groups or programs. Those who participate in such activities usually spend two hours doing them on a typical school day. Half of students who do activities believe that participating helps them do well in school.[156]

GIVING BACK

Get involved in at least one or two activities that sound interesting. It keeps you busy after school, and it's fun to make a difference for others in your school and community. It also can keep kids out of trouble.

—Ashley, 19

High school is a time to reach out, take a chance and give something a try—even if you won't experience instant success. Don't worry about what other kids think. If some activity doesn't capture your imagination or best use your skills, turn in a new direction.

The best advice I can offer is, "Give it a try!" I was a terribly shy teen, but I'd been writing stories since third grade, so a teacher suggested I write for the school newspaper. Me? Talk with people I didn't even know? I don't think so!

But I took a deep breath, gave it a try, and soon got hooked on the fun and adventure! If I hadn't enjoyed journalism back then, I could have stepped back and tried a myriad other opportunities at my big, lively, activities-packed high school. The atmosphere was so welcoming and full of encouragement.

Who knows what clues those high-school activities and classes could provide for future work, volunteer projects or life dreams? Today, when I hesitate about trying something new, I recall that little nudge in high school, and it propels me forward with new zest and enthusiasm to "give it a try"!

—Linda

When students work together to reach a common goal—especially when that goal involves helping others—they experience a sense of unity, personal worth and belonging.

—Allan L. Beane[157]

Doing service—
any act of kindness—for another
person is a great way to create a sense of
purpose and worth, build relationships, generate
goodwill, step out of a narrow focus on your
problems and generally feel good.

Think of someone who could benefit from
your time or talents, or someone you would just
like to help in some way. In the back of this book
is a blank "Service Certificate." Use it as a way
to say "I care." (You can also make
copies so you can spread
the joy around!)

WRITE ON AND RIGHT ON

I discovered writing as
an escape from a world of reality
in which I felt acutely
uncomfortable. It immediately
became my place of retreat,
my cave, my refuge.

—Tennessee Williams

I never had too
many problems socially because
I fell into a group of kids who had the
same interests and aptitudes, and similar
geopolitical knowledge and insights.
We were together for speech and
debate, model U.N., youth and
government, and Amnesty
International. These were all
student-motivated groups.

—Tara, 18

Involve yourself in an internship while
you're still in high school. Sometimes all
you have to do is ask. This is an opportunity
that will help you develop the professional skills
necessary for the "real world." It'll also
help guide you in choosing a life path.

—Joel, 21

Participating in extracurricular activities has been a major challenge for me. At the same time, they have also provided the best experiences and memories of my life. In ninth and tenth grade, I was a member of the ROTC Drill Team. I am proud to have competed in the National High School Drill Competition two years in a row. My drill team was like a family to me. Also, I did better in school, as no cadets were allowed to go to the Nationals if they failed a class. In eleventh and twelfth grade, I was a runner for the cross-country and track teams. I believe that without drill team, cross-country and track, I would have been depressed and bored.

—Amanda, 18

I've been keeping a journal since before junior high. There are a lot of times I have more feelings than I know what to do with, and nobody to talk to who will really listen to me. My journal has been a reliable, trustworthy outlet for me. I can get feelings out, work through problems and just be "heard" in a way I can't always get with my family or friends.

—Evonne, 18

I was getting involved with gangs and hanging out with the wrong crowd, so I didn't pay any attention to my schoolwork. I was one of those very bright kids who had to force myself to get a C in order to be accepted by my friends. I enrolled in every shop class imaginable. My counselors kept trying to put me in the college-bound courses, but I didn't want to do that because it wasn't cool.

I was also one of those kids who never needed a hall pass: If I didn't like your lecture, I just got up and walked out, and more than likely you were happy to get rid of me. I was always acting up in class. I was never a major danger, but always mischievous and just bright enough to get by.

One day I was out in the hallway, doing what I always did, just standing around talking to people. I was dressed in my gang attire then and trying to act "bad," you know, to the crowd. This one teacher came up to me, and she said, "You know, Lou, you're gonna wind up dead or in jail if you don't listen to me.

The school counselors were cool. Even though they were mostly good for venting, they truly were a comforting part of the sandpaper experience I call high school.

—Mark

I want you to take this class. I want you to tell me if you like it or you don't like it, but I want you to try it."

This class was called "Speech and Debate." I couldn't believe that young people in this class were getting grades to do what I was doing for free out in the hallway, talking and acting out. I remember sticking my hand in a hat, selecting a topic and defending it quite well. I said, "This is for me." And from that day on, I just soared like an eagle, went on ahead, went to college and did great.

—Louis

"And the award goes to . . . NIDA!!!" The camera pans to the shocked young lady, who is at a loss for words. She sits in her seat, stunned, in complete disbelief of what she has just heard. She cannot move, speak or think. She manages to stumble on stage and stand at the podium. Her mind is racing, yet she cannot put together words to form a sentence. But when she opens her mouth to speak, no words escape her. She can feel beads of perspiration form on her forehead. She looks up and sees the eyes of thousands staring at her, waiting for some sort of intelligible response. Her head begins to pound, and her heart races as time continues to waste away. Suddenly, there is an explosion of loud music that rips apart the silence, and she jerks up. She finds herself in her bed, listening to the radio. It was just a nightmare.

Public speaking is identified as the number-one fear in America. I shared this fear with many because I was an insecure and shy young girl. Whenever my teachers gave assignments that involved a presentation, I would have panic attacks. The thought of trying to explain things to my classmates, while they were staring at me, pointing at me and judging me was terrifying. Despite my timorous nature, my parents persuaded me to take debate class, and eventually join the team.

It was a dark and stormy afternoon as I walked into Room 220 of my high school and met my soon-to-be debate coach. I attended the team meetings wearily, and an overwhelming feeling of nervousness and anxiety grew. I was a very shy and chubby young girl, and starting high school was already a major obstacle. I could not even fathom getting up in front of a group of strangers and speaking intelligently about nuclear weapons, mental-health care or the oceans. My fears came true during my very first tournament. My partner and I were complete strangers and had never even practiced speaking. When the judge called upon me to speak, I felt as though I was going to vomit and came very close to tears. It was clear that my debate career was doomed for failure.

I somehow survived that weekend, and my parents encouraged me to continue with the debate meetings. The first month continued like this; I have honestly tried to block it out of my memory because it was very traumatic. But after struggling for a very long time, I began to get the hang of things. I became more comfortable speaking in front of people because I felt like what I had to say was worth listening to. I felt knowledgeable and worthy of someone else's time. The truth is that I felt inferior to many people that I was intimidated by, and debate changed this. And it was through debate that I realized what other people think doesn't matter because there will always be people who disagree with my ideas.

As I reflect upon my debate career, I realize that not only did I receive a wealth of information, but debate has also given me the self-confidence and composure that helped me survive high school. I had the courage to join other clubs and participate in sports. It gave me confidence to pursue leadership roles in other activities. Debate has given me the opportunity to travel all over the country. I have learned so much about the world and about myself. I have grown as a student and as a human being. I was exposed to many truths about the world and many unpleasant truths about myself. I am forever indebted to my coaches who held infinite forbearance for a very shy, unconfident, yet tenacious young girl. I am also very thankful

> I did something this year that surprised me: I ran for class president. I can't remember why I did it, but I did. Even though I didn't win, I made a lot of people laugh.
>
> —Chris, 14

to my parents because they supported me during my wins and my losses. Debate has taught me to present myself with poise and self-assurance to everyone, regardless of his or her beliefs.

—Nida, 17

Being an ESL student in high school was a good experience for me. I still remember my first day of school, going to my guidance counselor and asking for my schedule. At that time, I didn't even know what a schedule meant. Everything was different from what I was used to at the school I attended in Peru. The classrooms, students, teachers and administrators were all different.

I believe that taking ESL classes was very helpful to me in achieving in my studies because they were given by a teacher who knew Spanish and was able to communicate with me. From my own point of view, I believe that students who speak very little or no English at all should not be placed in a regular class because it can be frustrating. Not being able to communicate with the teacher and classmates can be very dangerous to the point where it pushes them to drop out of school.

In ESL classes, I met a lot of Spanish-speaking students from all over the world. This was good because I could communicate and relate with them.

Learning English wasn't easy at all. I think that being on the soccer team helped me to learn English, make friends, and to always keep busy with practices and games. Life is not easy, and you have to be willing to make sacrifices. This country gives you everything you need to become whatever you want to achieve. I will always be thankful to the ESL program at my high school.

—Francisco, 23

My whole life was falling apart. I felt like I was screaming, "Why doesn't anybody want to do anything about life?" It's really hard when you're a person who cares so much and has so many ideas about how things could be, but nobody wants to admit that there's anything wrong, and nobody can see where you're coming from.

> It is important to show up. Chances are, somewhere during your time in high school, something is going to be said that may have a major effect on your life. The more regularly you show up, the greater the chance that you will be there to hear it.

In eleventh grade, I pretty much dropped off the face of this school. I just blew off everybody. My advisor said I could go live with her or try to get into college early just to get out of my home situation. I found an emotional-growth boarding school that had workshops to help you work through your past and try and heal yourself. But it's a lockdown. You can't leave. You can't talk to anybody outside of the school. You can't wear your own clothes or wear nail polish or anything. It's very strict. There's no dating. You can't even talk about certain bands or kinds of music, or if a boy is cute. You can't speak to them or look at them. It's supposed to create a safe environment.

I went there voluntarily, and I was the only one there who did. Not a single other person who had come to that school had chosen to go there. They were blindfolded or tied up and taken there. I went there because I didn't have a better place to go. I knew I wouldn't be living much longer if I didn't go someplace that could straighten me out. It worked for me because I had to make it work.

—Simone, 21

FAMILY, FRIENDS AND FAITH

At school, I'm quiet and reserved, unlike at home or with my friends, where I'm a bit crazy. When I say crazy, I mean talking a lot, really fast, being a lot more outgoing and doing lots of fun things. I don't mean that I go out and drink, smoke and have sex. What keeps me away from those bad things is my faith in God. I grew up in a church filled with people who are strong in their faith. My parents helped me a lot in developing my faith. I thank them for that. Most all my friends are from my church family. We're a tight group, and we hang together. It's easier to stand up for what I believe and say no to bad things when I have my friends standing behind and supporting me.

> Having gone to an all-girl high school, I remember how much I enjoyed the camaraderie of my fellow girlfriends. They pulled me through the highs and lows of wanton hormones, the savage cliquishness of the other girls and a non-supportive family. We were a very creative bunch, always seeing the humor in absurd situations of which we had no control.
>
> —Nancy

I gave my life to God in the fourth grade. I remember giving God my heart, soul, mind and body. I love my Father God very much. If it wasn't for my faith in Him, I never would have made it through middle school, let alone high school. I truly feel that if I had not given my life to my heavenly Father when I did, I may be doing some of the terrible things I know other teens are doing. I only wish other teens knew that "happiness does not lie in things, but in the Maker of all things."

—*Ann, 18*

The way I deal with my fears is to make sure I fight against them every day to prevent them from coming true. Many times I think that I am in a dream world, and I am waiting to wake up. But when I go through the stresses of daily life, I realize that I am not in a dream world, that I am truly in the real world. My family and God are where I feel the safest. Anytime life starts to get too tough for me, those two roots are always the sources I return to. That is one of the main reasons why I have survived high school.

—Jordan, 17

I joined a B'nai Brith Youth group, an organization for Jewish kids, when I was a junior. I didn't find many outlets or groups in my high school that held much interest for me, but this group gave me a chance to develop leadership skills as an officer and newspaper editor, to perform in talent competitions, to play sports and to meet a lot of people. I think high school would have been unbearable otherwise.

—Ronnie, 19

Finding an identity outside of school is important because it allows for choices, variety and a break from school. For me it was my faith in Jesus Christ that was taught and encouraged at my church. It really allowed me to build relationships with young adults who listened to me and gave me advice, which I listened to because it was not coming from my parents.

—Sarah, 23

My mother and my good friends got me through high school. My mother always encouraged and supported me during my lowest moments and always let me know that I was a great person regardless of what was going on in the world. She loves me unconditionally. I had friends who I could confide in about high-school stuff. I had a great student advisor who helped with school stuff. There was a wonderful social worker who I felt comfortable talking to about my home life or insecurities at school. I also worked with a psychiatrist who is one of the most fabulous people I know. He allowed me to expose my feelings and fears and never judged me.

—Jena, 23

I had great parents who tried their best to encourage me to work hard in school and a God who gave me a conscience that kept me out of trouble—for the most part!

—Christa

SPORTS

I found that being involved gave me a positive identity, not only for myself, but for my school. Sports taught me to get along with all types of people and to respect and listen to adults other than my parents. Sports also taught me how to communicate and be a leader, skills that can be learned in any type of group setting, including the art club, chess club, etc. The main thing is to get involved!

—Sarah, 23

While most of my life during high school consisted of going to class, studying, attending Hebrew School, participating in a few clubs and waking up excruciatingly early, tennis was one of the few joys in life. I remember vividly winning the conference tennis doubles tournament. I had a wonderful relationship with the coach. Tennis always felt like a separate entity from high school. It was one of the very few outlets I had during an otherwise stressful time.

—Stephen, 22

Being involved in sports saved my life. That is how I made friends. I had good role models in my coaches as well as my parents. I did not give in to peer pressure too much. I had a strong sense of right, wrong and the consequences of both.

—Holly

I joined the wrestling team and got third place at one tournament. Once I threw up during practice. That's when I got one of my many nicknames: Ralph.

—Kristofer, 14

I played sports, so that helped a lot. Lots of funny memories around team events and road trips. It was hard, however, because I was not a typical jock and did not always fit in.

—Elena

Overall, my first year in high school was one of the most enjoyable, fun years of my life. This year wouldn't have been what it was without football. I excelled so much and had so much fun. I worked very hard and dedicated myself to the sport, and I am really happy with the outcome.

—Andrew, 14

THE ARTS

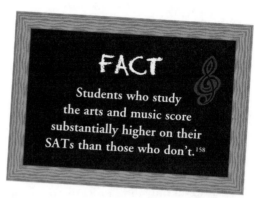

FACT

Students who study the arts and music score substantially higher on their SATs than those who don't.[158]

I was miserable almost the entire time I was in high school. The one thing that saved me was art. Anything to do with art. Drawing. Painting. Set construction. Fiber work. Ceramics. Sewing. Anything I could do with my hands. I could get lost for hours painting or making clothes. It was almost spiritual. It felt that grounding, that natural, that *right*. Nobody seemed to bother me when I was working on something, and it was a place I could be pretty successful. I wasn't cool, but boy, I could be creative. I don't think I would've made it otherwise.

—Gretchen

I still remember the day she came to observe our class. We were preparing for our Christmas concert, and she had come to watch as she was going to be taking over the position of band director at our high school. I remember not expecting much and thinking, *Boy, I wonder how long this one will last. None of our other band directors have ever cared. What makes anyone think she will?* Little did I know that our new band director was going to become a huge influence in my life in more ways than one.

The story of band in our district was not anything to brag about up until that point. We had been through four band directors in four years. The longest any of these directors ever stayed was for a grand total of two years. None of them really seemed to have the heart and the dedication to build the band program back up again, nor did any of them seem to care. And to make matters worse, we didn't help much either. We chased off most of the directors by playing cruel jokes on them and doing mean things to them. So really, it was no surprise that no one believed this new band director was going to last. But Mrs. Jacobs proved to be one tough cookie.

Through Mrs. Jacob's careful teachings and huge influence, I grew to love music—and not just the music I played in my CD player, but the music we played in band class. I loved the thrill of performing at concerts and contests. The sound of all of us playing together gave me a special feeling that I can't describe. Not only did I grow to love music, but also Mrs. Jacobs made me feel I was an important part of the band. She let me pick out music and do special jobs for her. When she needed another trumpet part player for a contest, I was the person she chose. She was always there whenever I needed her, and I was always there for her.

Just like that, band had become my life. Band had become the thing that, no matter how bad my day had been, offered an opportunity for me to do something I enjoyed and had fun doing. When those long days of high school were too much to handle, Mrs. Jacobs and band class became my shelter. I could get away from my world for a while and go into the world of music.

All too soon I was playing at my last high-school band concert, and in the blink of an eye it was over. But as I walked out of the doors of high-school band and high school itself and into the world of college, I realized I had come away with an even greater gift than I had previously thought. Not only had I come away with an appreciation for music and for the composers who wrote the songs I played with so much excitement, but I had also met one of the most influential people and biggest mentors in my life, which was a very valuable gift.

I joined school sports for the first time. I was on the frosh wrestling team. I really suck at wrestling, so I don't think I'm going to do that again. But then I joined swimming. That was fun. I got pretty good by the end of the year. I made varsity, so I got my letter and a patch as a swimmer. I loved this year. Too bad it went too fast.

—Erik, 14

I am now in college and still playing in the band. While it is nothing like high-school band class, I have come to the conclusion that nothing ever will be. The music and the memories will stay with me forever. I'm also proud to say Mrs. Jacobs has outlasted all of the bets and is in her fifth year as band director at my old high school.

—Lindsey, 19

High school is tough, and very few people will disagree with that. No matter what cliques you might have in your school, everyone finds high school stressful and hectic. But there are people who find salvation in activities, something that makes them want to go to school every day. Working in Sight & Sound really saved my high-school career from being a disaster.

In my first year of high school, I felt the need to be a part of something within the school. When I heard how fabulous the school musicals were, I knew I had to take a shot at it. My original intention was to get a lead role in the play, however, thinking about my audition now, I can see why I didn't make it my first try. I spoke with my mother, who always gives the best advice, and she told me to sign up for stage management. I laughed at that idea. I mean, what did the "techies" do exactly—run around with a headset on, speaking in a language that resembled gibberish? (I am very close to being fluent in "techie gibberish" now.) With no other choices, I signed up for stage management. I thought, *What did I have to lose?*

After the first meeting, and seeing the sets and props that I would be working with, I fell in love with the backstage life. A few of the older students who worked on previous productions showed me the ropes—literally! Being the youngest out of the management crew, I had to do the dirty work, and everyone made sure they didn't tell me that my job would be easy. Such jobs were crawling under the stage to hook cable mics, sweeping the stage before and after rehearsals, and putting away anything that was taken out. However, it all paid off. With my hard work and efforts, I received the position of assistant stage manager. Soon I was running around with a headset on and building the sets. As assistant stage manager for the school musical *Into the Woods*, I was so successful that my name was pasted around throughout the teachers' office as a hard-working person and a great leader. This was only the beginning of a wonderful year.

> **High school is not a predictor of the rest of your life. If you don't enjoy that moment in your life, there is a new world after high school.**
> —Jena, 23

Sadly enough, my busy schedule did not allow any fooling around because I had to keep up with my grades and schoolwork. If not, the consequences would be great, such as not being able to help with any performances. So I had to learn how to budget my time, not to fool around and to get my work accomplished. It may sound like a drag, but the rewards are unbelievable. Some people would complain about being at school longer then they have to, but it is a privilege for me. Also, with all of the activities I was involved in, I couldn't afford to miss a single day of school, so I made it a point to stay healthy and get to school every day. It didn't seem like a tedious job to go to school every day because I knew I had something waiting for me at the end, something that I enjoy.

School can seem like a torture chamber that will never end. Over the past few years, I have found that being active in your school can keep you somewhat sane. True, it can get stressful with the tests, the homework and the few difficult teachers who are "out to get you," but as long as you find something that is intriguing, high school won't seem so stressful, and it won't seem like forever. My crazy life of running about has showed me that high school is not one of the worst things that can happen to you, but really one of the best. These experiences have led me to a career that I wish to pursue, all thanks to high school.

—*Amanda, 16*

Throughout my lower education, I haven't had many hobbies. I didn't have many friends outside of the people in my classes in elementary school, and I wasn't very popular. This continued through middle school. I just didn't know how to relate to people. I had no idea that I was being annoying (and in some cases offensive) to the students around me. I was therefore very confused when my seemingly witty and relevant comments and actions were met with brush-offs and sometimes open hostility.

In eighth grade and early ninth grade, I got along by pretending I was crazy. (I was nothing of the sort, but it seemed to strike others as funny, and the teasing and loneliness let up a bit.) I've always sung in school choruses, way back from third grade, so when the announcement came for *Guys and Dolls* auditions, I signed up.

I met people there, and I hung out with classmates after school. It was very new to me. And most of the cast liked me because I could sing and read comfortably. (In ninth grade, good acting meant being loud and not stuttering.) School was still a struggle—I was always afraid of people making fun of me, or worse, of deserving their laughter.

> I take my life into perspective; I realize the short existence of high school will not affect my reputation outside. The cold prison in which we sacrifice four years of our lives is the gamble that we will be popular or a loser. The lottery ticket is not in your hands, but you do affect the numbers.
>
> —Chad, 17

By pure happenstance of conversation, two of my castmates from *Guys and Dolls* told me that maybe I should join the AARTS Academy. This seemed impossible. I didn't dance, I didn't act, I didn't think I could sing that well, and I didn't know if I wanted to keep performing. I thought of *Guys and Dolls*. I thought of how much it took my mind off of school and the loneliness I felt. I convinced my parents to let me join the AARTS Academy. Near the end of ninth grade, I hung out with some of the cast members from *Guys and Dolls* more frequently and sang with some of them in chorus. I almost felt popular. I started to open up—just a little bit. I stopped taking it for granted that I'd be laughed at in classes.

High school was tough—but not nearly as tough as junior high. I had a clean slate because I wasn't with most of the people from my younger years. But more than that—so much more than that—most of the people in my academic classes were people in the AARTS Academy. When I went to math and science and English, my classmates had a respect for me that they could only have learned to foster through listening to me in chorus, or by watching me in acting class. People started liking me. Several girls in high school wanted to go out with me. They liked my confidence, which I had received through singing and acting (and sometimes dancing) in my arts classes, in the three choruses I was in, and later, in the hallways and classrooms of high school. I could dance and sing in the halls! And people enjoyed it! I felt like a completely new person.

I spent four or five hours every day rehearsing. One hour in acting class, anywhere from one to three hours singing in my choruses, and countless hours at play rehearsal. Most people who performed at high school had schoolwork, rehearsal and downtime to recover. For me, rehearsal was my downtime, but it wasn't really downtime. It was high-octane fuel that made me so happy and proud of myself that I didn't know what to do. The sense of accomplishment after a good rehearsal, a great performance, even the pride that accompanies being asked advice on performing from older, more experienced students, all kept me going. I almost always had a smile—not because I felt that I had to in order to keep the taunts and jeers at bay, but because I was almost always happy with the work I was doing.

I don't think I've ever thanked my teachers enough for changing my life. They did, after all, make me into a completely new person, one who could dance and sing in the halls! In junior high, all I could do was look down at my shoes as I dragged my shoulder against the wall.

> What helped me get through high school was knowing that this time would soon be over and that I would have more control over my life.
>
> —Nancy

—Karl, 19

For four years (that's 208 weeks, 1456 days, 34,944 hours, 2,096,640 minutes or 125,798,400 seconds), you will be a high-school student. How will you use this time?

I want to spend more time doing _____

_____

_____

_____

I want to spend less time doing _____

_____

> The future belongs to those who believe in the beauty of their dreams.
> —Eleanor Roosevelt

_____

_____

_____

_____

HAVING A GOAL

Imagine, in the dead of night, a small, indistinct fishing boat starts its journey toward the possibility, not certainty, of freedom. It is crammed with sixty-four people, literally on top of each other. Their faces are ragged, and their clothes are torn. The smell is foul, and as the boat sways, the sound of someone moaning can be heard. Soon after, the stench of vomit starts a chain reaction. After twenty-three days of that monotonous routine, a voice exclaims, "Thuyen den roi!" which means that the boat has arrived. Everyone expels a sigh of relief. Freedom is no longer a dream, but a reality. Is this scenario a figment of my imagination, or did it really happen? On that boat was a family of three: a mother, a father and a baby girl. That family was mine.

On August 15, 1988, we had emigrated from communist Vietnam to Hong Kong. This was my parents' second attempt, and although the first ended in failure, they didn't give up. They believed that they could succeed, and they did.

Now, living happily in America, my parents have often recapped their escape to show me how difficult life was and how easy life is now. After dinner my parents would march into my room and begin the sojourn tale. "My daughter," they would start, "lately we have not seen you do very much studying. How are you going to be a doctor if you don't study? The only reason we came to America was so that you could have that bright future we dreamed of." And my usual response would be, "Yes, ba ma, I know." They'd ignore my comment and continue their long story. Their first attempt to leave was a failure. They had to go to prison for six months. At that time, my mom was pregnant with me, so she would explain about how hard it was to be pregnant in a prison that was filled with many diseased-ridden people who were missing more than a couple of teeth. "In prison," she would begin, "I was sick the whole time. Luckily, we were only there for six months. But when we got out, we didn't have a single penny to our name. It was all used up for that voyage to America. We had to work for two long years after you were born to try again." Then their story would turn to their second attempt. They'd say, "It was very hard to be granted asylum in America. Only one in a thousand families get this, and because we were very persistent and believed in ourselves, we were that tenth of a percent."

> The idea that I could craft my own future propelled me and gave me energy even when I was worn out. I didn't particularly hate high school, but I did think there was something better out there, and it was my goal to enable myself to find it. My friends, family and teachers, of course, also helped—spending time with people you love and enjoy makes any trying situation more tolerable.
>
> —Philissa, 19

Finally, they would get to the end. My dad or mom would look for a textbook, place it in front of me, open it to some random page and say, "You know how important it is that you go to college. You need to make our sacrifices and suffering worth it. Or else you won't get into Cornell. STUDY!" And off they went. I would stare at the textbook, contemplating the story I had just heard.

Although recounted many times, I never got tired of it. Why? It's a story

> When you have a dream and you recognize it as something you can actually strive to realize, I believe life opens up and offers opportunities.
>
> —Les Brown

about my life. If they had not succeeded, my life would be very different. I would be selling lottery tickets from dawn to dusk, with hips bruised from constantly carrying little brothers or sisters. But I'm not. I am a very intelligent teen who instead of a being high-school dropout in Vietnam, will be a bearer of not only a high-school diploma, but also a college diploma and, hopefully, an M.D. The idea that strength of will is stronger than strength of body has been hammered firmly into my head. Mom, Dad, I know what you're telling me: "Life doesn't always go to/The stronger or faster man/But in the end, the one who wins/Is the one who thinks he can." And I *know* that I can. I can succeed in high school, I can succeed in college, and I can succeed in life. Not only that, I will.

—Ngoc-Quynh, 18

Of everything that you go through in high school, you must have one thing that will keep you sane. You gotta have something to look forward to, at least one thing during your not-so-long stay at high school. Some teacher you like the most, some class you absolutely enjoy, some performance for the year that your school does, whatever floats your boat. After high school, you will have fewer chances to experiment with what you want to do. High school is all about experimentation, really, now that I think about it. After high school, the free ride that your local taxpayers have given you for a good thirteen or so years is up, and you are now fending from your own wallet.

—Michael, 18

High school is my future to college and to my profession. This is why I'm doing my best, because high school isn't forever. It's the first step of life.

—Eddie, 15

THE FACTS

YOUNG PEOPLE'S ASPIRATIONS[159]

Be in a career I like	Boys 86%	Girls 89%
Be in love	Boys 69%	Girls 75%
Make more money than friends	Boys 49%	Girls 39%
Be famous	Boys 27%	Girls 26%
Be my own boss	Boys 29%	Girls 21%

ADVICE

SET S.M.A.R.T. GOALS

Specific. Exactly what is it you wish to accomplish?

Measurable. How will you know when you have reached your goal?

Action-oriented. Describe the steps you will take to reach your goals.

Realistic. Choose things you can actually accomplish or learn to do.

Timed. Set deadlines for each of your goals. Adjust as needed.[160]

Live as if you were to die tomorrow. Learn as if you were to live forever.

—Mahatma Gandhi

GOALS

Living a life without conscious goals is like a driving a car with no idea where you want to go or the route you need to travel. You do not need to plan out every part of your life, but see what happens if you set some short-term, moderate-term and long-term goals.

Start with a simple goal, something you know you can accomplish. For example: clean your room, call a friend, write a letter, etc. From that success you can work on larger goals like improving your grade in math, exercising more, cursing less, etc. Try it, and see what happens!

This week, I want to accomplish:

_____

_____

_____

_____

This school year I am going to:

1. _____
2. _____
3. _____
4. _____
5. _____

By the time I turn twenty, I will:

1. _____
2. _____
3. _____
4. _____
5. _____

Studies have shown that students who set goals for themselves are more likely to suffer less stress and anxiety, and can concentrate, remember better and achieve more. Create a goal you want to achieve, and you increase the likelihood that the energy and resources you need will follow!

CHAPTER ELEVEN

Purpose, Perspective and Possibilities: Hanging In, Holding On and Looking Back

HIGH SCHOOL can feel like an out-of-control amusement-park ride that is never going to end, but the truth is, it will. How do you make it better now or just hold on until it ends? One strategy is to think about what you want your life to look like after high school. If you don't like how people have labeled you in high school, start to think about who *you* want to be. What do you want out of life, and what steps do you need to take to get there?

Here are flashbacks, feelings and feedback from those who have survived the four-year roller-coaster ride called high school. Maybe they have a tip to share that could make your own high-school journey a safer and smoother ride.

LIFE AFTER HIGH SCHOOL

> Things change.
> Just because life sucks
> at one moment doesn't
> mean it always will.
> —Laura Potash Fruitman[161]

I wish I'd had a college student's guidance—someone to say, "Yes, it sucks, but it'll all change in just a few months. Hold on!" This simple statement from a non-parent would have helped tremendously. Despite being at the height of the rebellious stage, I still think that I would have taken to heart the suggestions of people who had been through it. Most of the time, high-school kids are enamored by older, "cooler" college kids, wanting to seek out the secrets of their own future. I would not only have benefited from this important knowledge as far as staying in school goes, but I think I would have had a hint of perspective to realize "the world doesn't end here." It would have helped.

> I have this recurring
> nightmare: I'm back in high
> school, and I can't get out.
> —Ruthie

—Joel, 21

I had tried being the best at sports, at school, at being the most social person. I tried everything. I tried being a very giving person, going out of my way to make everybody feel good. I went through every way of being that I could, but nothing was fulfilling. Sometimes there is nothing you can do but wait. Things will happen. I believe in miracles. I did not believe in this before. I felt like there was absolutely no way to get out of that hole. But I found out that it's not when you think you can't take it anymore that it's the last straw—ten times *later* is the last straw.

Hang in there, and life changes for you. Everything goes through phases, and people grow and change without even trying. Everything comes in waves.

If you just hang out through the bad ones, a good wave is coming. I believe that God knows when you can't take anymore, not just when *you* think you can't take anymore. Something changes for people who hang in there. I just had to hang in there till I was twenty years old.

—*Simone, 21*

I wish I would have known that high school is not a big deal in the long run. I mean, academically it is important in terms of getting into college. But what happens in high school does not determine the course of your life. I do not see now most of the people I met in high school, and perhaps I will never see them again. I let so

> I am convinced I never would have received my doctorate if I had taken the results of standardized tests too seriously.
> —*Sen. Paul D. Wellstone*[162]

many things bother me that were just so little and stupid and not worth the time. I spent too much time feeling sorry for myself and worrying.

I think all of my friends now agree that if we had the choice to go back to high school, we never would, but we appreciate our time there and what we have learned from it. In retrospect, we look back at the things we have done, the things we said, and we laugh. During high school, I would never have been capable of doing that.

—*Jena, 23*

I wish I knew I didn't have to accept the way things were, and that I could have made a difference. I think if I had tried to be more active in changing things, I could have made a difference there for others.

—Josh, 20

You don't know which "nerd" might be the next Nobel laureate—or actor or billionaire. What you *should* know is that it all gets shuffled. Top dogs and underdogs sometimes change places. The elite clique doesn't stay on top forever, anymore than the school's untouchables stay on the bottom.

—Carol Weston[163]

How you rank in your high school shouldn't matter as long as you have your true friends there beside you. It will be all right, and there are way more important things to come in life besides what you wear or how you look. And remember that the hard times and the bad people you meet don't have a whole lot to do with the rest of your life. Believe me!

—Emily, 17

The biggest surprise for me after high school was realizing that high school doesn't mean everything, and who you were in high school doesn't mean all that much.

—Lynsey

My biggest surprise after high school is the hard decisions life brings. Making decisions for myself that will stick with me for the rest of my life is scary.

—Christa

I was most surprised by the fact I could actually enjoy life, and I didn't have to just watch as it goes by with me being stuck doing things I didn't want to do.

—Josh, 20

I was surprised to discover how easy real life is compared to the expectations of school.

—Nancy

It gets interesting! You finally get to challenge yourself intellectually, and you meet interesting people who have a passion for the same things that you do.

—Andreas

WHAT SURPRISED YOU MOST ABOUT LIFE AFTER HIGH SCHOOL?

Learning that education is *not* just about being able to regurgitate stuff a teacher feeds you in a form that the teacher wants or can understand. That the world isn't quite as black-and-white as I thought it was. That authenticity really *does* count more than a degree or designer label. That the world has space for me, and is far more accepting of what I have to offer and who I am. That the world is so much larger than I thought it was in high school, and that what was real and important there was real and important *only* there.

—Beverly

I think what surprised me is the fact that there is "life after high school." It is a new life. High school is this miniscule moment in time that is awkward, generally fun and confusing. After you're done with it, you start a new chapter in your life.

After high school you are given a clean slate. You can be whoever you want. You can start all over. People don't know you as "that girl from high school." You can be the person you always wanted but were afraid to be. People don't care about what you did or who you were in high school.

—Jena, 23

I was surprised at how unprepared I was to make decisions and manage my own life. I had very controlling parents, and throughout high school even the smallest decisions were made for me. I left home desperate for a sense of freedom and very little common sense—a bad combination!

When I got to college, I consistently got in trouble because there was no one there telling me what time to go to bed, nagging me to go to class or even

> I thought I would automatically gain maturity and insight when I graduated.
>
> —Elena

reminding me that if I didn't do laundry *really* soon, I wouldn't have anything clean to wear. I wish I had learned those skills at a younger age. I think I could have avoided learning many lessons the hard way from getting into the painful, dangerous and even illegal situations I often found myself in.

—Jeri

I found out very quickly that I wasn't the big fish in the little pond anymore! I proudly graduated in the top 10 percent of my senior class of about 550 kids at a top sub-urban high school. Suddenly, I was plopped down in the midst of a bunch of brilliant freshmen from all over the world in college! There I was, in classes with amazing kids who were National Merit scholars, kids at

> The tests in college are a lot more cumulative of everything you study. You need to know everything in the chapter, not just the definitions. Now that you're on your own, teachers don't check whether you come to class or not. So you have to do it on your own, and not just go to class to not get in trouble.
>
> —Matthew, 18

the very top of their classes, kids from the world's elite private schools. My professors were imposing and demanding, too. My French instructor was a French woman with an accent so strong she might as well have been speaking Chinese for all I could understand—even though I'd gotten As in high school!

It was a humbling and terrifying experience! What the heck was I doing there? But gradually through time, I found my own strengths. I also learned that these brilliant global students were just people, too—with some of the same interests, dreams and passion for life. That freshman year, with time and a lot of patience and new friends, I eventually found ways I could swim a little more freely in those bigger, scarier and much more challenging waters.

—*Linda*

HOW IS YOUR LIFE BETTER NOW THAT YOU'RE OUT OF HIGH SCHOOL?

It seemed like everything got better as soon as I graduated. I went off to college, where there were so many more people, and I could hang out with anybody. I had a lot more choices socially, and academically, too, which was important to me. I was challenged intellectually. Every class I took, every course I passed, took me one step closer to getting what I'd need to eventually start my own business and be my own boss. I have a wonderful husband, live in a place of my choosing, make my own hours, and though I always seem to be working, I'm doing something I love, which makes it not feel so much like work. I'm not trying to brag, honest. All of this is hard-earned. And none of it seemed possible back then.

—*Nikki*

> What surprised me most about my life after school is how many more people accepted others in college and in "real life." They weren't so cliquey. Rather, the judgmental and snotty people were the minority rather than the norm. I was also surprised at how popular I became at college, which was the opposite experience I had in high school.
>
> —Cheryl

I have more options to make decisions and don't have to worry about nonsense (like being made fun of) as much.
—Lynsey

My life is significantly better than in high school. I have a great job, a wonderful girlfriend, a car, strong relationships from college, a litany of experience, etc. In high school, I thought I was more of a follower than a leader. In college, I demonstrated many leadership characteristics. Compared to high school, my life has improved tenfold. Life does get better! Independence, freedom, flexibility and wisdom are just some of the benefits post-high school.
—Stephen, 22

In college, I feel like I'm doing schoolwork for something I'm gonna have a career in, not just classes you have to take. I feel like I'm living my life, not the life my school set for us. I'm doing things beyond the basics, for something I can use in my life. I get to live my own life.
—Matthew, 18

Since high school, I am free to pursue my own academic interests, and I do so with fervor.
—Lisa

My life is better now. I am married with three precious little girls who love and look up to me no matter who I was or what I did in high school.
—Christa

Once you get out, you can do whatever you want, and I like that. I also like being able to work and earn money. I'm pretty tight with my money, so it's not just about having stuff. Being able to work and have money gives me a lot of freedom.
—Jose

Overall, I would say that the only true thing that is better, now that I am out of high school, is the fact that I am out. I never ever got hurt bad, but the teasing was absolutely relentless! Surviving during high school was very hard, but I got through it. Sometimes I just don't remember how, but I must have waited it out. It hurt, but it was worth it.
—Mark

While I never felt oppressed by family, I do feel a greater sense of freedom now that I am not living in my parents' house. Making my own decisions about what to study, buy and do each day has given me a feeling of independence and an ownership over my successes—and failures. I've also been fortunate enough to find myself in a school where I feel intellectually and socially comfortable, and making friends has gotten easier and easier for me. Many of the greatest stressors of high school, though, have only been exacerbated—I still have no idea where my life is going!

> I'm no longer suicidal. I know my own worth, and I'm truly happy.
> —Jan

—*Philissa, 19*

THE FACTS

HAVING A TOUGH TIME AT SCHOOL?[164]

- Pablo Picasso's father pulled him out of school at age ten and hired a tutor who soon gave up and quit.
- Bill Gates dropped out of Harvard and went on to found Microsoft.
- Charles Mingus, jazz musician and one of the most important figures in twentieth-century American music, was beaten and verbally abused by teachers who pronounced him unable "to keep up with the white pupils."
- Albert Einstein didn't speak until age four, couldn't read until age seven, flunked all of his math classes, failed his college entrance exams, and generally disturbed his teachers with "unanswerable questions" and a tendency to smile "for no apparent reason."
- Thomas Edison ran away from school after being beaten with a cane for fidgeting and not paying attention.

- Malcolm X was told by his favorite teacher that Malcolm's dream of becoming a lawyer was "no realistic goal for a [black person]."
- Walt Disney was fired by a newspaper editor because he had "no good ideas."
- Werner von Braun, one of the world's first and foremost rocket engineers, failed ninth-grade algebra.
- Louis Pasteur was rated as "mediocre" in chemistry when he was at college. His work connecting germs with infectious diseases became the foundation of the science of microbiology and a cornerstone of modern medicine.
- Dr. Seuss's first book was rejected by twenty-three publishers.
- Abraham Lincoln was a captain when the Black Hawk War started. He came out as a lowly private. He also struggled with depression throughout his life.
- Oprah Winfrey failed as a reporter and was later reassigned to a local morning talk show, which was the beginning of her monumentally successful career.
- Jean Potter was referred to secretarial school by a high-school guidance counselor who assured her, "You'll never make it through college. Don't waste your father's money." She ignored this advice and went on to become a successful children's author and the Assistant U.S. Secretary of Education.
- Beethoven never learned to multiply or divide, and was told by his music teacher that he was "absolutely useless as a composer."
- Salma Hayek was expelled from her Catholic boarding school for setting all the clocks back in the nuns' quarters.
- Nicolas Cage was suspended for putting dead grasshoppers in the salad at a school picnic.
- Anna Kournikova got in trouble in school in Russia when teachers found out that her father was taking her take-home tests for her.
- Owen Wilson was expelled for cheating in geometry.
- Justin Timberlake won his high-school spelling bee, as did Barbra Streisand.
- Tom Cruise might not have had such a successful career as an actor had he not lost his position on his high-school wrestling team following a knee injury.

IF YOU BELIEVE IT, YOU CAN ACHIEVE IT

> You have powers you never dreamed of. You can do things you never thought you could do. There are no limitations in what you can do except the limitations of your own mind.
>
> —*Darwin P. Kingsley*[165]

ADVICE

BEING MORE POSITIVE

Positive people tend to be happier, have more friends and do better in school. Here are some ways to become a more positive person:

- Expect the best for yourself and others.
- Set goals and work toward them. Focus on what you want, rather than on avoiding what you *don't* want.
- Respect other people's dreams, even if they seem impossible.
- Keep trying, even if you make mistakes or encounter obstacles.
- Don't automatically expect negative outcomes. Imagine that your world can be even better than you can imagine.
- Look for the good that can come out of bad experiences.
- Fight fear with faith. Keep your thoughts positive.
- Develop "an attitude of gratitude." (See page 271.)
- Minimize the amount of time you spend with negative or pessimistic people. If possible, avoid them altogether.
- Minimize your exposure to negative or pessimistic news and entertainment. Seek out positive, uplifting sources of information and entertainment.

Even if you naturally think negatively, you can learn to change. Practice, practice, practice.

Don't feel deprived if you think you don't have enough of something because your soul is helping you to assemble a life that no one else will lead except you. One day your attention may be caught by a frog on the edge of a pond because you are meant to be a biologist, while your friend may notice only the water because he is meant to follow the sea.
—*Deepak Chopra* [166]

Always know in your heart that you are far bigger than anything that can happen to you.
—*Dan Zadra*

I was five years old when my father was shot and killed in front of my family and me. He was struck and killed instantly by a stray bullet while trying to break up an argument between two people. My life has been full of pain since I lost him. It has been especially difficult growing up without a father giving me good advice and keeping my life on track.

When he died, I thought that my life had ended, but with strength from God, I realized that if he were alive, he would want me to do what's right and to focus on school because education is and will always be the key to success. I thank God that even though my mother was devastated by my father's death, she was blessed with the strength to take care of her nine children. Her strength and wisdom were key to keeping us all on track and eventually freeing us from the manslaughter in Liberia.

When my family and I escaped from Liberia, we were forced to flee at night because leaving during the daylight hours meant being caught, tortured and/or killed for turning your back on your country. We escaped to the nearby country of Guinea where we sought refuge for seven years. During those seven years, I witnessed children die of starvation, lack of medicine and dehydration. After spending seven years in a refugee camp in Guinea, we moved to Ghana where we spent a year in a refugee camp as well. By this time, my older brother had already made his way to the United States and sent for us one by one.

The United States was a great contrast to life in Africa, especially the education. In Africa, the war prevented many children from going to school because it was very difficult to pay for school and buy food at the same time. Now being in the United States, I quickly realized that there are many opportunities here and was most amazed at the fact that school is free and there are many supplies here, unlike many African schools. However, I could never understand why so many students in this country take education as a joke and disrespect their teachers and don't take them seriously.

Academically, I am not the strongest student, but I am a very hard worker. I have disciplined myself to study hard all day in school and work just as hard immediately following school until the late evening on the soccer field. As a result I've maintained a B average, excelled in soccer and have led my team to many victories as a player and a captain. Where I'm from in Africa, there are not any opportunities. In this country, there are many opportunities, and you are able to make your life better.

—Yanquoi, 18

Some of God's greatest gifts are unanswered prayers.
—Garth Brooks

No pessimist ever discovered the secrets of the stars, or sailed to uncharted land, or opened a new heaven to the human spirit.
—Helen Keller

In order to be a realist, you must believe in miracles.
—David Ben-Gurion

ADVICE

DON'T THINK YOUR WAY INTO A CORNER

We have the power to sabotage the quality of our lives by the way we think. When we confuse what we want with what we need, it becomes almost impossible to ever be happy. Here are a few unhealthy thoughts and their healthier alternatives.

Unhealthy Thoughts	Healthy Thoughts
• I have to do it perfectly or I am a failure.	• I would like to do better, but if I know I have done my best, no one, not even me, can ask for more.
• If others would just do it my way, things would be fine.	• I may like things done my way, but there are many ways to get things done. People have the right to do things the way that feels comfortable to them even if it is not the way I would do it.
• If I don't get what I want (for example, an "A" in chemistry or a date with Jenny), my life totally sucks.	• An "A" in chemistry or a date with Jenny would be awesome, but each of those things is only a part of my life. Neither of them determines if my life sucks or is great.

Write down three of your unhealthy thoughts.

1. _____

2. _____

3. _____

Now write down three healthy thoughts that you can use to replace the unhealthy versions.

1. _____

2. _____

3. _____

"Education is the key to success," my mother kept telling me. Being educated means having the chance at a better life, a life in which you could be a part of a better society.

I was born in Monrovia, Liberia, into the heart of a civil war that lasted seven years. Seven years of bloodshed and killing, seven years of no place to live, seven years of hardship—no food, no water, no medicine for the sick, people dying of hunger, thirst, diseases, children separated from their family, brothers killing brothers because they were told to do so. Seven years of children watching their parent being shot, unable to prevent it from happening, babies missing, pregnant women being killed, people being raped, old, young, children, adults, their narrow lives became a rough road, a cup filled with pity, which allowed them to be infected with hatred and revenge. After seven years of civil war, children's lives had nothing to do with education. Their minds were filled with one thing—to kill. Little kids from eight to seventeen years of age were holding guns, like GMGs, AK47s, M1s, M16s. These are dangerous weapons, and they were in the hands of kids with nefarious minds, minds with no passion, no emotion, minds filled with nothing but the desire to kill. It was this time that changed my life forever.

I was separated from my parents and went away with my brother and sister. I became a refugee in Ghana, where I went to school. The school system in Africa is very different and difficult, but if you put your mind to it, you can achieve. With limited resources for schooling, students still manage to pursue their education and do so seriously with no playing around. Students go to school from 6 A.M. to 6 P.M. Monday to Friday, and most schools are also in session on Saturday. Many school materials are limited, like textbooks, chairs and teachers of high quality.

The disciplinary system in Africa is very, very different from the U.S.A. For example, if a student disturbs a class by talking when not permitted to do so, he or she can get beaten by the teacher or given the punishment of kneeling with heavy books in both hands, hands spread apart for the period. Can you imagine how that feels? Students in Africa can be beaten and/or expelled from the school if they fail two or three classes.

When my mother sent for me to come to the U.S.A., I knew it was going to be the start of a new life, a chance to make something of my life. My first day of school was like being with my friends at home, conversing with each other. The teachers' authority was not as powerful as in Africa. Students were sitting on the teacher's desk, talking back to the teacher in a rude manner. I was being taunted because of my accent, my pronunciation. It was different, but my mind was as sharp as a sword, and the lessons were easy because of the materials that were provided to me.

I had textbooks for every class without paying for them. I had the chance to eat free in school without paying. School to me seemed like a basket filled with bread that had been given to me. The time I spend in school is shorter and fun. Many opportunities are given to me, but most of my friends in the U.S.A. don't take these opportunities seriously, like I do. They don't know how blessed they are, how their lives are going to be incredible if they learn and grab the opportunities ahead of them. It was here my life began to change from worse to better. It was here I began to expand my learning abilities and my goals, all because of what I had provided to me in school.

I once heard the saying, "What is a dream if there is no dreamer?" I tend to dream big and work hard toward my dreams, to make this world a better place for people like myself, people who need education, people who will do anything to be educated. If kids knew the importance of education, they would focus on learning instead of thinking about what to wear to school the next day, thinking of what people may say about them if they're not dressed extravagantly.

Before I can do anything for my family and me, I have to focus on learning and striving to achieve better learning abilities. In doing this, I need to hope and struggle with myself. Being misjudged by others has to be none of my concern. I know who I am and where I came from. And it is in my heart always that "education is the key to success."

—Joe, 15

ADVICE

AN ATTITUDE OF GRATITUDE

E ven in times of stress and sadness, you have the power to create an "attitude of gratitude." In fact, it can even help you feel better. Here are some things you can do:

- Notice (and look for) the good stuff. Enjoy the beauty, comfort, love and opportunities you have in your life!
- Express appreciation to people who do or give nice things to you.
- Think of painful or disappointing events as opportunities for growth and learning. Deliberately look for silver linings!
- Pay attention to how much you complain or focus on what is lacking in your life.
- Accept compliments graciously. Just say "thank you."
- Start a personal gratitude journal. End your day by writing down at least three things you feel grateful for that day—or even three things that just didn't suck that day.
- If you appreciate the people in your life, let them know! On page 279, you will find an Angel Certificate that you can take to your local copy center and have duplicated to distribute to thank all the "angels in disguise" who are a part of your life.

Gratitude is a very personal experience. We all feel it and show it in different ways. Other people get to decide what they should feel grateful for, and so do you.

> If you're feeling really hopeless, *please* hang on. No matter how weird things get, it does get better. Simply turning eighteen gives you options you just don't have until then, options that offer *much* more freedom than you have in high school. Whether that means being able to go to college, get a job, get an apartment or go to another town, you will have a lot more choices available to you if you can just wait it out.
>
> —Clare

> The best way to predict your future is to create it.
>
> —*Stephen R. Covey*

HEY, IT'S YOUR LIFE

I would love to leave behind a beautiful legacy after I am gone. I want people to remember me for who I was in all parts of my life, and I want people to follow where I have left off and continue in my stead. Hopefully one day my name will be a constant reminder to everyone that you must fight for anything you believe in and that you must always make the best out of yourself. I think that I am much wiser now than I was five years ago, and I hope I grow in wisdom as I age.

—Jordan, 17

If I had known how difficult it was to be a high-school student, I would have skipped out on it long before I did. I was living with my sister in a different city because my folks kicked me out. I decided to view it as a chance to start over.

That hope was short-lived when I got into trouble the third day at my new school.

I was late for school and had to go to the office for a pass into class. I was tired from working the late shift, and I didn't get much sleep the night before.

When the lady at the counter asked me why I was late I said, "If I had my way, I wouldn't be here at all." I think that was the wrong attitude. She gave me detention for being insubordinate. What she didn't know was that there was no way in hell that I could miss work in order to serve detention. I decided to blow it off, go to work and make sure to never be late again. I figured that would take care of the "issue." Boy, was I wrong. The days of detention started piling up, and before I knew it I was missing my classes by getting called into the office during class time.

I wish this was the only thing that was wrong with my school life. I was lonely, I did not make any friends, I felt like no one understood me, and mostly I was sure no one really cared. My English teacher caught me cheating on a test. I was so embarrassed that I just wanted to die. You know what, though? He didn't say I was a bad person for cheating. He told me he was disappointed in my *behavior.* Until that day, I thought I *was* my behavior.

In January of my junior year, I decided to quit school. I thought it was the best thing to do because my teachers couldn't stand me, I was late all the time, I didn't have any friends in school, I had been in lots of trouble, and I was flunking all my subjects. I really just wanted to die. I hated my life and everyone in it. The day that I dropped out of school was one of the saddest days of my life. I could just imagine working in a dead-end job for the rest of my life. But the pain of staying in a place where I was a total failure was worse than the hope of something better away from school.

The road for a dropout is not an easy one. Over the next few years, I worked at a bunch of jobs—waitress, housecleaner, fast-food cook, movie theater attendant—all low-paying jobs. I could hardly afford a place to stay and food on a regular basis. One of two things happens to those who live like I did. Either they end up in trouble with the law, which happened to me once or twice, or they do whatever it takes to survive out on the streets. From the first experience I had with it, I made a very clear decision that jail was not a place for me. So at the lowest point in my life, hungry, lonely and lost, I made a decision to quit feeling sorry for myself and use the gifts and talents that I could pull together.

Just like my ninth-grade teacher indicated, *when you change your behavior, you change your life.* What really amazes me, in retrospect, is just how things begin to move in a positive direction when we make up our minds to change our attitude and behaviors.

—*Sandi*

> Growing up is a natural process intended not to curb our childhood fantasies of reaching the impossible, but to show us how much larger our definition of "possible" can be.
>
> —Adam, 18

I am an eighteen-year-old senior in high school, and I have been diagnosed with learning disabilities. I also suffer from some minor physical disabilities. I have not let these diagnoses hinder me in what I have accomplished or intend to accomplish in any way.

I try very hard to be a good person by treating all people as I want to be treated. I have many friends and try very hard to be a friend to people who may have more severe disabilities than my own. Most people shy away from them because they are "different." I feel this is all the more reason that they need a friend.

I have always worked hard, even voluntarily attending summer school and not taking a vacation from learning. I am interested in becoming a nurse so that I can help people. As someone who has received help most of her life, I know how important these people are.

—*Tashia, 18*

I turned sixteen in early January and dropped out of high school a week later. Eventually, I graduated through an independent correspondence program and went on to the local university where I again buried myself in books. I avoided having friends and, at first, avoided talking to professors. I struggled with depression and suicide during college, and I still battle myself for the right to breathe. I started tutoring fifth-graders and found that I could have an effect on someone. I realized that years of pain had prepared me to reenter schools and help others.

I would encourage you to look inside yourself, to see what you have to offer—and use that to give back to the world.

—Oprah Winfrey[167]

—Emily, 23

Try to stay in the harder classes. Even if you have to work harder rather than sleeping through an easier one, it is totally worth it. You are only cheating yourself by not taking all you can get. This does not mean to overbook yourself because chances are you will burn out sooner than your talents would normally carry you. That wouldn't do anybody good.

And you are probably thinking, "All right, this dude has made some sense so far, but I don't think he knows what he's talking about. He is done; I'm livin' it." For the most part, you are correct. Nobody else can be there for you more than you. All the lies you do or don't tell, all the friends you do or don't make, whatever, you are the one who has to wake up in the morning and face yourself in the mirror. And you will have to deal with your maker, if you believe in that sort of thing. Don't take what I write to be set in stone, just keep it in the back of your mind.

—Michael, 18

Remember, a mistake is just a decision that gets bad results.

—Carol Cassell[168]

One of the major events that shaped my life as a young teenager in a strict Catholic high school was my mother's visit to my school out of her concern over my studies, in particular, my state exam in English, which I did not pass the first time around. To be honest, I really don't remember if I ever passed the exam. What I do remember is my homeroom teacher, a Sister of Charity, telling my mother that I wasn't college material and that she would classify me as *educable retarded*. Needless to say, my immigrant mother told her off, and the rest is history. Today I am a school counselor with two master's degrees, one in education and the other in counseling and development. Ironically, I am also an adjunct college professor teaching a course on racism and sexism in education. This *educably retarded* child has come a long way.

—Nydia

ADVICE

MAKING BETTER CHOICES

Your life is and will be full of choices and decisions. What can you do to make sure that your choices are the best they can be?

- Be conscious and informed whenever you make a choice.
- Try to make choices that help other people, yourself or the world.
- Talk over your choice with people you trust, people who care about you and want what's best for you. Make sure to talk to at least one adult.
- After making a choice, review what you did and what happened as a result.
- Learn from your choice. When things don't work out the way you'd like, think of how you'll handle a similar situation differently in the future.[169]

MY SAFE ADULTS:

Name: _____

Phone: _____

Cell Phone: _____

E-mail: _____

Name: _____

Phone: _____

Cell Phone: _____

E-mail: _____

MY SAFE ADULTS:

Name: _____

Phone: _____

Cell Phone: _____

E-mail: _____

Name: _____

Phone: _____

Cell Phone: _____

E-mail: _____

I NEED TO TALK:

I need someone to talk to. Please call me or come find me to talk.

I NEED TO TALK:

I need someone to talk to. Please call me or come find me to talk.

I PROMISE I will not hurt myself. If I feel a desire to hurt myself I will call the numbers on the back of this card and seek HELP instead.

Signed: _____

I PROMISE I will not hurt myself. If I feel a desire to hurt myself I will call the numbers on the back of this card and seek HELP instead.

Signed: _____

I CAN LISTEN OR BE THERE FOR YOU.

I CAN LISTEN OR BE THERE FOR YOU.

MY SAFE ADULTS:

Name: _____

Phone: _____

Cell Phone: _____

E-mail: _____

Name: _____

Phone: _____

Cell Phone: _____

E-mail: _____

MY SAFE ADULTS:

Name: _____

Phone: _____

Cell Phone: _____

E-mail: _____

Name: _____

Phone: _____

Cell Phone: _____

E-mail: _____

Name: _____

School ID#: _____

Phone: _____

Cell Phone: _____

E-mail: _____

Name: _____

School ID#: _____

Phone: _____

Cell Phone: _____

E-mail: _____

Name: _____

Phone: _____

Cell Phone: _____

Name: _____

Phone: _____

Cell Phone: _____

Crisis Line Phone #: _____

Name: _____

Phone: _____

Cell Phone: _____

Name: _____

Phone: _____

Cell Phone: _____

Crisis Line Phone #: _____

Name: _____

Phone: _____

Cell Phone: _____

E-mail: _____

Name: _____

Phone: _____

Cell Phone: _____

E-mail: _____

Angel Certificate

A Special Thank-You to an Angel in Disguise

This certificate acknowledges

_____

As an Angel in Disguise. A special thank-you for:

_____

_____

_____

_____

*Your kindness and thoughtfulness
are appreciated.*

Signed: _____ Date: _____

Service Certificate

A GIFT OF SERVICE

This certificate entitles

_____

To the following gift of service:

_____
_____
_____
_____
_____

Signed: _____   Date: _____

RESOURCES

ADULTS, MENTORSHIP

Communities in Schools

www.cisnet.org/index.html

Helps schools connect with community resources to guide youth to stay in school, prepare for life and learn. Also matches teens with mentors.

Big Brothers and Sisters of America

www.bbbsa.org

Matches at-risk youth with caring adult mentors.

Save the Children

www.savethechildren.org

Matches adult mentors with youth; provides access to mentoring organizations in your area.

100 Black Men of America

www.100blackmen.org

National alliance of leading black men who share their skills and resources with African-American youth. Works to improve the quality of life for young people by empowering them through various initiatives, including mentoring.

YMCA and YWCA of the USA

www.ymca.net and *www.ywca.org*

YMCAs and YWCAs are at the heart of community life in neighborhoods and towns across the nation. Check your local Y to see what programs are offered.

VIOLENCE, BULLYING, BUILDING RESPECT AND TOLERANCE

Anti-Defamation League of B'nai Brith

www.adl.org

Devoted to stopping defamation of Jewish people and securing justice and fair treatment to all.

Center for Democratic Renewal

www.publiceye.org/cdr/cdr.html

Community-based coalition fighting hate group activity and providing resources to respond to incidents of hate-motivated violence and intimidation.

National School Safety Center

www.nssc1.org

Serves as an advocate for safe, secure and peaceful schools worldwide, and as a catalyst for the prevention of school crime and violence. Offers quality information, resources, consultation and training services, and identifies and promotes strategies, promising practices and programs that support safe schools for all students as part of the total academic mission.

LEARNING, ACHIEVEMENT AND MOTIVATION

Academic Therapy Publications

www.academictherapy.com

Publishes a directory of facilities and services, and offers numerous resources for the learning disabled, their parents and teachers, psychologists, speech therapists and testing personnel.

Aspira

www.aspira.org

The only national nonprofit organization devoted solely to the education and leadership development of Puerto Rican and other Latino youth.

American Vocational Association

www.avaonline.org

Supports secondary, postsecondary and adult vocational education, education for special population groups and cooperative education.

Learning Disabilities Association of America (LDA)

www.ldanatl.org

LDA is the largest non-profit volunteer organization advocating for individuals with learning disabilities, building public awareness, encouraging research, establishing career opportunities, promoting teacher training, and advocating for individuals and their families.

Council for Exceptional Children

www.cec.sped.org

The CEC is the largest international professional organization dedicated to improving educational outcomes for individuals with exceptionalities, students with disabilities and/or the gifted.

National Dropout Prevention Center

www.dropoutprevention.org

Serves as a research center and resource network for practitioners, researchers and policymakers to reshape school and community environments to meet the needs of youth in at-risk situations so students receive the quality education and services necessary to succeed academically and graduate from high school.

The International Dyslexia Association

(IDA, formerly The Orton Dyslexia Society)

www.interdys.org

A non-profit organization dedicated to helping individuals with dyslexia, their families and the communities that support them. IDA is the oldest learning disabilities organization in the nation, devoted to providing the most comprehensive forum for parents, educators and researchers to share their experiences, methods and knowledge.

STUDY HELPERS: BRAIN BOOSTERS AND SENSORY STIMULATORS

Educational Kinesiology Foundation
www.braingym.org
Information on Brain Gym, exercises to help wake up your brain. Also includes research and classes.

Trainer's Warehouse: Fidget Toys and other learning resources
www.trainerswarehouse.com
In addition to resources for teachers, they've got markers, storage materials and lots and lots of "fidget" toys.

JOB SEEKING, ALTERNATIVE WORK OR STUDY PROGRAMS

Youth Venture
www.youthventure.org
Support network for launching ventures that will bring positive change to your school and community. Encourages young people to define goals and create plans for achieving them.

Organized from the Inside Out for Teens
www.organizedteens.com
Julie Morgenstern and Jessi Morgenstern-Colon offer invaluable tips adapted

from their book, *Organizing from the Inside Out for Teens* to organize your space, your stuff, your time.

SEXUALITY, GLBT-RELATED

Parents, Families and Friends of Lesbians and Gays (PFLAG)
www.pflag.org
A national non-profit organization dedicated to celebrating diversity and envisioning a society that embraces everyone, including those of diverse sexual orientation and gender indentities.

OutProud
www.outproud.org
An organization for GLBTQ youth. The site has a huge amount of information and a wide variety of resources, including a forum to talk with other teens, a resource library, true teen coming-out stories, and a special page for transgender teens.

Young Gay America
www.younggayamerica.com
If you want to read about what other GLBTQ teens across America are doing, this is the place to go. Chat, check out articles, post questions, and read about Benjie and Mike's adventures as they drive across the country interviewing GLBTQ teens.

Coalition for Positive Sexuality
www.positive.org
An excellent sex information site for teens. Down-to-earth in tone and thorough, it answers many questions about sex and offers information (in English and Spanish) about safer sex and contraception. It also offers a discussion board where teens can learn with and consult each other about sexuality issues.

Go Ask Alice

www.goaskalice.columbia.edu

In a Q-and-A format, Columbia University's Go Ask Alice provides factual, in-depth, straightforward and nonjudgmental information about sexuality, sexual health issues and relationships.

EMOTIONS, SUICIDE, ANXIETY, MENTAL HEALTH

National Hospital for Kids in Crisis

www.kidspeace.org

Offers a wide range of community and residential services, free-standing psychiatric children's hospital, juvenile justice programs and specialized foster care, to give hope, help and healing to children facing crisis.

American Foundation for Suicide Prevention

www.afsp.org

Exclusively dedicated to funding research, developing prevention initiatives and offering educational programs and conferences for survivors, mental health professionals and the public.

Anxiety Disorders Association of America (ADAA)

www.adaa.org

Promotes early diagnosis, treatment and cure of anxiety disorders and is committed to improving the lives of the people who suffer from them.

Emotions Anonymous

www.emotionsanonymous.org

A 12-step program composed of people who come together for the purpose of working toward recovery from emotional difficulties.

Covenant House Nineline
(800) 999-9999
www.covenanthouse.org/nineline/index.html
Twenty-four-hour hotline focusing primarily on homeless youth (runaways and abandoned kids), but also helps young people who are suicidal. The hotline will help you find a crisis center nearest you.

DRUG ABUSE, TOBACCO, ALCOHOLISM

National Institute of Drug Abuse
www.drugabuse.gov/students.html
Includes research information about the effects of drug abuse on the brain and interactive activities to help you learn more about various drugs and how they affect how your brain works.

S.A.F.E. (Self Abuse Finally Ends)
www.selfinjury.com
Network and educational resource base committed to helping you and others achieve an end to self-injurious behavior (any form of self-mutilation or deliberate self-harm).

The Truth
www.thetruth.com
The truth about BIG TOBACCO, smoking and tobacco related issues.

Campaign for Tobacco-Free Kids
www.tobaccofreekids.org
The country's largest nongovernnment initiative to protect children from tobacco addiction.

Alateen
www. al-anon.alateen.org
Part of Al-Anon, Alateen helps families and friends of alcoholics recover from the effects of living with a problem-drinking relative or friend.

Narcotics Anonymous

www.na.org

Narcotics Anonymous is an international, community-based association of recovering drug addicts.

Alcoholics Anonymous

www.alcoholics-anonymous.org

Alcoholics Anonymous® is a fellowship of men and women who share their experience, strength and hope with each other so that they may solve their common problem and help others to recover from alcoholism.

EATING DISORDERS AND FOOD SENSITIVITIES

Feingold Institute

www.feingold.org

Includes information and resources about allergies and sensitivities to certain foods and food additives. Also information in their newsletters about light sensitivities, sensitivities to certain school products and supplies, environmental sensitivities in schools—plus the potential impact of these sensitivities on behavior and learning.

National Association of Anorexia Nervosa and Associated Disorders

www.anad.org

Seeks to alleviate the problems of eating disorders, especially anorexia nervosa and bulimia nervosa. Resource center for information about eating disorders and facilities for treatment.

National Association to Advance Fat Acceptance (NAAFA)

www.naafa.org

Dedicated to eliminating discrimination based on body size and improving the quality of life for fat people.

American Dietetic Association

www.eatright.org

The country's largest organization of food and nutritional professionals, ADA promotes optimal nutrition, health and well-being.

Overeaters Anonymous

www.oa.org

Offers a program of recovery from compulsive overeating within a fellowship of experience, strength and hope. OA addresses physical, emotional and spiritual well-being, not just weight-loss, obesity or diets.

The Body Positive

www.bodypositive.com

Teaches young people to creatively transform the conditions in their lives that shape their body image and relationship to food.

SEX AND PREGNANCY

Planned Parenthood

www.plannedparenthood.org

Supports people who make their own decisions about having children without government interference, providing contraceptive counseling and services through clinics throughout the United States.

Rape, Abuse and Incest National Network (RAINN)

www.rainn.org

The nation's largest anti-sexual assault organization, carrying out programs to prevent sexual assault, help victims and ensure that rapists are brought to justice.

National Sexual Assault Hotline
(800) 656-HOPE
The hotline, operated by RAINN, offers free, confidential counseling twenty-four hours a day.

Project Reality
www.projectreality.org
Encourages sexual abstinence and teaches teens that saying "no" to premarital sex is their right and is in the best interest of society.

RELATIONSHIPS, VIOLENCE, SAFETY

National Domestic Violence Hotline
1-800-799-7233 (SAFE)
www.ndvh.org
A twenty-four-hour phone line with information and resources to end domestic violence, offer referrals to over 4,000 shelters and help people in violent relationships find safety. Bilingual operators and services for hearing-impaired available.

Center for the Prevention of School Violence
www.cpsv.org
This center focuses on ensuring that schools are safe and secure, creating an atmosphere that is conducive to learning.

The Giraffe Project
www.giraffe.org/giraffe
Helps teachers and youth leaders build courage, caring and responsibility in kids from 6–18 years old, then guides kids in designing and implementing their own service projects.

NOTES

Some of the contributions in this book were adapted from material in Jane Bluestein's other books, including *Mentors, Masters and Mrs. MacGregor* and *Creating Emotionally Safe Schools.*

1 Ralph Keyes, *Is There Life After High School?* (Boston: Little, Brown and Company, 1976), 13.

2 Keyes, 182.

3 Denise Clark Pope, *Doing School: How We Are Creating a Generation of Stressed Out, Materialistic and Miseducated Students* (New Haven, CT: Yale University Press, 2001), 4.

4 Deepak Chopra, *Fire in the Heart: A Spiritual Guide for Teens* (New York: Simon and Schuster Books for Young Readers, 2004), 187.

5 Quoted in Al Desetta and Sybil Wolin, eds., *The Struggle to Be Strong: True Stories by Teens About Overcoming Tough Times* (Minneapolis, MN: Free Spirit Publishing, 2000), 52.

6 Quoted in Desetta and Wolin, 52.

7 Kelly Huegel, *GLBTQ: The Survival Guide for Queer and Questioning Teens* (Minneapolis, MN: Free Spirit Publishing, 2003), 5.

8 Quoted in Jim Delisle and Judy Galbraith, *When Gifted Kids Don't Have All the Answers* (Minneapolis, MN: Free Spirit Publishing, 2002), 212.

9 Quoted in Carol Weston, *For Teens Only: Quotes, Notes & Advice You Can Use* (New York: HarperTrophy, 2003), 12.

10 Barbara Mayer, *How to Succeed in High School* (Lincolnwood, IL: VGM Career Horizons, 1997), xii.

11 Amanda Lenhart, Lee Rainie and Oliver Lewis, "Teenage Life Online: The rise of the instant-message generation and the Internet's impact on friendships and family relationships." Available: Pew Internet and American Life Project Web site, *www.pewinternet.org/pdfs/PIP_Teens_Report.pdf*

12 Ned Vizzini, *Teen Angst? Naaah . . .* (Minneapolis, MN: Free Spirit Publishing, 2002), 73.

13 Character in the movie *13 Going on 30,* quoted in Liam Lacy, "Garner Grows in Big Role," *The Globe and Mail* (Apr. 23, 2004): R.

14 "The State of Our Nation's Youth." Available: Horatio Alger Association Web site, *www.horatioalger.com/pdfs/state03.pdf*

15 Quoted in Gayatri Patnaik and Michelle T. Shinseki, eds., *The Secret Life of Teens: Young People Speak Out About Their Lives* (San Francisco: HarperSanFrancisco, 2000), 19.

16 Vizzini, 41.

17 Quoted in Ruth Bell, *Changing Bodies, Changing Lives* (New York: Three Rivers Press, 1998), 170.

18 Quoted in Chérie Carter-Scott, *If High School Is a Game, Here's How to Break the Rules* (New York: Delacorte Press, 2001), 13.

19 Emily White, *Fast Girls: Teenage Tribes and the Myth of the Slut* (New York: Scribner, 2002), 11.

20 Quoted in Weston, 13.

21 Huegel, 80–81.

22 Huegel, 80–81.

23 High-school student quoted in Murray Milner, Jr., *Freaks, Geeks, and Cool Kids: American Teenagers, Schools, and the Culture of Consumption* (New York: Routledge, 2004), 43.

24 Quoted in Livia King, "Bridging Cultures," *Albuquerque Journal* (Jan. 4, 2000).

25 Quoted in Patnaik and Shinseki, 62–63.

26 Quoted in Desetta and Wolin, 32.

27 Told to ABC News broadcaster Jonathan Dube, quoted in Linda Jacobs Altman, *Racism and Ethnic Bias: Everybody's Problem* (Berkeley Heights, NJ: Enslow Publishers, Inc., 2001), 46.

28 Jodee Blanco, *Please Stop Laughing at Me* (Avon, MA: Adams Media Corporation, 2003), 139.

29 Adapted from Pat Palmer and Melissa Alberti Froehner, *Teen Esteem: A Self-Direction Manual for Young Adults* (Atascadero, CA: Impact Publishers, Inc., 2000), 67–71.

30 Terry Dunnahoo, *How to Survive High School: A Student's Guide* (New York: Franklin Watts, 1993), 19.

31 Chopra, 112.

32 Altoosa Rubenstein, "Lots More to Learn in High School," York Daily Record (May 18, 2004): 1D.

33 Alex J. Packer, *Bringing Up Parents* (Minneapolis, MN: Free Spirit Publishing, 1993), 105, 108–111.

34 Chopra, 30.

35 Mayer, 74.

36 Mayer, 74.

37 Blanco, 111.

38 Keyes, 108.

39 Barbara Lewis, *What Do You Stand For? A Kid's Guide to Building Character* (Minneapolis, MN: Free Spirit Publishing, 1998), 72.

40 Kelly Bagnaschi and John Geraci, eds., "Love and Romance and America's Youth," *Trends and Tudes* (Feb. 2003). Available: Harris Interactive Web site, *www.harrisinteractive.com/news/newsletters/k12news/HI_Trends&TudesNews2003_V2_iss2.pdf*

41 Quoted in Huegel, 11.

42 Bell, 223.

43 Quoted in Patnaik and Shinseki, 75.

44 Quoted in Barbara Moe, *Understanding the Causes of a Negative Body Image* (New York: The Rosen Publishing Group, 1999), 7.

45 Quoted in Lenhart, Rainie and Lewis.

46 Adapted from Alex J. Packer, *How Rude: The Teenagers' Guide to Good Manners, Proper Behavior and Not Grossing People Out* (Minneapolis, MN: Free Spirit Publishing, 1997), 246–248.

47 Lenhart, Rainie and Lewis.

48 Bagnaschi and Geraci.

49 Huegel, 42, 45.

50 Quoted in Huegel, 37.

51 Huegel, 59.

52 Allison Bloom, "Not Your Parent's Prom," In Focus, May 30, 2003. Available: teenwire Web site, *www.teenwire.com/infocus/2003/if_20030530p230_prom.asp*

53 Lenhart, Rainie and Lewis.

54 Marlin S. Potash and Laura Potash Fruitman, *Am I Weird or Is This Normal?* (New York: Fireside Books, 2001), 46.

55 "Youth Risk Behavior Surveillance—United States, 2003." Available: Centers for Disease Control Web site, *www.cdc.gov/mmwr/PDF/SS/SS5302.pdf*

56 Adapted from Packer, *How Rude*, 260.

57 "Youth Risk Behavior Surveillance—United States, 2003."

58 "Youth Risk Behavior Surveillance—United States, 2003."

59 Vizzini, 201.

60 Quoted in Amy L. Best, *Prom Night: Youth, Schools and Popular Culture* (New York: Routledge, 2000), 91.

61 Huegel, 107.

62 Vizzini, 212.

63 Quoted in Don Nardo, *Teen Sexuality* (San Diego, CA: Lucent Books, Inc., 1997), 50.

64 "National Youth Risk Behavior Survey: 1991–2003," *Trends in the Prevalence of Sexual Behaviors*, Available: Centers for Disease Control Web site, *www.cdc.gov/HealthyYouth/YRBS/pdfs/trends-sex.pdf*

65 Quoted in Nardo, 31.

66 Nardo, 30.

67 Jill Nelson, "Black Teens' View of Sex Sounds Alarms," *USA Today* (Mar. 19, 2004): 19A.

68 Victoria Sherrow, *Dropping Out* (New York: Benchmark Books, 1996), 44.

69 "School Violence Prevention," Available: U.S. Department of Health and Human Services Web site., *mentalhealth.samhsa.gov/schoolviolence/*

70 "Initiation Rites in American High Schools: A National Survey." Available: Alfred University Web site, *www.alfred.edu/news/hazing__study.pdf*

71 "Education: People's Chief Concerns." Available: Public Agenda Web site *www.publicagenda.org/issues/pcc_detail.cfm?issue_type=education&list=18*

72 "Initiation Rites in American High Schools: A National Survey."

73 "Initiation Rites in American High Schools: A National Survey."

74 Quoted in Huegel, 32.

75 Character in the movie *Mean Girls.*

76 "Just the Facts" (1998). Availability: Blackboard On-Line, the GLSEN (Gay, Lesbian and Straight Education Network) Web site, *www.glstn.org/pages/sections/library/reference/006.article*; also, the 2001 GLSEN (Gay, Lesbian and Straight Education Network) National School Climate Survey in Huegel, 30, 61, 74; also Rose Arce, "Classes Open at Gay High School," Sept. 8, 2003. Available: CNN Education Web site, *www.cnn.com/2003/EDUCATION/09/08/gay.school/index.html*

77 Thanks to Jo Ann Freiberg, bully-prevention specialist, Co-Founder, Director of Education and Programs for Operation Respect CT.

78 Irene M. McDonald, "Expanding the Lens: Student Perceptions of School Violence," in Juanita Ross Epp and Alisa M. Watkinson, eds., *Systemic Violence: How Schools Hurt Children,* (London: Falmer Press, 1996), 83.

79 William Goodwin, *Teen Violence* (San Diego, CA: Lucent Books, Inc., 1998), 11.

80 Kelly Bagnaschi and Dana Markow, eds., "Feeling Safe: What Girls Say," Trends and Tudes (Oct. 2003). Available: Harris Interactive Web site, *www.harrisinteractive.com/news/newsletters/k12news/HI_Trends &TudesNews2004_v3_iss03.pdf*

81 Thanks to Peter Volkmann, MSW, Fordham University. Representative to the United Nations through the International Critical Incident Stress Foundation, a non-governmental organization in special consultative status with the Economic and Social Council of the U.N.

82 Peter Volkmann.

83 Thanks to Jo Ann Freiberg, bully-prevention specialist, Co-Founder, Director of Education and Programs for Operation Respect CT.

84 Denise M. Bonilla, *School Violence* (New York, NY: The H. W. Wilson Company, 2000), 18.

85 "Just the Facts"; also, the 2001 GLSEN (Gay, Lesbian and Straight Education Network) National School Climate Survey in Huegel, 30, 61, 74; also Rose Arce, "Classes Open at Gay High School," Sept. 8, 2003. Available: CNN Education Web site, *www.cnn.com/2003/EDUCATION/09/08/gay.school/index.html*

86 Jo Ann Freilberg.

87 Quoted in Bell, 214.

88 "Controlling Anger—Before It Controls You," ©2000 by the American Psychological Association. Contact info: *http://www.apa.org/about/contact.html*

89 Quoted in Cindy Maynard, "How to Make Peace with Your Body," *Current Health 2*, Sept. 1998, Vol. 25, No. 1, page 6(6) ©1998 Weekly Reader Corporation.

90 Alan Greene, "Eating Disorders in Teens" (Mar. 29, 2001). Available: Dr. Greene's Web site: Caring for the Next Generation, *www.drgreene.com/21_343.html*

91 "How to Make Peace with Your Body."

92 Bill Hewitt, et al., "Juiced Up," *People* (May 31, 2004), 92–95.

93 "Steroids (Anabolic-Androgenic)," *NIDA InfoFacts,* March 2004. Available: National Institute on Drug Abuse Web site, *165.112.78.61/Infofax/steroids.html*; also Bill Hewitt, et al., "Juiced Up," People (May 31, 2004), 92–95.

94 Keyes, 20.

95 Potash and Fruitman, 136.

96 Tim Wendel, "The Teen Brain," *USA Weekend* (May 16–18, 2003): 24.

97 Peter L. Benson, Judy Galbraith and Pamela Espeland, *What Teens Need to Succeed* (Minneapolis, MN: Free Spirit Publishing, 1998), 163.

98 "The MetLife Survey of the American Teacher 2002," Available: MetLife Web site, *www.metlife.com/WPSAssets/11738669411033654558V1FBook%20v.3.pdf*

99 Maynard.

100 Maynard.

101 Kelly Bagnaschi and Dana Markow, Ph.D., eds., "Obesity, Nutrition and Physical Activity," *Trends & Tudes,* Vol. 3, Issue 8, Aug. 2004.

102 Carter-Scott, 3.

103 "National Youth Risk Behavior Survey: 1991–2003," *Trends in the Prevalence of Selected Risk Behaviors.* Available: Centers for Disease Control Web site, *www.cdc.gov/HealthyYouth/YRBS/pdfs/trends.pdf*; "Youth Risk Behavior Surveillance, United States, 2003."

104 Quoted in Eleanor H. Ayer, *Teen Smoking* (San Diego, CA: Lucent Books, Inc., 1999), 37.

105 Quoted in Ayer, 68.

106 Ayer, 22, 31.

107 Institute of Medicine, quoted in Eleanor H. Ayer, *Teen Smoking* (San Diego, CA: Lucent Books, Inc., 1999), 38.

108 Hayley R. Mitchell, *Teen Alcoholism* (San Diego, CA: Lucent Books, Inc., 1998).

109 "Fact Sheet: Alcohol-Related Traffic Fatalities" (Dec. 5, 1997). Available: Centers for Disease Control Web site, *www.cdc.gov/od/oc/media/fact/alctrfa.htm*

110 "Youth Risk Behavior Survey of High School Students Attending Bureau Funded Schools." Available: Bureau of Indian Affairs/Office of Indian Education Programs Web site, *www.oiep.bia.edu/docs/hsyrbs_ 2001.pdf*

111 Lisa Wolff, *Teen Depression* (San Diego, CA: Lucent Books, Inc., 1999), 16.

112 Janet Kolehmainen and Sandra Handwerk, *Teen Suicide: A Book for Friends, Families and Classmates* (Minneapolis: Lerner Publications, Co., 1986), 21.

113 Wolff, 16.

114 From "Why Am I So Sad?" Copyright 2000 The Nemours Foundation. Contact info: *http://www. nemours.org/internet?url=no/info/contact_us.html&setPid=3*

115 Wolff, 50.

116 Quoted in Patnaik and Shinseki, 106.

117 Evelyn Leite and Pamela Espeland, *Different Like Me: A Book for Teens Who Worry About Their Parents' Use of Alcohol* (Minneapolis, MN: Johnson Institute Books, 1987), 7.

118 Quoted in Mitchell, 35.

119 Quoted in Gail B. Stewart, *Teen Addicts* (San Diego, CA: Lucent Books, Inc., 2000), 8.

120 Quoted in Wolff, 19.

121 Quoted in Gail B. Stewart, *Teen Alcoholics* (San Diego, CA: Lucent Books, Inc., 2000), 100.

122 Quoted in Ayer, 21.

123 Earl Hipp, *Fighting Invisible Tigers: A Stress Management Guide for Teens* (Minneapolis, MN: Free Spirit Publishing, 1995), 3.

124 "Seven Sleep-Smart Tips for Teens." Available: National Sleep Foundation Web site, *www.sleep foundation.org/PressArchives/seven.cfm*

125 Nancy Tipton, "All Those Heavy Textbooks Can Be a Pain in the Back," *Albuquerque Journal* special "Back to School" insert (Aug. 8, 2004): 6.

126 "At a Glance: Suicide Among the Young." Available: National Strategy for Suicide Prevention Web site, *www.mentalhealth.samhsa.gov/suicideprevention/young.asp*

127 Packer, *How Rude*, 310.

128 Adapted from Packer, *How Rude*, 307–309.

129 Quoted in Patnaik and Shinseki, 14–15.

130 Excerpted from *When Gifted Kids Don't Have All the Answers: How to Meet Their Social and Emotional Needs* by Jim Delisle, Ph.D. and Judy Galbraith, M.A. ©2000. Used with permission from Free Spirit Publishing, Inc., Minneapolis, MN; 1-866-703-7322; *www.freespirit.com*. All rights reserved.

131 Miriam Elliott and Susan Meltsner, *The Perfectionist Predicament* (New York: William Morrow and Co., Inc., 1991), 168.

132 Potash and Fruitman, 222–223.

133 *Reach for the Stars.*

134 "The MetLife Survey of the American Teacher 2002," Available: MetLife Website, *www.metlife.com/ WPSAssets/11738669411033654558V1FBook%20v.3.pdf*

135 Quoted in Rebecca Greene, *The Teenager's Guide to School Outside the Box* (Minneapolis, MN: Free Spirit Publishing, 2001), 42.

136 Sherrow, 67.

137 Sherrow, 61.

138 Vizzini, 43.

139 Roarke O'Leary, "Sit Up Straight and Pay Attention," *Albuquerque Journal* (Dec. 11, 2001): B1.

140 Kelly Bagnaschi and John Geraci, eds., "What Does It Mean to Be a Girl or a Boy Today?" *Trends and Tudes* (Jan. 2003). Available: Harris Interactive Web site, [Internet, WWW], Address: *http://www. harrisinteractive.com/news/newsletters/k12news/HI_Trends&TudesNews2003_V2_iss1.pdf*

141 Roarke O'Leary.

142 Greene, 15.

143 "The MetLife Survey of the American Teacher 2002."

144 Sherrow, 72.

145 Dunnahoo, 63.

146 Beverly K. Bachel, *What Do You Really Want? A Guide for Teens* (Minneapolis, MN: Free Spirit Publishing, 2001), 97.

147 Lewis, 71.

148 Quoted in Dotson Rader, "My Fear Fuels Me," *Parade* Magazine (July 11, 2004): 5.

149 Margi Trapani, *Inside a Support Group: Help for Teenage Children of Alcoholics* (New York: The Rosen Publishing Group, Inc., 1997), 19, 24–25.

150 Wolff.

151 Leite and Espeland, 51.

152 Packer, *Bringing Up Parents,* 46.

153 Carter-Scott, 71.

154 Packer, *Bringing Up Parents,* 105, 108–111.

155 Greene, 64.

156 "The MetLife Survey of the American Teacher 2002."

157 Allan L. Beane, *The Bully-Free Classroom* (Minneapolis, MN: Free Spirit Publishing, 1999), 73.

158 Quoting a 1997 College Board study in Benson, Galbraith and Espeland, 139.

159 "Then (1966) and Now (2002): How Have Teens Changed?" Available: Harris Interactive Web site (*Trends and Tudes,* Nov. 2002), *www.harrisinteractive.com/news/newsletters/k12news/HI_Trends& TudesNews_05.pdf*

160 Adapted from "Setting Goals." Available: Northwestern University, Student Affairs, University Career Services. *www.northwestern.edu/careers/students/started/goalset.htm*

161 Potash and Fruitman, 252.

162 Jay Matthews, "Bad Scores Good Company," Analysts and Achievers Say SAT Results Don't Dictate Success (June 23, 2004). Available: The Washington Post Web site, *www.washingtonpost.com/wp-dyn/articles/A61961–2004Jun22.html*

163 Weston, 83.

164 Bluestein, *Creating Emotionally Safe Schools*, ch. 12; also Lewis, 128–129, 184–185; also Wolff, 21; also Jay Matthews, "Bad Scores Good Company," *Analysts and Achievers Say SAT Results Don't Dictate Success* (June 23, 2004). Available: *The Washington Post* Web site, *www.washingtonpost.com/wp-dyn/articles/A61961–2004Jun22.html*; also Jo Piazza and Chris Rovzar, "Celebs in Tales Told Out of School" (Sept. 5, 2004). Available: *The Daily News Front Page* Web site, *www.nydailynews.com/front/story/229213p–196831c.html*; also "Tom Cruise Biography." Available: tiscali.film&tv Web site, *www.tiscali.co.uk/entertainment/film/biographies/tom_cruise_biog/2*

165 *Reach for the Stars* (White Plains, NY: Peter Pauper Press, Inc., 2002).

166 Chopra, 79.

167 Quoted in Carter-Scott, 160.

168 Adapted from Carol Cassell, "Making Decisions Step by Step." Paper presented at the Ben Franklin Institute Summit for Clinical Excellence: Third Conference on Adolescence, April 2004.

169 Lewis, 30.

ABOUT THE AUTHORS

Dr. Jane Bluestein has worked as a classroom teacher or counselor with kids of all ages. For the past several years, her work has focused on helping teachers and parents improve the ways they connect with kids. She is the author of numerous books, including *Creating Emotionally Safe Schools* and *Parents, Teens & Boundaries*. She heads Instructional Support Services, Inc., a consulting and resource firm in Albuquerque, New Mexico. Although Jane had a few positive experiences and a number of good teachers (a few with whom she's still in touch) in high school, she's very glad to have those days behind her.

Eric D. Katz, MSAC, is a psychotherapist and a New York state certified school counselor who works on the front lines in a diverse high school in Newburgh, New York. He is a consultant to the College Board's Equity and Excellence Program, an advisory board member for Long Island University's Graduate Program for School Counseling and the coauthor of the advanced series of school counselor workshops for the College Board's Pathways to Excellence Program.

Mr. Katz is a trained crisis intervention counselor and provided assistance to students and staff in New York City after September 11. He is a featured speaker at the state and national level and is deeply committed to helping teens succeed not just in high school but in life. After all, high school's not forever.

MORE TIPS

Want even more great stories, tips and facts?
Visit our website at *www.highschoolsnotforever.com*

High School's Not Forever is alive and well on the Internet. Visit our site to see how teens like you are responding to this book and to learn how even more of you are facing the daily grind we call high school.

Got something you want to say?
Please send your comments, questions and feedback to us at *editor@ highschoolsnotforever.com*. If you wish to have your comments published on the Web site please complete the permission form on our Web site.

Share your story of high school survival:
We are looking for the good, the bad and the real. What have you had to face, how have you dealt with it? Share your experiences so that others can learn.

1) Send your comments or your original story, experience, observation, poem or artwork to *editor@highschoolsnotforever.com*. You can also mail your submission to *High School's Not Forever,* 1709 Father Sky Court NE, Albuquerque, NM, 87112, or fax it to us at 505-323-9045. Please include your name, age and contact information (address, phone and email address). **No names will be used without your permission and contact information is never shared.**

2) If you want your name included with your submission, you will need to sign and return a release giving us permission to do so. You can go to our Web site at *www.highschoolsnotforever.com/permit.html* and download a simple permission form. If you are under eighteen, a parent or guardian must also sign the form. Send this form to the same e-mail, mail or fax listed above. **Material submitted without a permission form will be used anonymously.**